The Boy Detectives

ALSO BY
MICHAEL G. CORNELIUS

*Nancy Drew and Her Sister Sleuths:
Essays on the Fiction of Girl Detectives*
(McFarland, 2008)

The Boy Detectives
Essays on the Hardy Boys and Others

Edited by
MICHAEL G. CORNELIUS

McFarland & Company, Inc., Publishers
Jefferson, North Carolina, and London

LIBRARY OF CONGRESS CATALOGUING-IN-PUBLICATION DATA

The boy detectives : essays on the Hardy Boys and others / edited by Michael G. Cornelius.
    p.   cm.
    Includes bibliographical references and index.

    ISBN 978-0-7864-6033-5
    softcover : 50# alkaline paper

    1. Detective and mystery stories, American — History and criticism. 2. Detectives in literature. 3. Boys in literature. 4. Stratemeyer, Edward, 1862–1930 — Characters — Hardy Boys. 5. Hardy Boys (Fictitious characters) 6. Children's stories, American — History and criticism. 7. Young adult fiction, American — History and criticism. I. Cornelius, Michael G.
    PS374.D4B69   2010
    813'.087209 — dc22
                                            2010020982

British Library cataloguing data are available

©2010 Michael G. Cornelius. All rights reserved

No part of this book may be reproduced or transmitted in any form or by any means, electronic or mechanical, including photocopying or recording, or by any information storage and retrieval system, without permission in writing from the publisher.

Cover image ©2010 Pictures Now

Manufactured in the United States of America

McFarland & Company, Inc., Publishers
  Box 611, Jefferson, North Carolina 28640
  www.mcfarlandpub.com

I'd like to dedicate this book, as all things are, to Joe.
And to all the boy sleuths, both in this book
and reading it now: this one's for you.

In memory of Hilda Jackson.

Contents

Acknowledgments ix
Introduction: The Nomenclature of Boy Sleuths
    MICHAEL G. CORNELIUS 1

1. A Hardy Boys' Identity Narrative and *The Tower Treasure*
    LARRY T. SHILLOCK 19
2. Hardy Camaraderie: Boy Sleuthing and Male Community in the Hardy Boys Mysteries
    C. M. GILL 35
3. Terminal Immaterial: The Uncertain Subject of the Hardy Boys Airport Mysteries
    CHRISTOPHER SCHABERG 51
4. Strategies of Adaptation: The Hardy Boys on Television
    BRIAN TAVES 62
5. Natural Detective Work: Ideas About Nature in the Early Tom Swift Books
    ELIZABETH D. BLUM 86
6. Tim Murphy: Superhero Without a Cape
    FRED ERISMAN 108
7. Adventures and Affect: The Character of the Boy Detective and Orphan in Astrid Lindgren's *Rasmus and the Tramp*
    CHARLOTTE BEYER 120
8. The Power of Three: Alfred Hitchcock's Three Investigators Series
    ALAN PICKRELL 132

9. Clashing Genres: (No) Sex and (No) Violence in the
    Christopher Cool, TEEN Agent Series
    MICHAEL G. CORNELIUS   143
10. "The Perfect Hero for His Age": Christopher Boone and the
    Role of Logic in the Boy Detective Narrative
    NICOLA ALLEN   167
11. Has the World Outgrown the Classic Boy Detective?
    JOHN FINLAY KERR   180

About the Contributors   199
Index   203

Acknowledgments

This book was completed with the generous support of the Paul Swain Havens Research Scholars Award. I would like to thank Lorraine Hamilton Havens and the entire Havens family for their continuing support of the faculty of Wilson College. I would also like to thank all of the contributors for their excellent work. Thanks also to Nicole Twigg, Joseph Garcia, Larry Shillock, and anyone else who had a hand in putting this collection together.

Introduction: The Nomenclature of Boy Sleuths

Michael G. Cornelius

Rover: "One who roves or wanders, *esp.* to a great distance; an adventurer"
Swift: "moving, or capable of moving, with great speed or velocity; *coll.*, intelligent, clever"
Sturdy: "Impetuously brave, fierce in combat; characterized by rough bodily vigor; solidly built; stalwart, strong, robust, hardy; robust in mind or character"
Fearless: "Unaffected by fear; bold, intrepid; confident"
Cool: "assured and unabashed where diffidence and hesitation would be expected; calm, composed; attractively shrewd or clever; sophisticated, stylish, classy; fashionable, up to date"
Quest: "In chivalric romance: an expedition or search undertaken by a knight or group of knights to obtain some thing or achieve some exploit; search, pursuit"
King: "The usual title of the male sovereign ruler of an independent state; something to which there is attributed supremacy or chief excellency in its class"
Power: "Ability to act or affect something strongly; physical or mental strength; might; vigor, energy; effectiveness"
Hardy: "Bold, courageous, daring; capable of enduring."

—*The Oxford English Dictionary*

The list above is a significant sampling of what are known as emblematic names. Emblematic names, according to Juliet McGrath, "either reflect the outcome of the action with regard to various characters, or they are indicative of the essential qualities of these characters" (McGrath 334). In other words, with an emblematic name, the moniker of a character is designed to encapsulate some kernel of truth, some aspect of identity, that said character espouses, usually in a wholly earnest (though sometimes quite ironic) manner. Boy detectives' last names often tend to reflect "essential qualities," characteristics that are masculine, strong, and desirable. The use of such emblematic names is derivative, in a sense, of the mechanics and directives of boy detective series as a whole; quite literally, for boy detectives, their names recount much indeed.

A character's name can tell us a lot about the person, such as gender, family interrelatedness (in the case of juniors, thirds, or fourths) or ethnic origin. Names also have particular connotations. A name can sound snooty (such as Little Lord Fauntleroy, whose name, despite the noble sentiment of its origins, has now become tantamount with snobbery and pomposity) or utterly common (as with "plain" Janes, or every Tom, Dick, and Harry, where the name itself has become synonymous with the gender). Names can suggest economic status, especially in the case of the rich (think of the Carrington family from the television series *Dynasty*) or a racial, ethnic, or geographic background: Umbeke, Shaniqua, José, Mohammed, and Bjorn suggest traditional African, African American, Hispanic, Muslim or Arabic, and Scandinavian ethnicities, respectively. Names can create allusions to historical, mythological, or popular cultural personages. The main character in Larry Gelbart's *M*A*S*H* shares both his given name and his nickname with differing historical and literary personages — Benjamin Franklin Pierce suggesting both a famous founding father and a pre–Civil War U.S. president, and the nickname Hawkeye referring back to the protagonist of James Fenimore Cooper's *The Last of the Mohicans*. A name can even suggest utter anonymity — Jane Doe, John Smith — names that, in our culture, have become synonymous with obscurity, mystery, and nothingness.

In all of these cases the name is the beginning point for a character's subjectivity — it marks an activation in a literal sense, a foundation on which to build, a foundation that may be built in an earnest relationship to the character or an ironic one. This can be illustrated by the same example. Buffy Summers, the main character from the 1992 film *Buffy the Vampire Slayer* and the subsequent television series (1997–2003) has a name that is emblematic of the initial fashioning of the character herself. "Buffy Summers" implies a beach-bred California social princess, upwardly mobile and aspirant, popular and vacuous. The character as depicted in the film and played by Kristy Swanson fits that description. The character as re-imagined for the television series and played by Sarah Michelle Gellar does not; in the series, the name becomes ironic, as Buffy is an outcast, as far from being socially mobile as possible. In the film, the name is used as a way of grounding the audience with the subjectivity of the film's protagonist; while Buffy may grow as a character (as dynamic figures are wont to do in literature and film) she never truly abandons her roots. In the series, however, the name becomes an ironic reminder of what Buffy has given up to become the protector of her society; though she defends it nightly from all manner of threats, it has rejected her because her actions, while necessary, belie the social conformity that teenaged social motility requires. She acts "weird," and though her actions save lives, Buffy is viewed as a pariah by the elevated cliques within her social strata. In the film, Buffy's movement away from social motility and her cheerleader-clique demonstrates growth, the dynamism the character embraces as the film progresses. In the series, when Buffy tries out for the cheerleading squad again, the audience views that re-embracing of desire for teen-aged motility and normativity as regressive, as against the growth she has previously demonstrated. Thus in both the film and the series, Buffy's name represents a place wherein subjective motility can begin; it provides the filmmakers with a place to move away from and go towards, depending upon the development of the character.

Emblematic names, however, are often designed to relate *all* or nearly all a reader needs to know about a character; in short, they "establish character" (McGrath 334). This is because, in most instances, emblematic names reflect flat characters, literary constructions who eschew a dynamic, more well-rounded subjectivity in favor of a simplistic, adroitly-fashioned identity designed to establish a character in order to extend the generic boundaries of text, and not subjectivity. For example, the use of emblematic names in Renaissance and, even more commonly, Restoration dramas by authors such as William Shakespeare, Ben Jonson, William Wycherley, John Wilmot, and James Shirley are designed to establish a typology of character to then satirize the generic or societal conventions that produced such typologies in the first place. Jonson's character of Morose, for example, in his play *Epicœne, or the Silent Woman*, is an apt illustration of the emblematic name in action. *Epicœne* tells the tale of a young rapscallion who finds himself in a financial quagmire when his uncle, Morose, proposes to marry, thus cutting him off from a considerable allowance and inheritance. Rather than seem offended, the young man offers to find his uncle a suitable wife. Morose is advancing in years and the idea of corporeal companionship — in both the comfortive and sexual connotations of the word — appeals to him. Yet Morose cannot abide frivolity of any kind, and noise even less, and he views women as endless purveyors of both. In the play, Morose is a gloomy, sullen man who prefers calmness, stillness, and silence. He is, in short, a *morose* man, and having thus established his character, Jonson focuses on using the man as a means to critique the society and the medium that has spawned them both. Morose's nephew, Dauphine (also an emblematic name), finds his uncle a wife ideally suited to his exacting specifications — a woman so quiet that, when she speaks (as she rarely does) she oft cannot be heard. Elated, Morose marries the woman his nephew has found him — only to find that, after the wedding, his formerly silent bride now talks, and talks, and talks. Beside himself, Morose acquiesces to his nephew's demand to fully restore him and make him his heir if he can find some way to release Morose from his matrimonial bonds to this woman — which Dauphine does, when he reveals that Epicoene is really a man, as all "women" were on the Jacobian stage.

In *Epicœne*, Jonson wishes to waste little time in establishing the character of Morose; while his typology is cynosure to the *action* of the play, it is not integral to the play's culminative meaning. This is typical of emblematic names in these time periods: think of Mr. Pinchwife, Mrs. Dainty Fidget, and Old Lady Squeamish from William Wycherley's *The Country Wife*, or Jonson's trio of grotesques of Nano, the dwarf, Androgyno, the hermaphrodite, and Castrone, the eunuch, from *Volpone*, whose names reflect the type of individual they are.[1] Thus emblematic names are designed as a jumping off point for the author; rather than taking the time to develop a fully-fleshed figure, only to burlesque him or her, authors rely on stock social constructions to facilitate the development of a work's conventions, meanings, and themes. The end result is that characters with emblematic names are generally meaningless in the development of the central thematic function of the narrative itself; they are important in establishing plot, conflict, and resolution, but they are generally less significant when deciphering the commentative meaning of the piece, meant to act only the part their names ascribe to them, and nothing more. We ultimately learn nothing from Morose, nor are we meant to; he is merely a tool — an important tool, but a tool nonetheless — Jonson utilizes to establish other significant conclusions elsewhere.

Thus it seems unusual that an entire class of literary figures — boy detectives — are typified by individuals whose names are emblematic of their characters. This would seem to suggest that these characters are irrelevant to the functioning of entire series that are, in fact, named for them, series that are *emblematic* of the ideal held in the boy sleuth's name. Yet in the context of the boy detective, emblematic names — such as the *Rover* Boys, Tom *Swift*, Christopher *Cool*, Don *Sturdy*, Bret *King*, Tom *Quest*, Dave *Fearless*, the *Power* Boys, and, most significant of them all, the *Hardy* Boys — both reflect more than these types of names would otherwise seemingly suggest, while still functioning as they do in other literary contexts. This is not quite a binaristic opposition — less yin and yang, and more six of one, three of another — but it is key to understanding the very nature of boy detectives themselves. For, in many ways, boy sleuths are nothing more and nothing less than what their names suggest, and this single facet of their identity has proven key to both their commercial and generic success.

The essential act of detection — of uncovering, or rediscovering, some lost truth or knowledge — is an act as old as fiction itself. Gilgamesh, in the earliest Mesopotamian epics, sought to learn the truth behind the oldest question of all — the meaning of life — when he journeyed the far reaches of the world to seek out Utnapishtim and pursue his own desire for immortality. His quest for immortality involved, in a roundabout way, tracking down witnesses, taking their statements, seeking out tangible clues, and sifting through all of the gathered material to reach relevant conclusions — in short, the very acts that hallmark a good detective. Literature and stories from every ancient and modern culture abound with tales of ordinary men and women thrust into extraordinary circumstances that require detection: Arthur must seek out the Holy Grail; Hamlet must ascertain the truth behind his father's murder; Jane Eyre must uncover the secret madwoman of Thornfield Hall; Harry Potter must determine who is trying to steal the Sorcerer's Stone. All of these famous examples represent acts of detection; all represent the essential activity of uncovering something that is unknown, or unknowable, to the seeker.

Detectives, however, are a much more recent literary construct. The notion of a character whose main, functional literary identity is predicated on this notion of discovering truth — who acts, as it were, as a full-time truth seeker — elevated the act of detection from merely something characters *did* to a type of subjectivity that defined the characters themselves. The detective genre is "directed at resolving contradictions that emerge between personal desire and social law, between the individual and the collective, in short, in the archetypal conflict between nature and culture" (Ibarra 412). The detective functions within this conflict as "a model of subjectivity released within a contrived but meaningful environment ... [acting as a] symbol for certain perplexities of the social" (Ibarra 413.) What is encoded within all this is that it truly is the *villain* who enacts the generic codes of the detective novel; it is the villain's "personal desire" — the motive for committing the crime that establishes the genre — that generates the proper auspices for the genre of the work itself. The job of the detective — the very reason for his/her subjectivity — is to mediate these personal desires and bring them back into the fold of the social will. In most significant ways, this renders the protagonist less imperative to the tale than the antagonist. Without the antagonist villain, there would be need for the detective sleuth; without crime, there would be no mystery to solve.

This relationship between villain and detective is key to understanding the nature of the detective genre as a whole. For while the genre itself rests on the actions of the villain, the reader is generally asked to identify with the actions of the sleuth, and not the scoundrel. In essence, we are being asked to identify and adhere to social norms and conventions, even at the peril of our own individual will and desires. Detective tales are stories of social conformity, where the discursive element is tracked down and purged and the social order restored. The fact that detectives are able to comprehend these social discursives might unnerve us if they were not so keenly on the side of law and, more significantly, order.

Hence the role of the detective lends itself to a flat representation, to a character whose purpose is all that is needed to understand his or her subjectivity. This is likely why authors have been crafting detectives with odd or unusual quirks or character features as cynosure to their fashioned identities since the emergence of the figure. These more peculiar aspects of their characterizations are designed to achieve dynamism. Thus Sherlock Holmes has his cocaine and his violin; Hercule Poirot his mustaches; Miss Marple her fussy Victorian ways; Nero Wolfe his gluttony. Today's detectives are no different: Janet Evanovich's Stephanie Plum is a former underwear saleswoman turned bounty hunter with bad hair, a reformed prostitute for a partner, a crazed gun-toting grandmother, and a nasty habit of getting every car she has ever owned blown up. A character like Stephanie is, in fact, the sum product of her quirks, perhaps because the true defining aspect of her subjectivity — the act of detection — does not lend itself to any sort of well-rounded fashioning in the first place. Hence adult detective figures today are an endless parade of odd traits and unusual habits; as the song says, "you gotta have a gimmick."

This, however, is not the case with most juvenile detectives, and especially boy sleuths, who have embraced the flat dictates of their detective subjectivity and rejected the eccentric characterizations of their adult detective colleagues. In juvenile series literature, quirks are for sidekicks: the main detectives are always stalwart, brave, stolid, and true, or, to put it another way, Hardy, Fearless, Sturdy, and Cool. This may have something to do with the origins of the figure itself. Adult sleuths are the by-product of late eighteenth century gothic fiction and adventurer's tales; their earliest forebear, Edgar Allan Poe's C. Auguste Dupin, the very model for the Gold Age gentleman detective, solved his crimes with a hyper-developed intellect and an imagination that allowed him to project himself into the mind of the criminal. Like his successor Holmes, Dupin was so good at observing people and understanding the psychology of crime and human behavior that he could seemingly read an individual's mind and presage what that person would or would not do. All adult detective fictions are, in many ways, a response to, or a redaction of, Poe's Dupin, from Conan Doyle to Christie to even modern takes on the detective like the popular television franchise *CSI*, whose famous "interior" shots, which actually show the viewer the projection of the gunman's bullet inside the human body or the breakdown of a victim's cellular tissue due to poisoning, are just a special-effects driven offshoot of Dupin's famous creative imagination. Boy sleuths, however, do not originate with Poe, and are not simply a juvenilization of these adult progenitors. Rather, the genre of the boy sleuth series was a juvenile outgrowth of the popular dime novels of the latter half of the nineteenth century. A significant progenitor of boy sleuth books were the popular tales of Horatio Alger, Jr., who popularized boys' and girls' "rags to riches" tales. The Alger hero, a boy who, through "hard work and belief in American ideals," rises above his own fortunes to achieve material success, became the stock figure for children's novels (Axe 10). This figure was adapted around the turn of the century by Edward Stratemeyer, founder of the famous Stratemeyer Syndicate, and others. John Axe believes that "Edward Stratemeyer deserves the credit he gets for inventing the modern concept of juvenile series fiction" (10). This modern concept still hearkened to the American ideals of the Alger books, but now, the heroes were usually from a middle or upper-class background. Thus they had access to new technologies and transportation devices (such as automobiles, airplanes, and speedboats) and were not generally hampered by a lack of financial resources. In many ways, twentieth-century boys' series books were the direct progeny of the Alger series, in that these books seemed to take place after the trials and tribulations of the "rags to riches" story were concluded. Now financially secure and part of the larger material and social continuum, the boys could have adventures limited only by their roles as pseudo-adults and the social mores contained within the genre itself.

Boys' and girls' sleuthing stories, in general, are designed to uphold the status quo and confirm patriarchal American values. Boy sleuth books create characters that reflect the best in boys of their time: hard-working, socially conscious, justice-oriented young men who work to right wrongs, restore order, and maintain civil peace in their hometowns and abroad. This is all reflective of the flat subjectivity that hallmarks a true detective; most boy sleuths never alter from this identity, and thus never change. As such, boy detective texts are robustly self-conscious of their genres; genre is both the means through which the boy sleuths interact with their world and their reason for said interaction. These sleuths always long for mystery and adventure; when one ends, they consciously cannot wait for another to begin. In many ways, boy sleuths are sleuths first and boys second; they live to detect, and the act of detection, in turn, is what has given them life.

This obsession with genre creates a formulaic pattern for the books, one that Stratemeyer himself had keenly constructed as part of Syndicate practice. Critics have long noted that Stratemeyer Syndicate books were based on a "safe and sane" formula that the would eventually launch dozens of successful children's series, including the Rover Boys, the Bobbsey Twins, Bomba the Jungle Boy, the Dana Girls, Nancy Drew and the Hardy Boys (Herz 12). The formula was codified in 1899 with the inception of the Rover Boys series, and has been simply described as "good mystery and lots of action, with some educational material" (Herz 8). While the "educational material" could be information about the places the characters visited or the objects encountered during the story, the "action" was always to be "tension without violence" (Herz 12). In the series, "tension is created through the *possibility* that something catastrophic may happen" (Herz 12). It was considvered vital that "the books contained nothing prurient or off-color, and even the sanitized 'violence' involved no blood. It is true that the boys and the villains repeatedly got tied up, hit on the head, or nearly drowned, and that they tumbled down cliffs or fell through trapdoors, but they never died brutal deaths ... by the standards of the late twentieth century, the series books were remarkably tame and included no tobacco and not the slightest hint of sex, even on the part of the villains" (Greenwald 36). Ultimately, the books were intended to reflect "good, wholesome adventure and suspense" (Herz 13). More than one hundred years later, this formula has remained relatively intact, and even current boy sleuth series in print tend to uphold its values.

One perhaps unforeseen result from establishing such a successful formula was the notion that the characters within the Syndicate's books must also adhere to the rigid, essentialist confines of the series' formula as well. The heroes and heroines of Stratemeyer works had to be figures who could reasonably be expected to fulfill the dictates of the Stratemeyer formula. This is perhaps the most significant factor in the fashioning of the boy detective's literary subjectivity. Yet, in many ways, this flies in the face of how protagonist identity is generally viewed and constructed. Paul Smith, for example, argues that identity is always created or fashioned in opposition to some other:

> The "subject" is generally considered epistemologically as the counterpart to the phenomenal object and is commonly described as the sum of sensations, or the "consciousness," by which and against which the exter-

nal world can be posited. That is to say, the subject as the product of traditional western philosophical speculation, is the complex but nonetheless unified locus of the constitution of the phenomenal world. In different versions the "subject" enters a dialectic with the world as either its product or its source, or both. In any case, the "subject" is the bearer of consciousness that will interact with whatever the world is taken to consist in [xxvii].

Smith adds, "The human species is not prone to think of itself except in some version of that opposition" (xxviii). David Morley and Kevin Robins are a little more specific than Smith: "[I]dentity must be defined, not by its positive content, but always by its relation to, and differentiation from, other [identities]" (10). Thus Smith and Morley and Robins argue that what is essential in fashioning subjectivity is not what a figure stands for, but rather, what a figure is against, or, on some perverse level, who a character is *not*. This suggests a richness and complexity of subjectivity that is clearly lacking in a boy detective who, seemingly, is often little more than what his name would suggest. If a character is supposed to be viewed by the reader as being essentially "hardy," for example, how does this fashion a subjectivity — a protagonist identity — necessary to sustain over eighty years of publishing success?

I realize it is something of a *reductio ad absurdum* to suggest that the Hardy boys are nothing more than "hardy," just as it is ridiculous to suggest that the fashioning of literary identities is always given such due consideration as Smith implies. And yet, in many ways, both Smith and the construct of the emblematic name present useful methodologies for interpreting and comprehending the boy detective identity. In reducing such series to a stock formula, the Stratemeyer Syndicate has established only two key personages necessary to populate boy detective texts — the protagonist and the antagonist. The result is that such stories are set up as a continuing parade of solitary oppositional relationships, namely the boy sleuth(s) versus the villain(s). All other relationships — familial, fraternal, romantic — work only to enhance the primary relationship between the detective and his foe. Thus social outings always lead to clues, and family vacation destinations become the coincidental hideout of a nefarious gang of rogues or thieves. For the Hardy boys, their father, Fenton Hardy, is often the source of a case; he acts, first and foremost, as the purveyor of mystery and not as a paternal figure, since boy sleuths such as the Hardys are usually well beyond needing supervision in any parental sense of the word. Parents provide mysteries and those things boy sleuths lack that can aid in solving mysteries — usually financial resources. Friends assist with detection — they can be helpers, acting as lookouts or tailing suspects, or they can be victims, the initial source of the difficulty, but the relationship only extends as far as the mystery does. In many instances, after the case is solved, the friend is never heard from again. In other instances, where a group of friends are reoccurring figures in the series, they will only appear again when mystery rears its head. As for girlfriends, as Mark Connelly has pointed out, boy detectives are generally "sexless" individuals (140). When they do have girlfriends, their presence is only designed to reassure the reader of the normative sexuality of the boy detective; their appearances are usually quite brief, designed to "provide moral support ... and display the widely accepted sex roles" generally found in boy detective narratives (Connelly 142).

Thus the most significant figures found in boy detective narratives, other than the sleuths themselves, are the villains. These antagonists are, by design, shallow, flat figures who exist only to disrupt the social order and then be detained by the series protagonist. Unsurprisingly, they remain generally interchangeable, usually motivated by base profit, and are always caught in the end. And yet, through their sheer acts of villainy, through their personal motivations and selfish desires, the series' criminals often enact a grander sense of subjectivity than the sleuths do. The villains act as men sometimes do; they want, they need, they feel desire: desire for things, desire for power, desire for prestige or money or revenge. It is these selfish acts that constitute the only real character development in any boy sleuth book. Perhaps most telling, series villains almost never have emblematic names. It is true that their names often denote their supreme villainy; no one would ever mistake men named Vilnoff (from the Hardy Boys mystery *The Sinister Sign-Post*) or Long Shadow (from the Rick Brant Science-Adventure Story *The Caves of Fear*) or Dr. Death (from the Christopher Cool TEEN Agent adventure *Mission: Moonfire*) of being a proverbial "Boy Scout." Yet even the individualistic, identificatory nature of their names is telling; while their names mark them as villains, they also allow them to stand out from the rest of the book's crowd because no one else is so marked. The books' antagonists are created, in fact, as Smith suggests — namely, in opposition to someone else, in this case, everyone else in the book in general and the boy sleuth in particular. Thus the series' authors are careful never to mark their antagonists as too interesting; they are villains, and nothing more, but their villainy makes them more well-rounded than the boy sleuth himself.

Still, the subjectivity of series antagonists is as wanting as that of the protagonists. Nevertheless, as characters created in opposition to such undeveloped subjectivities, there is no need for boy sleuths to develop a dynamism beyond what their last names entail. As long as they balance the villainy of the series antagonist, they serve their formulaic purpose. Complicating the sleuth would only complicate the formula, something that would be seen as antithetical to the sleuthing and commercial success of the boy detective himself (at least until quite recent times.)

Thus the figure of the boy sleuth emerges quite early on, a subjectivity fully if perhaps ill formed: boy sleuths are young, healthy, athletic, and strong, physically and mentally fit. They capably represent the mid-century American values of Mom, Old Glory, and apple pie. They possess an "aw, shucks" charm that enables them to successfully navigate the world they inhabit, both logistically and temporally. They are smart but not overly intellectual; they are technologically savvy and highly mobile, embracing the latest in vehicular innovation, whatever it may be (automobile, motorcycle, motorboat, airplane.) According to Fred Erisman, technology in boys' series literature is designed to proffer "the picture of American youth as mechanically competent" (Erisman 14). Erisman adds that technology and a technical education were ways to become "universally acknowledged and respected" (Erisman 15). Competent? Respected? These are qualities reflected in all boy detectives. Or, to put it another way, boy sleuths clearly are Swift, Sturdy, Hardy, Cool young men.

Of course, not all boy sleuths have emblematic names. Yet those who don't still have names that are abbreviated (usually monosyllabic), powerful, and masculine. Sleuths and adventurers like Rick Brant, Ken Holt, and Ted Scott embody the same characteristics as their emblematically-named brethren, and their characterizations are similarly flat. Yet I hope I am not seeming dismissive of the boy sleuth's subjectivity. Far from it; indeed, there is something utterly heroic about being so devoted to the values of social justice and standing in such firm opposition to villainy that everything else — all other relationships and interests — fall by the wayside. Boy sleuths have, in most instances, even eschewed aging, even avoided that final transcending act of actually reaching adulthood, in order to forestall college, occupation, marriage, responsibility — all in the name of pursuing not fun or frivolity, but justice. In some very real way, I am reminded of Michel Foucault's construct of subjectivity and exomologesis. A conceptualization of the self that is bound in self-contemplation, exomologesis "designates an act meant to reveal both a truth and the subject's adherence to that truth; to do the exomologesis of one's belief is not merely to affirm what one believes but to affirm the fact of that belief; it is to make the act of affirmation an object of affirmation, and hence authenticate it either for oneself or with regard to others" (81–82). An act of faith, exomologesis creates a process of disclosing and comprehending an individual or subject's sense of self-identification. The key aspect here is meant to hinge on Foucault's equilibrium between the concept of knowing one's self (revealing a truth) and accepting and embracing that self (adherence to that truth). For Foucault, it is not enough to simply *be*; it is just as important to embrace the act of *being* and the *being* crafted by said act. Boy detectives are, in many ways, an extreme vision of exomologesis. Not only are they what their names suggest they are, they embrace this seeming dichotomy; by embracing their names, they are emblems of themselves and of the best in their own society as well.

Though boy detectives predate their female counterparts, and though girl sleuths were not specifically created in opposition to their male forbears, understanding the nature of subjectivity in the girl sleuth can be advantageous to aid in further comprehending the nature of subjectivity in the boy sleuth. This is partly because girl sleuths have been more commercially and critically successful than boy detectives; however, it is also because girl sleuths must also navigate their complex relationships to their own gender. Women in mid-century America, the height of the girl sleuth phenomenon, were obviously more socially disenfranchised than their male counterparts; likewise, their appeal and their construct differed from boy detectives because of the hurdles and advantages their gender created. In the companion book to this study, *Nancy Drew and Her Sister Sleuths: Essays on the Fiction of Girl Detectives*, I describe the identity formation of girl sleuths as being based on a series of contradicting notions that suggested a tension between the inherent "girl" sleuth and the womanhood she is on the verge of attaining but will never quite reach:

> Girl sleuths are fearless but cautious; they are intelligent but undereducated; they are bold but decorous; they are physical yet cerebral; they are unbound yet always contained. Girl sleuths navigate the world of adults with the greatest of ease; police chiefs flock to them for aid, and criminals are generally subdued with a minimum of fuss and muss. However, they remain ever young, always eager to attend a dance or go to the malt shop with a "special" friend. Girl sleuths are impossibly feminine, perfectly appointed and impeccably dressed, yet they are downright feminist, barging through barriers that their adult female counterparts would not get through for decades to come. She enjoys a cadre of loyal friends but often prefers to act alone, saving the denouement of the mystery solely for herself ["Introduction" 2].

Thus the girl sleuth has often been described critically as a forever girl, a feminist figure who at her heights nonetheless embodies the full zenith and potentiality of girlhood (a condition I once labeled "hegemonical girlhood," an apt moniker for the girl sleuth figure herself) ("Configuring" 37). This tension between her "girlness" and womanhood denotes the popularity of the figure; she received much of the benefits of being a progressive, mid-century female without the crushing social conscriptions that accompanied it. Ultimately, girl sleuths are neither "girls" nor "women," and yet, in many ways, they are both.

Boy sleuths, on the other hand, must delicately balance boyhood *and* manhood; rather than being both man and boy, they fall somewhere in the nether regions between boyhood and manhood. Generally, as white, middle-class (or higher) young males they stand on the cusp of full-fledged patriarchy, looking in to the promised land that will someday be their domain. This creates both a privileged class of individuals, whose freedoms, on the surface, far outrank those of their female colleagues, yet also individuals who already feel the full oppression of the social conscriptions of adulthood and masculinity. Whereas girl sleuths can forever be girls, boy sleuths must begin their career on the cusp of manhood; as such, their behavior is far more scrutinized, and rigid social conformity becomes a natural part of their varying endeavors. This is seen in the fact that many girl sleuths tend to work alone: Nancy Drew, Cherry Ames, Vicki Barr, Judy Bolton, Trixie Belden and their like may have many friends who share in their cases, but it is the girl sleuth who takes credit for solving the mystery. Even her series is eponymously named only for her. Boy sleuths, on the other hand, share their adventures more readily with peer groups; they practice their male social interaction as a furtherance of the adult ideals that now creep into every facet of their existence. Mysteries solved with chums are preparation for further careers in the world, in business, law, medicine, or politics, areas dominated by men in mid-century America. Thus many boy detectives work in teams: the Hardy Boys most famously, but also the Power Boys and the Three Investigators, and numerous other boys series featured groups, including the Rover Boys, the Motor Boys, the Radio Boys, the Racer Boys, the Fairview Boys, and the X Bar X Boys, just to name a few. Even those series that focus on an individual boy hero, such as Rick Brant or Ken Holt, feature secondary characters that are often as important as the titular character himself; fans of each series could not imagine Rick without trusty pal Don "Scotty" Scott, and Sandy Allen was as integral to the Ken Holt series as its eponymous hero. In the Christopher Cool juvenile spy series, Chris' partner Geronimo Johnson is so vital to the action that, at times, the narrative is told from his perspective; despite the solitary nature of the name of the series, the series really features two espionage agents, not one.

One interesting result of this "practiced manhood" is the general avoidance of adolescence altogether. Unlike their female counterparts, boy detectives seem to transition from post-pubescence directly onto the cusp of adulthood, all in an effort to avoid adolescence. By doing this, they eschew the hallmarks of American male adolescence: developmental sexuality, explorations with and understanding of the nature of violence, the pressures of rigid gender constructions, social awkwardness, uncontrollable hormones and urges, maturing forms and bodies, isolation, and the navigation of the group/pack mentality. Any of these would work to both complicate the subjectivity of the boy sleuth (thus complicating the emblematic nature of his last name) as well to humanize, or make more dynamic, the figure. This is anathematic to the construct of the series formula. To avoid this, boy sleuths emerge from a protected cocoon of childhood on the verge of fully fledged American male adulthood. This can be seen in sleuths ranging from the very young Encyclopedia Brown, who is still technically a child, to the Hardy boys themselves. All of them achieve, through the act of detection, a level of social responsibility and privilege that is usually attained only through the successful completion of adolescence without having to actually traverse the dangerous and discomfiting waters of transitional youth. For most subjectivities, complications, whether internal or external, create character growth. Yet boy detectives avoid complications in favor of plain conflict. Heralding only an unadorned "man versus man" sensibility of narrative structure allows a boy sleuth series to craft figures that are fully formed only through that very conflict in the first place. This creates figures with enormous and unique privilege: all the benefits of surviving the teen years without the messy acne and psychological scars. Yet rather than elect to exercise their privilege for their own gains, boy sleuths choose to work for law and order, embodying a man's role (usually better than the fully fledged male adult law enforcement officials in the series) while still navigating a boy's world (the first brushes with sexuality, economic freedom and responsibility, violence, the larger community around them). It is this post-pubescent/cusp of adulthood shift that truly hallmarks the figure of the boy detective. Though unhampered by traditional roles to the extent the girl sleuth is, the boy sleuth must still balance boyhood and manhood, pleasing parents and embracing patriarchy, scheduling sleuthing/spying activities and first dates, balancing government spy work with harmless soda shop romances. Ultimately, the boy sleuth is neither man nor boy, and yet, he must enact both roles on varying occasions, and thus be able to successfully navigate both temporal subjectivities while truly never belonging to either one.

This brings us back to names, to the earnestness of the appellative in the boy sleuth series that reflects the nature of the series itself, and to the search for subjectivity. For indeed, what unites the various essays in this collection is the search for a boy sleuth identity, for a fuller picture of this rich and flat literary construct. This quest begins with Larry T. Shillock's "A

Hardy Boys' Identity Narrative and *The Tower Treasure*." In his essay, Shillock continues exploring the notion of formula in the most famous boy detective series of all, examining the relationship between the boys and their father and the formation of identity that results from identifying both with and against the paternal figure (and, in some larger extent, the patriarchy as a whole.) This thread is continued by C. M. Gill in "Hardy Camaraderie: Boy Sleuthing and Male Community in the Hardy Boys Mysteries." Gill explores the relationship between maleness and the juvenile mystery, expanding upon notions of sociality and male "bonding" in the series. For Gill, male identity hinges upon achieving a social group that reflects one's values, beliefs, and activities; it is, in some ways, the essence of exomologesis as practiced by those who reflect the subjectivity of the boy sleuth himself.

The Hardy Boys series is, of course, the epitome of the boy detective story, and thus it is no surprise that considerations of these works dominate the first half of this collection. Christopher Schaberg examines the ways in which airports can disrupt subjectivity by creating "uncertain," oft transitioning spaces that can also render the subject of the text uncertain as well. "Terminal Immaterial: The Uncertain Subject of the Hardy Boys Airport Mysteries" demonstrates a limitation, then, to the emblematic nature of boy sleuth identity; setting, which often seems wholly incidental and yet utterly significant to the juvenile detective, can imprint its own strictures on even the firmest of literary fashionings. Brian Taves concludes this section of the collection by recounting the history of the Hardy Boys series on film. Though never the subject of major motion pictures (unlike their female counterpart Nancy Drew) the Hardy boys have been adapted for television in five significant incarnations, and in "Strategies of Adaptation: The Hardy Boys on Television," Taves examines the ways in which these varying adaptations altered subjectivity and, perhaps just as interestingly, impacted the future fashioning of America's most famous boy sleuths.

Of course, the figure of the boy detective pre-dates the Hardy boys, and as such, the emblematic nature of his subjectivity was also in formation (if not fully developed) from the earliest incarnations of the boy sleuth as well. Elizabeth Blum looks at one such figure, Tom Swift, and examines his relationships to nature in "Natural Detective Work: Ideas About Nature in the Early Tom Swift Books." In exploring Gilded Age and Progressive Era attitudes about the natural world, Blum challenges the identity-marker of a boy sleuth who is determined to conquer and commercialize the world around him. She questions the source of his values, an important query as it relates to understanding the nature of the sleuth himself. Fred Erisman also examines the question of identity and values in the boy sleuth though, in this case, Erisman finds much to celebrate in the boy sleuth figure. His essay, "Tim Murphy: Superhero Without a Cape," suggests aspects of the superhero identity made popular in the later 1930s can be found in earlier series like Tim Murphy. Erisman explores notions of shifting subjectivities (i.e., the "secret" identity) while examining the values inherent to early boys' series like Tim Murphy and those that succeeded him.

The 1960s saw a resurgence of interest in the boy sleuth. However, not all new works about him reflected commonly-held notions of emblematic subjectivity. Famed children's author Astrid Lindgren, for example, complicates the identity of the boy detective by casting as her sleuthing protagonist a figure marginalized by society. Charlotte Beyer, in "Adventures and Affect: The Character of the Boy Detective and Orphan in Astrid Lindgren's *Rasmus and the Tramp*," explains that by using the character of Rasmus, a runaway orphan boy, as the protagonist sleuth, Lindgren is beginning to complicate the otherwise static identity of the boy detective-figure itself. Other 1960s series also took unique approaches to the subjectivity of the boy sleuth. Alan Pickrell, in his essay "The Power of Three: Alfred Hitchcock's Three Investigators Series," shows that in the famous Three Investigators series it takes all three detectives—Jupiter Jones, Pete Crenshaw, and Bob Andrews—to make one idealized boy sleuth subjectivity. In splitting up the "perfect" boy sleuth, the series seems to suggest the impossibility of such a figure actually existing, and thus utilizes three separate characters to make what Pickrell labels one complete whole. My own essay, "Clashing Genres: (No) Sex and (No) Violence in the Christopher Cool, TEEN Agent Series," likewise complicates the relationship between identity and the boy sleuth. Like Schaberg, who notes that setting can disrupt the nature of the boy detective's subjectivity, I explore here how genre can do the same. The Christopher Cool series blends aspect of the boy sleuth series and spy genre; if on the surface these two genres seem to have much in common, in reality their differences caused great conflict within the books as the series tries to maintain the auspices of both, failing to do either capably or well.

Still, while the three previous examples complicate the boy sleuth identity, they do not entirely disrupt or displace it. Beyer demonstrates that Rasmus is, in fact, the ideal boy sleuth; it is only those around him, who judge him by his social class, who cannot always see this. Pickrell may argue that it now takes three individual sleuths to make one whole boy detective identity, but the end result is a success, commercially and critically; subjectivity, while splintered, is still honored. As for the Christopher Cool series, it is ultimately the dictates of the Syndicate "formula" and the emblematic, iconographic nature of the boy sleuth himself that dooms the series; the tension between the conflicting genres cannot be resolved in part because of the intractable nature of the boy sleuth's identity. Truly, it is not until post-modern explorations of the boy sleuth that this subjectivity is really challenged, though even then it is only shaken and not destroyed. Nicola Allen is the first to explore this concept in her essay "'The Perfect Hero for His Age': Christopher Boone and the Role of Logic in the Boy Detective Narrative." In an examination of Mark Haddon's *The Curious Incident of the Dog in the Night-Time*, Allen explores how the book's protagonist's Asperger's syndrome impacts his subjectivity as boy sleuth, suggesting that it truly affects the way readers look at his boy-ness, and not his detective-ness, which is actually enhanced by his disability. Thus Allen suggests that disrupting boy sleuth subjectivity may truly begin with disrupting the boy and not the sleuth. Likewise, John Finlay Kerr explores several postmodern takes on the figure in "Has the World Outgrown the Classic Boy Detective?" In his essay, Kerr explores Haddon's work, Joe Meno's *The Boy Detective Fails*, and the updated versions of the Hardy Boys series to explore how a post-modern society views an emblematic subjectivity like that of the boy detective. Ultimately, Kerr seems to conclude that while we can no longer imagine the classical boy sleuth existing in our time, we still — "secretly," to use his word — wish they did.

And yet why not? Cast forever as the eternal prince, suffused with the nobility and privilege that the moniker suggests, boy detectives remain the inheritors of the kingdom. Though they are, as the title "prince" suggests, not quite ready to ascend the throne to full-fledged manhood, they remain forever young and forever questing, rescuing fair damsels, slaying heartless beasts, and bringing countless scoundrels and villains to justice. Perhaps the great achievement of the boy sleuth is the very nature of his existence itself, the simple fact that he is what the emblematic nature of his name suggests: Hardy, Daring, Sturdy, Fearless, and Cool. As the old maxim poses, what's in name? For a boy detective, the answer is — just about everything.

Notes

1. Emblematic criticism has generally fallen out of favor amongst academic circles as being too limiting a field, save for in restricted ways regarding sixteenth- and seventeenth-century literature. This is interesting because boy detectives have, as well, fallen out of favor, and certainly the emblematic nature of their names resonates the "old-fashioned" construction of their subjectivities.

Works Cited

Axe, John. *All About Collecting Boys' Series Books*. Grantsville, MD: Hobby House Press, 2002.
Blaine, John. *The Caves of Fear*. New York: Grosset & Dunlap, 1951.

Connelly, Mark. *The Hardy Boys Mysteries, 1927–1979: A Cultural and Literary History*. Jefferson, NC: McFarland, 2008.
Cornelius, Michael G. "Configuring Identity and Flights of Fancy in the Vicki Barr, Flight Stewardess Series." *Clues* 27.1 (2009): 33–48.
_____. "Introduction: The Mystery of the 'Moll Dick.'" Eds. Michael G. Cornelius and Melanie E. Gregg. *Nancy Drew and Her Sister Sleuths: Essays on the Fiction of Girl Detectives*. Jefferson, NC: McFarland, 2008. 1–11.
Dixon, Franklin W. *The Sinister Sign-Post*. New York: Grosset & Dunlap, 1936.
Erisman, Fred. *Boys' Books, Boys Dreams, and the Mystique of Flight*. Fort Worth: Texas Christian University Press, 2006.
Foucault, Michel. *Ethics: Subjectivity and Truth*. Ed. Paul Rabinow. Trans. Robert Hurley et al. New York: The New Press, 1994
Ibarra, Peter R. "Dislocating Moral Order and Social Identity in Cinematic Space: The Inverted Detective Figure in 'Tightrope' and 'Cruising.'" *The Sociological Quarterly* 39.3 (Summer 1998): 409–433.
Lancer, Jack. *Mission: Moonfire*. New York: Grosset & Dunlap, 1967.
McGrath, Juliet. "James Shirley's Uses of Language." *Studies in English Literature* 6.2 (1966): 323–339.
Morley, David, and Kevin Robins. "Spaces of Identity: Communications Technologies and the Reconfiguration of Europe." *Screen* 30 (1989): 10–34.
The Oxford English Dictionary. Oxford: Oxford University Press, 1987, 2007.
Smith, Paul. *Discerning the Subject*. Minneapolis: University of Minnesota Press, 1988.

1

A Hardy Boys' Identity Narrative and *The Tower Treasure*

LARRY T. SHILLOCK

> *A literary work ... predisposes its audience to a very specific kind of reception by announcements, overt and covert signals, familiar characteristics, or implicit allusions. It awakens memories of what was already read, brings the reader to a specific emotional attitude, and with its beginning arouses expectations for the "middle and end," which can then be maintained intact or altered, reoriented, or even fulfilled ironically in the course of the reading according to specific rules of the genre or type of text.*
> — Hans Robert Jauss

Few words are more insulting to modern authors than "formulaic." To slur someone's work in this way implies that it was somehow made by an assembly line rather than a craftsperson. While Romantic originality is relevant, even in these "po-mo" times, it is less ascribable to authors who create a literary series in an established genre, since making an enduring formula often requires writers to prize design over innovation. At base, such a formula must be concrete enough — in its characters, relationships, and settings — to generate "like stories" over time; it must then be flexible enough so that each new narrative derives and marks some distance from the originating formula. Readers trade up from earlier books in a series to later ones — thereby making the series *serial* to them — precisely when authors know their audience's horizon of expectations (Jauss) and work in concert with it. Given as much, it is not surprising that the Nancy Drew and Hardy Boys mystery series are formulaic; rather, it is surprising that such formulae can be sustained for any appreciable time. Today, as the success of the Harry Potter books and the ascendance of *Twilight* hysteria indicate, readers crave continuity, finding in their relations to characters an uncanny index of themselves — sans magic and vampires, of course. It would thereby be useful if scholars could show why young readers identify with characters and tell which aspects in the design of a series enable identification to occur. The Hardy Boys franchise is a logical starting point for such a re-telling. Young readers can expect to find in its mysteries a formulaic conflation of Oedipal anxiety, as felt by Frank and Joe Hardy, amateur detectives, and Oedipal plotting. To interpret the Hardy Boys series using psychoanalysis and narrative theory is to risk treating its embedded critique of adulthood as a universal rather than local phenomenon. It is a risk work taking, however, since criticisms of adults joined to a plot type linked to Oedipus, the first detective, structure *The Tower Treasure* and later volumes in the series. Over time, the Hardy Boys formula instantiates its own masterplot: a father-and-sons double plot that treats the ambivalence associated with love and the perils of identity formation as among its first principles.

The Mystery of Father-Love

The story of how the Hardy Boys series came to be written has been well told. Edward Stratemeyer, its originator, was a successful, turn-of-the-century writer of children's books. Striking out on his own in 1906, he formed a syndicate that hired writers to produce genre stories following his models and plots. The writers were paid piece-meal, and even the most successful ones worked relatively anonymously in a system of Stratemeyer's devising. Following Stratemeyer's outlines, Leslie McFarlane wrote the first three books in the Hardy Boys series and thereby contributed to its formula. Despite helping to establish the series, McFarlane and his subsequent work were credited to Franklin W. Dixon, a pseudonym. Stratemeyer's approach was efficient, timely, responsive to readers' interests — and successful. As Robert L. Crawford observes, "The result was a torrent of books and series; by 1930, tens of millions of books had been published representing over 700 titles" (10). That success was due to giving young readers what they sought — excitement and mobility — rather than what Meghan O'Rourke calls the "Sunday-school moralism" that reflected what adults considered to be proper juvenile literature (123).

The first book in the Hardy Boys series, *The Tower Treasure* (1927), begins notably. McFarlane drops readers into a familiar discussion between Frank, the dark-haired elder brother, and his fair-haired brother Joe. The boys are reminiscing about an idea they gave their father that enabled him to solve a forgery case. Fenton Hardy, "an internationally famous detective who had made a name for himself in the years he had spent on the New York police force and who was now, at the age of forty, handling his own practice," used his sons' insight but refuses to take their dream of becoming detectives seriously (2). Their mother, Laura Hardy, is even less enamored with their ambition. As Frank remarks, "She comes out plump and plain and says she wants one of us to be a doctor and the other a lawyer" (3). Like their father, the boys want to make "a name" for themselves — securing, that is, an identity as detectives — by solving a case of their own. To do so they must overcome parental resistance, a fact signaled by how often and how passionately the boys speak of their dream. Indeed, seven of the first ten paragraphs in the book are about that ambition, an obsessive emphasis that works against the opening chapter and its responsibility to exposition. In all, Frank and Joe are anxious "to follow in the footsteps of their father," bring criminals to justice and, in Frank's words, "show that Fenton Hardy's sons are worthy of his name. Oh, boy, but what wouldn't I give to be as famous as dad!" (2, 4). Here a desire to become a detective evinces considerable egocentrism. It also signals an identity conflict, since making a name one's own can refer to reputation — to being "as famous as dad" — but also to creating a new relation to the name ascribed to a boy at birth. Such a relation extends to separating from the father whose last(ing) name one carries.

The problem facing the boys, beyond parental resistance, relates to age and opportunity. Frank and Joe can talk about detecting but, at sixteen and fifteen years old, they are mere high school students — and impatient ones at that. "Perhaps Dad may give us a real case some time," Frank muses. "Some time! I want to be on a real case *now*!" Joe retorts (5). His wish begins to be granted after a driver almost runs their motorcycles over and then, further along the road, wrecks the car. The unknown man escapes the accident unharmed and flees the scene by stealing a yellow roadster owned by Chet Morton, a friend of the boys. A crime spree takes shape when he tries to rob the Bayport steamboat office at gunpoint, only to be frightened off when a customer intrudes upon the robbery.

After trying to follow the criminal, the Hardy boys return home to tell their father about the experience. When he learns that they were, in Joe's self-important word, "investigating," he replies, "in mock surprise. 'So my sons were investigating, eh? What was it? A murder? A plot to blow up the White House? A train wreck? Something big, I hope'" (34). It is hard to deny the elder Hardy his humor, since the boys are at best precocious. By contrast, "Mr. Hardy is an ideal father — strong, manly, athletic, and knowledgeable" (Connelly 8). Generous with his sons and a loving, if sometimes absent, figure, Fenton is also an idealized detective. His status is considerably higher than that of the private eyes imagined by Dashiell Hammett, Raymond Chandler, James M. Cain, and Horace McCoy during this period of American literary history. As a father-detective, therefore, Fenton is both idealized and an ego ideal.

In Freud's tripartite model of the mind, compromised of an ego, a super-ego, and an id, the ego is the center of reason and perception. It would seem to follow that self-control is centered in the ego and linked to consciousness. As Freud observes in *The Ego and the Id* (1923), however, awareness is vexed because perceptions come from the world and emotion and cannot all take form as thought. Having taken form, the thoughts which enable awareness can shift from consciousness to a state of preconscious—nearly unconscious—latency. Such a shift occurs when a perception becomes tied to words. What Freud calls "word-presentations" (10) are an unstable mix of perception, image, representation, and memory that may become available to consciousness again. Many memory traces do not re-emerge, and some change in the process of escaping repression.

The ego is charged with the task of self-control, especially in relation to the unconscious drives. Yet the ego is limited and its control of the drives are analogous, in Freud's terms, to how a rider on horseback feels when trying to "check the superior strength of the horse" (15). Matters are further complicated because the ego is divided into an ego ideal or super-ego, a part of the mind that is less firmly allied with consciousness, cathected by aggression, and tied to a child's resolution of the Oedipus complex. To say that the ego is burdened by its responsibilities is thus an understatement.

Although a great deal has been written about Freud's foundational complex, comparatively little of that discourse was actually produced by him. It is therefore best to hear how he defines "the triangular character of the Oedipus situation":

> At a very early age the little boy develops an object-cathexis for his mother, which originally related to the mother's breast and is the prototype of an object-choice on the anaclitic model; the boy deals with his father by identifying himself with him. For a time these two relationships proceed side by side, until the boy's sexual wishes in regard to his mother become more intense and his father is perceived as an obstacle to them; from this the Oedipus complex originates. His identification with his father then takes on a hostile colouring and changes into a wish to get rid of his father in order to take his place with his mother. Henceforward, his relation to his father is ambivalent; [and] it seems as if the ambivalence inherent in the identification from the beginning had become manifest [21–22].

What is important here for masculinity — beyond desire being mobile and triangulated — is that love and identification vie for a boy's attention. A boy must give up his mother love to become a youth and, later, a man, by replacing it with "either an identification with his mother or an intensification of his identification with his father" (22). In both cases, life begins with love, but it is identification that generates identity. Laura Hardy is marginal to *The Tower Treasure* and the early works in the series. Unnamed for several chapters, she seems to exist to make sandwiches so that the boys can go on long, unsupervised adventures without getting hungry. Identification with her — or with other females, in the case of girl-avoiding Joe — is little in evidence. Thus, prompted by the opening chapter, readers focus on the boys and their identity quest.

Fenton is at the center of Frank and Joe's concerns, so much so that friendships, sports, and attending school recede in importance. To say that the brothers have resolved their Oedipus complexes by intensifying their identification with him and his profession is true, and yet it understates how difficult it is to become a man. In response, *The Tower Treasure* inaugurates a model of plot that triangulates the boys' ambivalence — as excited by the too-good, too-understanding, too-unthreatening, and yet still-authoritative father — by displacing the threat to others. It does so because anxiety is in the service of identity, and Fenton is simply too loving of a father to be much of an Oedipal foil to his sons. Even at his most masterful, he excites insufficient ambivalence, and thus what Freud calls "Oedipus situations" must ramify beyond the home.

The first of these displacements occurs in relation to the criminal. Wearing (and not wearing) a red wig, which is a sign of his mobile identity, John "Red" Jackley encounters the boys on the road from Bayport to Willowville. Frank and Joe are carrying legal papers, an errand that they have mixed feelings about, since it demonstrates the confidence Fenton has in them but is not quite like being on a case. Our "errand" boys hear a car approaching at great speed and see that they and their motorcycles might be driven by it from the rutted road and over one-hundred-foot-tall cliffs. Thus aggression — in the person of an adult male — intrudes on their shared fantasy of becoming detectives. Hence the scene foregrounds identification while building to the kind of episodic climax that nineteenth-century serialized fiction made popular.

The second chapter begins with the boys, now off their bikes, immobilized and servile at the embankment's edge. As the "viciously" driven car misses them by mere inches, the driver "shouted something they could not catch at them and shook his fist" (9). Despite the treble threat posed by car, voice, and fist, Frank and Joe observe that the driver is hatless and redheaded. When, shortly thereafter, they come upon the crashed vehicle, learn of Chet's stolen roadster, and encounter Ike Harrity, an "inoffensive old chap" who works for the steamboat company and was unnerved by the near-robbery, the boys infer that one person might have done the crimes (26). Here the boys act as detectives do — moving from initial perception to investigating the crashed vehicle and on to interrogating Callie Shaw, who was also nearly hit by the man in Chet's roadster. Beyond almost killing the boys, the unknown criminal has taken a car that is the centerpiece of a friend's identity and reduced Callie, Frank's almost-girlfriend, to tears. Hence the criminal enacts an Oedipal threat to love more broadly.

The Tower Treasure represents adults in ways that will shape the series as a whole. First, as readers may quickly intuit, it isolates the Oedipal anxiety posed by a father who was once a representative of the law and displaces it onto a criminal or, in later stories, criminals. Next, it mocks adults who are peripheral to the plot but happen upon it. The first of these adults gets introduced in chapter three, just after Frank and Joe persuade Chet to join their search for his car. After returning to the wrecked car and studying it for clues, the boys encounter a "lanky old farmer" and some farmhands. A question posed by Frank — "Didn't see a yellow roadster pass here within the last hour, did you?" (19) — elicits their considerable confusion. The narrative spends three pages parodying the ineffectual men, even as the criminal widens the gap between himself and his now-stalled pursuers. The forward movement of the plot is arrested, too, as Frank waits for an answer — and to what end? The structural point is that adults do not form a coherent group. Readers know that one adult — Fenton Hardy — is exemplary. Another adult, a professional criminal, is life-threatening. And still other adults may be laughable or intrusive or both. Among the laughable ones are "Lem Billers — the laziest man in nine counties," who is baffled by Chet during an ensuing six-page set-piece; Constable Riley, who tries to resolve a conflict between a chauffeur and Billers and soon becomes "vastly puzzled" doing so; and Rocco, the Italian-American owner of a fruit stand who speaks in dialect and, in a later scene, will think a disguised clock is a ticking bomb (39, 43). Readers and characters alike must negotiate a world of such adults. For the most part, the Hardy boys move more thoughtfully through it than do their elders — precisely what the narrative predisposes its audience to think. Younger readers are thus amused and reassured even by plot points that are at odds with the plot.

Readers encounter the intrusive kind of adults when Frank, Joe, and their father interact with persons who bear upon the narrative and compete with them to shape it. Such characters synthesize traits associated with the criminal and the ineffectual adults. They are linked to the criminal because they have a symbolic authority that may enable them to solve the crime; they share with the arguing farmhands a capacity to create obstacles to the generative force of plot. The Bayport chief of police, his detective, and his constable are among those in this third category. The narrator introduces Chief Ezra Collig as "a burly, red-faced individual, much given to telling long-winded stories" (26). The chief spends most of his time in the office, often "with his feet on the desk, reading the comic papers or polishing up his numerous badges" (26). Pompous, he insists upon being the center of attention: readers see that he will interview Harrity; he will name what is and is not a clue for all concerned; he will deduce that the person who stole a yellow roadster and tried to rob the steamship office was the same man — a conclusion that the Hardy brothers arrived at more quickly. Detective Smuff and Policeman Riley attend to the chief throughout the scene, "both trying their best to look important and composed" (26). If there is a plot function associated with these inadequate foils, it could be termed "obstructing justice." To a man, they do not know that they do not know, and thus make wrong-headed decisions. Enjoying the security conferred by adulthood, they treat Frank and Joe with disdain. The chief puts the matter succinctly: "You boys don't know what you're talking about" (31).

Despite his self-satisfaction, the chief has a point. Fenton echoes part of it when, soon thereafter, he tells his sons that their "powers of observation have not been trained" (36). He follows this unflinching point by characterizing the local high school's superintendent, a man whom he has never met. His deductions amaze the boys. "You must train yourselves to be observant," Fenton counsels, "so that in time you will automatically remember little details about people you meet and places you've visited" (37). Instructive and inclusive, Fenton's speech indicates that Frank and Joe cannot simply become detectives; they must consciously school themselves in detection. Fenton, in his role as father and detective-ideal, now appears ready to help them.

Despite his expertise, Mr. Hardy does not define observation fully. He is correct about accruing and storing details; but the relation between observations and clues is more complicated in mysteries. An observation might tell detectives and readers alike something about a character or an event. A clue, by contrast, reveals an aspect of a crime. The Hardy Boys series treats clues in two main ways. There are the clues that announce themselves as such — the red wig, for instance. There are also observations that are not immediately seen as relevant; the image of the red-headed (or is that brown-haired?) criminal who tried to rob the steamboat office is this type of clue. While all clues are synecdochic, and thus signify larger units of narrative, some go more or less unobserved and get stored in memory. These observations, ideas, details, or raw events then become latent to the mind. The unconscious mulls a clue over until it escapes repression and returns to consciousness. Now at the service of the ego, the clue is thus a deferred interpretation—a prior fact that predicts future knowledge. Fenton's account shows that he lacks an understanding of what Freud called returning a "word-presentation" to awareness. Such a return is rarely automatic for the most important clues in the series.

Gratified by their father's instruction, Frank and Joe are still no nearer to solving the crime spree and becoming detectives than before. They decide to take a day off and play. While doing so, Joe, "an amateur naturalist," stumbles upon a tire track far from the nearest road (47–48). Recalling his father's instruction, he commits its tread to memory. A chance comment to Chet by him and further study among the trees reveals the stolen roadster. Elated, Chet studies his car for damage and finds none. Despite having just been instructed on the value of observation, Frank and Joe leave the work to Chet and exit the scene without looking for evidence. Returning to Bayport, the boys encounter Detective Smuff, who condescends characteristically to them and then reports that "the Tower Mansion has been robbed" (52).

Now that another serious crime has taken place—a theft of $40,000 in bonds and jewels from a locked safe—the police return to the narrative in force. Complicating matters, Hurd and Adelia Applegate, the owners of the Tower Mansion, hire Fenton. For their part, the Applegates are difficult to typify. The narrator is clear that they are rich, eccentric, and unconcerned with others' points of view. Are readers to see them, then, as quirky crime victims, or as adults who have a claim on the narrative and thus may play a role—obstructive or helpful—in its resolution? In response to the new crime and its mysteries, the plot effectively splits, with the primary investigators maintaining their own plot lines.

Mysteries are at base hero narratives and, from the first scene with Frank and Joe, *The Tower Treasure* has been clear that Fenton is that hero. Mysteries are also Oedipal narratives, insofar as they are based on a desire to know and reveal. As Teresa de Lauretis observes, "Oedipus solves the riddle, and his answer, the very meaning and content of the riddle, is—man, universal man, Oedipus therefore" (111). Despite her tortured diction, de Lauretis makes two points: first, that Oedipus becomes himself by solving a riddle posed by a monster. The act of detecting thus consolidates his authority as a speaker and a man. Secondly, his individual, gendered identity, as well as the identity of interpreters who will model themselves after him, is contingent upon "the hero as mover of the narrative, the center and term of reference and consciousness and desire" (112). If identity for boys can hinge upon intensified identification with a father, it must, following de Lauretis's psychoanalytic rereading, also hinge upon the capacity to narrate — to drive a plot forward, overcome its obstacles, solve what is elusive and mysterious about it, and then, in an act of advanced language competence, explain the events through narration.

In *Reading for the Plot: Design and Intention in Narrative*, Peter Brooks extends de Lauretis's observation by first criticizing the narratologists whose work she elucidates, since, in his terms, they have "neglected the temporal dynamics that shape narratives in our reading of them, the play of desire in time that makes us turn pages and strive toward narrative ends" (xiii). For Brooks, desire is immanent in the text, felt in the act of reading, experienced through identification, and ultimately productive of selfhood. Here his emphasis on "play" is telling. Children "play" by modeling themselves after others and thereby help to construct their own identities. A door with loose hinges has a certain serial "play," or repetitive variability, in its motion. To be in a "play" is to perform as a character and to collapse the distance between self and other. Readers, finally, "play" with their selves and worlds by reading, and writers "play" with order while writing, since the faculty of the imagination enables both parties to sympathetically project themselves into other characters' circumstances and experiences. "Reordering by narrative may therefore have as its function," J. Hillis Miller asserts, "the affirmation and reinforcement, even the creation, of the most basic assumptions of a culture about human existence, about time, destiny, selfhood, where we come from, what we ought to do while we are here, where we go — the whole course of human life" (71). For Miller, such creation is necessarily incomplete, and sense-making in the service of selfhood is vexed:

> The universality of this form of "the same in the different" in narrative has two implications. It implies that we want stories for something they can do for us, something we inexhaustibly need. It implies that this function is not performed primarily by the characters, the true-to-life setting, or even by the "theme" or "message," the "moral," but by the sequential structure of events, the plot [71].

Despite their nuanced differences, De Lauretis, Brooks, and Miller hold that self-formation is contingent upon plot and narration. It follows from them that masculine identity, seen in narrative/Oedipal terms, might be construed as a process that begins with love, becomes marked by a process of modeling one's self after others, and then changes once a boy learns to tell stories about *himself* and his circumstances that supersede the stories that a family tells about *itself* and its history. Such stories are at base serial; they tell and re-tell — often obsessively — what has happened and also imagine what might happen. Thus persons enact self-knowledge and thereby individual identity by playing at becoming detectives of the world around them — precisely the process that the Hardy Boys series presents to its legions of young readers.

The Towering Riddle of Identity

Upon being hired, Fenton invites the boys along on a visit to the Applegate residence, a "palatial" building that overlooks the bay and town "like some ancient feudal castle" (53). "Well," he says to them, "if you are so anxious to be detectives, I suppose it is as good a chance as any to watch a crime investigation from the inside" (57). Anxious is the right word, since the boys are moving into the adult domain where their father, the police, clients, and criminals hold sway, a domain at once threatening and exciting. The boy-detectives understand that they are mere observers. Hurd Applegate, however, isn't persuaded that anyone can detect for him, since he "*know*[s] who took the stuff" (58). Apparently Fenton has been hired less to solve the crime than to provide evidence for what Hurd already knows: "Henry Robinson — the caretaker. He's the man" (58). Here readers see a second crime impinge upon Frank and Joe, since, like the roadster stolen from Chet and Callie's near-accident, the new crime threatens a friend, Slim, Slim's father Henry, and his family's circumstances. The police agree with Hurd's conclusion and arrest Robinson promptly. The Hardy boys thus face a dilemma: they are situated as observers of an investigation, not as its actual detectives, but they can't just watch their friend and his family get destroyed. For his part, Slim dreams of attending college, and such dreams are to be realized, not crushed, in a series devoted to youthful readers and successful identity-formation.

Without seeking permission, the boys investigate a new, more serious crime by returning to the scene of a previous one. Their motivation is both altruistic and self-interested, at once protective of a friend's identity and devoted to their own ambitions. Frank and Joe have a "hunch" that they did a shoddy job evaluating the crime scene and its wrecked car. Thus the boys experience a return to awareness of a forgotten word-presentation, and it compels them to re-investigate. They soon find a piece of the red wig, a synecdoche of the criminal's doubled identity. Their self-interest then comes to the fore when they learn of the $1000 reward for the return of the bonds and jewels. "That's a lot of money, Joe," observes Frank. "And there's no reason why we haven't as good a chance of getting it as any one else does" (78). Actually, there are a lot of reasons — including their age, observational shortcomings, and investigative inexperience. That their father and the Bayport police force are investigating as well further reduces the odds that the boys will solve the crime first. In a flush of youthful egocentrism, Frank and Joe decide "to plug away at this affair until we get to the bottom of it" (81). When they tell Fenton their decision — again, without seeking permission — he observes that they are on their own: "But you can't ask me to help you any more than I've done. It's my case too, remember. So from now on, you are part of my opposition" (83).

As feminist psychologists have often observed, becoming a youth and, later, a man requires males to differentiate themselves from most things "feminine." At this point in the narrative, the Hardy sons are successfully — and excessively — differentiated from their mother and feminine love; now, however, they feel ambivalent about their father, since he concurs with their goal of earning the reward but has marked their relationship as competitive. Recognizing that they must best their father if they are to achieve their ambitions, the brothers see, in Frank's apt words, that "Dad sure took the wind out of our sails that time" (83). In this way, they experience the aloneness associated with male adolescence as well as the unclear pathways that will lead them to adulthood (see, e.g., Gurian).

Young readers know that parents pose obstacles to their identities, and a series that focused on stories showing powerful adults repressing youth would not interest them. They also know that parents are essential to their processes of becoming. The Hardy Boys series offers a fine solution to the real competition between fathers and sons by first providing ways for Frank and Joe to move about unimpeded by either parent. After investigating the wrecked car, the boys realize — in a second return of a memory trace — that they "didn't take much time to look around when that roadster was found," and so that is what they do (84). Investigating the scene alone produces the criminal's full wig, a hat, and a coat. When the boys share the new clues with their father, he agrees to share what he knows with them. Their portion of the plot leads to discovery; his part leads to travel. The double plot upon which the series is based thus sends the father away — out of the domestic sphere and to New York, where he interviews wigmakers and spends a week reading police files. Fenton's departure is a regression, for it returns him to the police work he did before his boys became young men. It thus gives center stage to Frank and Joe. Unsupervised, they can detect more or less unhindered, and readers are free to identify with them and not the novel's purported hero.

The double plot also speaks to a double logic that will inform the Hardy Boys series. Under its terms, the boys have several Oedipal relationships — with their father, to be sure, but also with criminals that they pursue and even the police chief and his men. The perils associated with adults are made literal when the boys, in later stories, encounter thugs who tie them up and threaten their lives, acts which signal repression, unrestrained aggression, and even death. How the series characterizes adults speaks to the boys' manifest ambivalence about the psychic struggles that youths undergo. Specifically, the series splits the father-imago into a benevolent one (Fenton) and a threatening counterpart (criminals or policemen). Fenton is shown as being "hardy" enough, as a man, for the boys to love; the criminals, as being aggressive enough to hate. Such a compromise formation displaces the boys' Oedipal hostility from their father and his unassailable authority onto what Freud, in "The Uncanny," calls the characters who comprise a "father-series" (384) — i.e., other adult males. Some of these men will be hapless ones, like the farmhands, Billers, and the police, and some will be considerably more dangerous figures, like the criminal whose shifting identity means that he is unknown and could thus be lurking anywhere.

A mobile criminal is dangerous, and so Fenton goes after him. The boys find themselves part of a fatherless household, which creates an authority gap that they can play at filling. Their Oedipal energies get turned to the less dangerous pastime of investigation, since it is unlikely that they will meet a criminal when studying prior crime scenes. Danger still remains, however, since such criminals experience being detected as a form of aggression and respond to it aggressively. Indeed, criminals protect the riddles that their actions pose and the narratives that their crimes coalesce to form from anyone's interpretation. Lawbreakers especially do not want to be revealed to the police by mere boys — the successors to Oedipus or not — and end up being jailed. Young readers struggle with their own ambivalence about adults, and so it is understandable that they identify with Frank and Joe and with the Oedipal process of detecting. That the boys traverse the public sphere freely and succeed in showing adults to be dangerous and even criminal is felt by boys and readers alike as sweet indeed.

Holding three clues, Fenton believes that it will be "but a matter of hours before he ran the owner of the red wig to earth" (97). Aptly, this particular metaphor aligns Fenton with the criminal, and his vicious driving, and reminds readers that fatherhood and detection are played for real stakes. The boys are also confident that their father will succeed. Yet Fenton does not succeed, and his overconfidence leads him to feel temporarily "defeated" (105). Only after more work than anticipated does he discover Jackley's identity. Fearing that he may have been exposed, Jackley leaves the city and leads Fenton and the police on a chase that ends with another crash. Hospitalized, he lies near death. Given the logic of a Depression-era detective series, criminals will eventually be punished, whether by a private or institutional superego or both.

The boys again revert to being boys — a tactical error. As amateur detectives, they are competing with a professional criminal, an even more professional detective, and the police; greater focus on detection is demanded of them if they are to be equal to their ambitions. Specifically, Frank and Joe fail to seize the authority — and accompanying plot line — made available by their father's absence because Frank comes under Callie's feminine influence and goes with her to visit the Robinsons, who have relocated to a poorer section of town. Generosity, not the crime spree, is now his chief concern. As a result, Fenton may solve the mystery and apprehend the criminal — eventualities that young readers might understand and even predict but would not relish. Such readers want Frank and Joe to succeed — earning a reward of their own for investing in the plot — so that their success can be read as a sign that other youth may overcome obstacles, understand "affairs" that escape the grasp of the ego, and thus accede to a name that they share but do not as yet possess. Prowess — even at the remove in which readers experience it — is allied to narrative self-affirmations.

Fenton returns to Bayport discouraged, since Jackley may die before he can be interrogated, and the police intend to speak to the thief as well. When Collig and Smuff arrive at the Hardy residence to find out what Fenton knows about the case, the detective requests that his sons be present too. Collig agrees, saying, "Can't do no good and they can't do no harm" (123). A blanket statement, the claim strips the boys of their agency, now and in the future. From Collig's adult perspective, they are incapable of affecting the case and how the police conceive of it, a doubly wrong prediction. First, the boys concoct a scheme that distracts the police so that they miss the train to their interview with Jackley. Speaking to him unimpeded, Fenton learns that the criminal was responsible for the failed robbery at the steamboat office and the successful theft at the Applegate residence. Jackley confesses to stealing the bonds and jewels and hiding them "in the old tower," which is the last thing he says before dying (143). Upon his return to Bayport, Fenton tells Laura the case is "practically solved" (142).

Frank and Joe search the old and new towers at the Applegate mansion and find nothing; a second search also fails. Hurd Applegate exults in their failure, since it affirms that his caretaker was guilty. The police agree and re-arrest Robinson. Rather than finding the stolen goods, earning the reward, and proving the innocence of their friend's father, Frank and Joe, by dallying, have made matters worse. Their father's authority is compromised too, since the police spread word that "Fenton Hardy was made to look ridiculous by believing a false confession," assertions the townspeople repeat (168). No longer great, the great detective admits to having "exhausted every line of action in this case" (179). In effect, he resigns his plotline and thus passes the mantle of detective to Frank and Joe, as they have long desired. Given the boys' false starts, readers should be predisposed to think them unequal to the task, much as the Collig did. Moreover, readers could be expected to take the plot reversal that leads to such father-failure and son-frustration personally, recognizing in it their own adolescent powerlessness. However much authors may cue readers to interpret in particular ways "by announcements, overt and covert signals, familiar characteristics, or implicit allusions," authors also conceive of reading as a domain where expectations can be "reoriented" (Jauss 23).

The boys decide to go play — to regress as their father has done before them. Mrs. Hardy "had been tolerantly amused by her son's activities in the Tower affair, but she was glad to see them return to their boyish ways" (186). The domestic sphere is where the boys belong, not the greater world of cases, police, criminals, and anxious danger. But the id of a young detective never sleeps; and so as Frank and Joe get on their motorcycles and head along the railroad and over to Chet's house, retracing part of the route that began the novel, a latent word-presentation again returns to grab the attention of their egos. Specifically, the boys recall that the Bayport and Coast line once employed Jackley. Stopped in their tracks near its tracks, they reflect on "every incident of the mysterious affair" and scan the horizon (188). Of course "affairs" are mysterious to virginal boys; as a metaphor for a case and a repetitively voiced replacement for the word "crime" in *The Tower Treasure*, they are also Oedipal at base. What Frank and Joe wish to know, working "from the inside" on the "Tower affair," is thus forbidden knowledge (81). Like Oedipus before them, they will risk their identities to solve a vexing riddle: when is an old tower not an old tower? The answer is when it is not a part of the family house that was originally robbed, but is a railroad tower adjacent to a village known as the "Junction" (202). Looking in its direction, the boys see "the spindly legs and squat bulk of a water tank, painted a bright scarlet" (189–90). The personified and eroticized source of moisture, the tank that squats in full view is in the "far distance," which is the narrative future (189). A second tower is a mere couple of hundred years away: "But this tower — one of the old style built before the modern tanks came into use — was not freshly painted" (190). It is "weather-beaten," the narrator observes, "and although the old structure had not been torn down, it was not now used" (190). Rapt, the boys stare at both structures and experience the kind of unconscious memory trace that the series will treat serially: the old tower clue must refer to the older of these two towers.

In *The Pleasure of the Text*, Roland Barthes names reading as "an Oedipal pleasure (to denude, to know, to learn the origin and the end)" and hypothesizes that "every narrative (every unveiling of the truth) is a staging of the (absent, hidden, or hypostatized) father." If that is the case even some of the time, it follows that repetition contributes to the "solidity of narrative forms" (10) — what others might call the formulae that structure popular genres. Throughout, *The Tower Treasure* offers its own variation on Oedipus and his masterplot. Driven to get to the bottom of an affair whose forbidden knowledge has remained tantalizingly out of reach, Frank and Joe seek to understand narrative itself, what Barthes calls "the origin and the end" and what readers would name as the full story of Jackley's crimes. The book of which the boys are a central part has staged the removal of the modern family's central authority: their father and Mr. Robinson. Fenton is absent, an "old structure" not in use, which leaves the terrain of detection to the boys and the hapless police. Mr. Robinson is hidden in jail, which forces his family into poverty and his son, Slim, from school and into menial labor. While chasing criminals can be dangerous, not catching them can apparently be devastating to the identity of a family too. From the beginning of the novel that begins the Hardy Boys series, Frank and Joe have sought to earn their father's approbation and prove equal to his name — without, of course, desiring to triumph over him as the police have analogously triumphed over Robinson. The truth that risks being unveiled now is that fathers, too, were once young boys and, like sons who struggle to traverse masculinity, are still vulnerable. To its credit, the Hardy Boys series looks at this monstrous truth directly. Readers looking on cannot help but be doubly anxious in the face of a double plot and its potentially double devastation of two loving fathers.

Two towers — their implied vulgar Freudianisms notwithstanding — arrest the gaze of two boys who are not easily kept in place. Frank and Joe choose the masculine old tower to search rather than the feminine new tower, despite its "scarlet" allure. Their choice dispels the anxieties of readers when, under some old boards, the brothers find a different kind of treasure, a different kind of family jewels. Elated, Joe exclaims, "*Now* I'd like to see dad tell us we're not cut out to be detectives!" He adds, "Wait til Hurd Applegate sees his bonds back. And wait til Chief Collig and Detective Smuff hear about it!" (198). The metaphor of being "cut out to be detectives" is both serial — in the sense of paper cut-outs made by children — and anxiety-provoking, since it speaks to touching and disfiguring, if not castration. When Fenton, his sons, and the Applegates bring the recovered bonds and jewels to the police station, Collig responds with disbelief and anger. The narrative, however, reserves the best response for Adelia, a shrill eccentric, who culminates the scene's criticism of adults by calling the boys "real detectives, both of them! Smart lads." Hurd adds that Frank and Joe "showed some real detective work, and I hope they grow up to follow in their father's footsteps" (206). *The Tower Treasure* thus ends as it began: ambivalently. The boys have done some "real detective work" and they may "follow in their father's footsteps" but they are still followers, not adults. In a wonderful compromise formation, the series grants them authority and success, thereby pleasing its young readers, without allowing the brothers to become what they desire to be. Thus does it give the father-and-sons masterplot both its force and future design. A "hardy" boys' identity narrative, it will henceforth enable Frank and Joe to obsessively repeat their performances as "amateur detectives," which is to say that they will continue investigating—and identifying with their father—in the service of masculine love.

WORKS CITED

Barthes, Roland. *The Pleasure of the Text*. Trans. Richard Miller. New York: Hill & Wang, 1975.
Brooks, Peter. *Reading for the Plot: Design and Intention in Narrative*. New York: Vintage, 1985.
Connelly, Mark. *The Hardy Boys Mysteries, 1927–1979: A Cultural and Literary History*. Jefferson, NC: McFarland, 2008.
Crawford, Robert L. "Rewriting the Past in Children's Literature: The Hardy Boys and Other Series." *Children's Literature Association Quarterly* 18.1 (1993): 10–12.
De Lauretis, Teresa. *Alice Doesn't: Feminism, Semiotics, Cinema*. Bloomington: Indiana University Press, 1984.
Dixon, Franklin W. *The Tower Treasure*. New York: Grosset & Dunlap, 1927.
Freud, Sigmund. *The Ego and the Id*. 1923. Trans. Joan Riviere. New York: Norton, 1962.
_____. "The Uncanny." *Collected Papers*. Vol. 4. Trans. Joan Riviere. New York: Basic, 1959. 368–407.
Gurian, Michael. *A Fine Young Man: What Parents, Mentors and Educators Can Do to Shape Adolescent Boys into Exceptional Men*. New York: Putnam, 1998.
Jauss, Hans Robert. *Toward an Aesthetic of Reception*. Trans. Timothy Bahti. Minneapolis: University of Minnesota Press, 1982.
Miller, J. Hillis. "Narrative." *Critical Terms for Literary Study*. Eds. Frank Lentricchia and Thomas McLaughlin. 2d ed. Chicago: University of Chicago Press, 1995. 66–79.
O'Rourke, Meghan. "Nancy Drew's Father: A Critic at Large." *The New Yorker* 8 Nov. 2004: 120–29.

2
Hardy Camaraderie: Boy Sleuthing and Male Community in the Hardy Boys Mysteries

C. M. Gill

Since its inception in 1927, the original Hardy Boys series has been a best-selling staple of juvenile literature. Although it was not the first series to present the boy sleuth protagonist, this particular series remains among the most famous and highly successful of such depictions within children's literature. In fact, even in the twenty-first century (over eighty years after their debut), the books continue to sell more than a million copies per year in the United States alone (Connelly 3). The ability of the books to virtually transcend time and engage generation after generation of readers is indeed remarkable. The Hardy Boys books have remained extensively read and known, their characters' names instantly recognizable by virtually all young American readers, and their titles are still widely available on bookstore shelves. The incredible power of these particular stories to remain at the forefront of the cultural consciousness points to their importance as a cultural text. Indeed, the immense and continued esteem of the books and characters is simply too compelling to ignore; clearly, the Hardy Boys are a force to be reckoned with.

Yet, in spite of this pervasive influence, there is remarkably little scholarship examining the Hardy Boys, or the figure of the boy sleuth in general. In spite of the considerable influence of the Hardys, few scholars seem interested in the boy detectives, and their significance within our literature and culture has gone largely unrecognized. This article seeks to correct such oversight and present a discussion on the ways in which these books construct the figure of the boy sleuth and the world he occupies. This examination, in fact, ultimately reveals a great deal about twentieth-century ideology concerning the nature of mystery, adventure, and the unknown and the perceived connection(s) of each with and to gender. Indeed, this essay seeks to address and answer this central question: What is the unique nature of male adventure, mystery, and sleuthing as presented and defined within the original Hardy Boys series?

The fundamental essence of the Hardy Boys is, of course, mystery, and indeed the Hardy name is synonymous with mystery, detection, and sleuthing. In fact, the Hardys enjoy references in multiple genres and texts, including books, film, music, theatre, and various forms of popular culture. At the heart of each of these replicas, regardless of genre, stand the two title characters — the Hardy boys, Frank and Joe. The boy detectives remain consistently present within each of their legacy series (The Hardy Boys Casefiles, The Hardy Boys Digests, The Clues Brothers, and The Hardy Boys: Undercover Brothers, to name a few), and the characters' ability to garner such interest as detectives is indeed impressive. Thus, the embodiment of the boy detective within Frank and Joe Hardy is of particular distinction when considering the figure of the boy sleuth and why the image offered within the pages of the Hardy Boys books is so enduring.

Perhaps the answer lies within the sister series of the Hardy Boys books: The Nancy Drew Mystery Stories. Indeed, to properly consider the *boy* sleuth in particular and to examine his world as uniquely boy or male-oriented, one should first look at the parallel world of the girl sleuth. No other mystery series has enjoyed the success of the Hardy Boys books, except, of course, the Nancy Drew books, and the striking similarities of the two series indelibly link them. In addition to the shared publisher and creator, the book series bear a virtually identical physical appearance and format, and the plots and stories are often parallel as well. This congruency highlights the fact that the books' creator, Edward Stratemeyer, and publisher, Grossest & Dunlap, likely sought to encourage connections between the two series. The Nancy Drew books, advertised and viewed as the "girl" version of the Hardy Boys series, seems to exist on the one hand as its antithesis, offering readers a parallel detective, story, and world to that offered within the Hardy Boys books. Yet, the Nancy Drew books also serve as the companion, "sister" series to the "boy" version. Readers clearly see and enjoy the connections between the two, for several crossover series emerge in which the world of the Hardys and that of Nancy Drew merge. Two books series (Nancy Drew and the Hardy Boys Super Sleuths! and Nancy Drew and Hardy Boys Super Mystery Series) as well as a television program (*The Hardy Boys/Nancy Drew Mysteries*) present a world in which the three sleuths join forces to solve mysteries. If Nancy Drew was not originally conceived as a twin or sister series of the Hardy Boys, it seems readers (and, later, viewers) came to see it as such, and indeed it seems virtually impossible to discuss one fully without considering the other, particularly when discussing the gender distinctions of the sleuths and their connections to the worlds they inhabit.

In considering the strangely interconnected and yet separate nature of the two series, one may wonder as to the purpose in creating a separate series at all. To do so is to cast Nancy's adventures as inherently different — and separate — from Frank and Joe's, and vice versa. This separation of mystery and detection into supposedly boy "versus" girl territory illustrates an underlying belief that male detectives and readers want or need one series, and female detectives and readers another. This divergence seems to suggest that boys possess an inherent fascination with and/or need to inhabit a certain type of space and story, and girls another. The splitting of the Nancy Drew and Hardy Boys books into two separate series thus seems to reflect two major ideologies: 1) girls' and boys' inner natures as detectives or clue seekers are different; and 2) the inherent nature of mystery is in some way connected to gender.

In spite of the separation of the two series, the dangers faced by the girl and boy sleuths are remarkably similar. Both Nancy and the Hardys must retrieve and return stolen property, physically escape from being locked up, bound, and/or left for dead, rescue their kidnapped fathers, and face dangerous criminals who seek to silence (and often kill) them. Sally Parry points out that Nancy Drew has "survived innumerable threats, capsizing boats, and various traffic accidents. Despite the obstacles in her way, however, she is usually able to restore missing valuables, reunite families, and send villains to prison. Her success thus lies in being able to see what others fail to and in combining common sense with observation and intuition" (147). Yet, all of this could be similarly noted about the Hardys and their adventures. In fact, the two series seem like virtual mirror images in terms of plot and structure. The series open with the same type of mystery, placing their detective protagonists in virtually identical situations. In Nancy's first adventure, *The Secret of the Old Clock* (1930), she faces a speeding car that almost runs her off the road, encounters people whose rightful inheritance has been stolen, and then helps to rightfully restore the stolen goods. Frank and Joe's first adventure, *The Tower Treasure* (1927), also includes an encounter with a speeding car that threatens to run them off the road; they, too, discover a theft of property and must restore stolen materials to their rightful owner. Many of the consequent books share these similarities in story line, plot, and chapter division as well.

One may begin to wonder, then, as to the distinction between the two series, particularly in terms of the ways in which they connect their protagonist's gender to mystery. In examining the Hardys to see what characteristics they embody as boy sleuths, one would likely note their resourcefulness, bravery, intelligence, logical thinking, and cunning. They are physical and cerebral, both actors and thinkers; they ponder clues and think through their cases, but they are also willing and able to act, or react, quickly when the situation necessitates it. They also prove themselves selfless and noble, often endangering their lives for the sake of others' safety and benefit. However, to cast these characteristics as solely belonging to the boy sleuth would not be accurate, for Nancy Drew possesses them as well. Nancy, too, repeatedly demonstrates her bravery, intelligence, cunning, and logical thinking abilities. She reacts quickly in dangerous and fearful situations, and she, too, risks her own life for the sake of solving a mystery or helping others.

Yet another connection between the sleuths' depictions is the exaggerated gender separation of the textual worlds they inhabit. As boy sleuths, the Hardy boys navigate a world populated almost entirely by men and boys. Frank and Joe work exclusively with their father and male friends; the police are men; the competing detectives are men; and the villains are men. The reverse is similarly true in Nancy Drew. Although the gender division in Nancy's world is not as distinct as it is in the Hardy Boys books, Nancy also navigates a world largely filled with members of her own gender; although her father, boyfriend, and male police officers appear in the novels, they do not play pivotal roles. Her involvement in cases typically requires her to interact almost exclusively with females: female victims, female companions, and of course the series often includes female villains as well (*The Secret of the Old Clock*, *The Mystery at Lilac Inn*, *The Clue in the Diary*). Ultimately, men and boys play minor roles in the Nancy Drew books, as do women and girls in the Hardy Boys books, though the extent to which females are written out of the script is much more pronounced in the Hardy Boys books than the omission of males is within the Nancy Drew books.

Why the books engage in this gender segregation is indeed an interesting point to consider. The reasons for excluding men from Nancy's world are a bit more understandable; that is, the inclusion of men in the novel would likely disrupt the female-centric nature of the series; this, in turn, could create an eroto-romantic tension that could threaten Nancy's career and create "a space around her over which she no longer exerted ultimate autonomy" (Cornelius, "Blinded Her" 78). The reverse certainly cannot be said for the boy detective; the presence of females in Frank and Joe's fictional space would certainly not threaten their careers or autonomy, yet the women and girls in the Hardy Boys series remain trapped in constricting, insulting roles that exclude them from the adventure and mystery of the novels. Marty Roth argues detective fiction must necessarily engage in such exclusion because the very presence of women signifies sexuality, and thus serves as a distraction to the male protagonists: "A good deal of Western fiction consists of games women cannot play.... Women enter the adventure to distract the privileged players, or they play so badly that a lot of time is taken up helping them to their feet. In general, they are said to interfere with the process of male satisfaction" (113). This point certainly seems to hold true in the Hardy Boys books, for the very title points to the importance of being both *hardy* and a *boy*. Though their ages vary slightly throughout the series, Frank and Joe do indeed remain boys who are, at least theoretically, under the authority of their parents, though this authority is rather tangential. The boys discuss and visit colleges occasionally, but they do not actually move out of their family home, and thus they do not grow into independent, self-supporting men. Their depiction similarly casts them as *hardy*, meaning they are robust, courageous, and daring; they inherently possess the strength to withstand hardship, danger, and mystery solving.

These abilities contrast starkly to those of the books' females — including and especially their mother. Laura Hardy's characterization deems her utterly incapable of understanding and coping with the mysteries that her teenage sons can easily handle and understand. In fact, the boys act as her authority figure by taking charge of the nature and type of knowledge to which she has access. The boys often decide to keep her out of the loop, even when her husband's life is in jeopardy; her teenage sons thus have the ability to decide what information she can or should have concerning her husband. Usually, the books cast Laura as a virtually impotent member of the Hardy household; her only functions are to cook for and worry about her sons and husband. Bobbie Ann Mason notes that Laura Hardy is in fact "hidden so successfully that the reader never suspects she has any power" (50). The inclusion of Aunt Gertrude serves to further strengthen the notion that women are simply incapable of solving, or for that matter gaining involvement in, mysteries. Aunt Gertrude's only function in the novels seems to be expressing concern over and doubt about the boys' safety and to attempt to talk them out of their dangerous vocation. She is virtually useless as a character, except of course to highlight the belief that women have and deserve no place in mystery solving.

In terms of girlfriends or companions for the Hardy boys, females again play a limited role. Mark Connelly notes the odd sexlessness of Frank and Joe in the first fifty-eight books; although they are heterosexual teen boys,

Frank and Joe rarely date or have romantic connections with females. Connelly argues the primary reason for this lack of even suggested sexuality in the books is a direct result of Stratemeyer himself and his belief that "presenting both male and female characters in books might raise parental concerns" (140). Yet although the Hardy boys "have retained their virginity for eighty years," they have not "been without at least superficial female companionship" (140). Frank and Joe's relationships with girls are indeed limited; Callie Shaw and Iola Morton are pseudo girlfriends who merely "play an important role in the wish fulfillment theme.... Callie and Iola cheer the Hardy Boys on, fall victim and require rescuing, and affirm their manhood" (141).

Indeed, the all-male world of the Hardys helps underscore not only the power and importance of men, but also the primary way in which men both attain and maintain this power: male community. The Hardy Boys books' promotion of collaborative efforts between and among exclusively male groups illustrates the importance of men working to help and support each other, and, at the same time, excludes women from this adventure and camaraderie. In case after case, Frank and Joe immediately call upon their male friends' aid, disregarding the potential help and input of the women and girls in their lives. Their first adventure, in fact, makes clear both their inability to handle the case on their own and also their willingness to include their friends in their work:

> Frank shrugged. Several ideas were brought up by the brothers, but one which Joe proposed was given preference. They would get hold of a large group of their friends. On the theory that the thief could not have driven a long distance away because of the police alarm, the boys would make an extensive search in the surrounding area for Chet's jalopy.
> [Joe] "We'll hunt in every possible hiding place," he stated.
> Early the next morning, Frank hurried to the telephone and put in one call after another to "the gang" [Dixon *Tower Treasure* 41].

This all-male "gang" (Chet Morton, Allen "Biff" Hooper, Jerry Gilroy, Phil Cohen, and Tony Prito), or some combination of representative members, virtually always accompanies the Hardy boys on their adventures, particularly in the first fifty-eight books in the series. The boys, in fact, frequently note the willingness of their friends to help them, and this help proves highly valuable to the Hardys and their mysteries.

The Nancy Drew books attempt to create a collaborative effort with the addition of two female friends, Bess Marvin and George Fayne, but the girls certainly do not achieve the community that the Hardys and their friends do. Indeed, Bess and George could hardly be called sleuths; they merely tag along with Nancy on her adventures, acting as mere accompaniments for Nancy. The girls rarely do any actual work, and in fact they often fall asleep and/or end up hurt during peak mystery-solving moments; thus, Nancy faces the climax and solves the mystery herself. In fact, Sally Parry labels Nancy Drew "a proactive person who seeks out mysteries to solve" but "seems to work best alone in trying to restore the status quo" (145). Although her desire for and success in promoting the status quo is debatable, Nancy does indeed seem to work best alone. She does receive a degree of help from Bess and George in solving some cases, but the addition of her companions to the stories seems to have been a mere afterthought. Nancy's supposed partner sleuths George and Bess do not appear until the fifth book in the series, *The Secret at Shadow Ranch* (1931), and the addition is not an overly compelling one. In spite of their presence, Nancy remains largely a solitary practitioner, and obviously so to a greater degree than her male counterparts who, at the very least, have each other, as *brothers*. An only child, literally and metaphorically, Nancy enjoys no such sisterhood, and indeed the books point out that Nancy is largely an aberration; there are not many women like her — women who willingly risk their lives to restore stolen property, right wrongs, and punish wrongdoers. Michael Cornelius points out that although a girl sleuth such as Nancy Drew enjoys a cadre of loyal friends, she "prefers to act alone, saving the denouement of the mystery solely for herself" ("Introduction" 2). The implication here that Nancy *chooses* to solve the cases on her own is an interesting one. Parry, on the other hand, sees Nancy's role as problem solver not necessarily as a chosen one, for Parry argues that George and Bess are largely unable (and perhaps unwilling) to help Nancy — and thus she must solve the mystery herself. Although Bess and George accompany Nancy on her travels, they often "place eating, shopping, or going out on dates as a higher priority than solving a mystery, thus limiting their effectiveness in aiding Nancy" (149). In fact, the books' story lines often find excuses to remove Bess and George from the climax of the mystery. In *The Haunted Showboat*, George attempts to explore the riverboat and look for clues; when she ascends the stairway that leads to the boat's hold (the very space that later proves to be a key location of the mystery — the spot where Nancy later discovers the hidden gold), the step gives way and plunges George into darkness. This removal of George from the case is significant, for it illustrates George's prohibition from walking in Nancy's footsteps, from literally solving the mystery, since it is in the hold of the boat that Nancy later discoveries the hidden gold that helps catch the book's villain, Alex Upgrove, and thus ultimately solves the case. Similarly, in *The Clue in the Diary*, Bess and George again reveal their inadequacy as sleuths. When the girls must await the appearance of suspect Felix Raybolt, Bess and George literally fall asleep on the job, and it is Nancy who "had taken matters into her own hands" (Keene 163). Yet, Nancy willingly leaves her friends and rarely seems upset or bothered by their inadequacies in helping her to solve cases; in fact, the narration notes in this particular case that Nancy "felt a glow of pleasure as always when she made lasting friends of people *she* had helped" (174, emphasis mine). Thus, Nancy does indeed seem to enjoy working on and solving cases herself, and though she does have access to others' help, she seems to view the accompanying credit and rewards as belonging to her. Nancy also keeps boyfriend Ned Nickerson at a distance from both her and her cases. He lifts heavy items or forces open doors occasionally, but he usually remains neatly tucked away at college or work, and when he does assist her, his help is minimal. Indeed, Nancy needs — and accepts — little help from either men or women, for it is she who finds the clues, tracks down the villains, and solves the case, often even beating her father to the punch.

The Hardys, on the other hand, repeatedly rely on and solicit the help of others, and indeed they have a large pool of willing male help from which to draw. In fact, it often takes both brothers, their friends, and their father to conclude a mystery similar to those Nancy Drew solves almost entirely on her own. Although her father and friends may often weigh in on her cases, the cases are indeed *hers*, and others offer mere voices of assistance. Fenton Hardy, however, often has a pivotal role in the mysteries of the Hardy Boys series, and even in his absence, Frank and Joe can and do often call upon the help of their male friends, most notably Chet, who is noted as "their staunch friend who had joined in the sleuthing as an invaluable ally" (Dixon *The Secret of the Caves* 7). From the beginning of the series, "the gang" is intimately involved in the cases of Frank and Joe, and Fenton himself notes the value and necessity of the boys' ability to form a network of men with whom to work. In fact, readers likely get the impression that without their friends, the Hardy boys would not be as effective as detectives as they are with their friends' assistance. Fenton Hardy himself echoes this belief, particularly when the boys and their friends' ability to work together saves his life. In *The House on the Cliff* (1927), Fenton is kidnapped by drug smugglers, and the brothers — working together with "the gang" — not only solve the case but also rescue Fenton. Fenton acknowledges and praises the boys' cooperation and professes gratitude for and belief in the value of the community the boys have established: "I want to thank each of you boys individually for what you did. Without the seven of you, this case might never have been solved and I might not have been found alive" (180). Throughout the series, Fenton expresses his belief in the ability of his sons and their friends to solve cases, and he encourages the boys to build such a community with their male friends. He notes his confidence in their trustworthiness even with confidential information: "I know I can trust your special friends. Call them up" (*House on the Cliff* 4). Thus, the "famous detective" himself assures the boys of the value of their male friends' assistance and community. Although Fenton is included within this community, Frank and Joe occasionally compete with him for cases as well; *The Tower Treasure* (1927), their first case and adventure, highlights the potential for competition among the Hardy men. Yet, as Connelly notes, any competition or conflict that may arise within the Hardy men's detective work is resolved "by a cooperative rivalry that demonstrates mutual dependence as a requirement for success" (151). In fact, the narrator often directly remarks on the powerful camaraderie between the three Hardy men to ensure the reader does not miss it: "Ever since the brothers had been old enough to engage in sleuthing, there had been a great camaraderie among the Hardy 'men folk'" (Dixon *Secret Caves* 14).

The books' covers reflect both the importance of this community for the male sleuth and the autonomy of the female sleuth; the Hardy brothers appear together on virtually every book cover in mid-mystery, working together to solve the particular riddle they must face. Several covers also include their friends and/or father (*The House on the Cliff, Footprints Under the Window, The Secret Warning, The Secret of Skull Mountain*). The Nancy Drew book covers — even after the addition of Bess and George — remain focused on Nancy; most covers depict her alone, mid mystery, facing and solving the case on her own. The titles of the series, of course, make this point as well: to name a series the "Hardy Boys Mystery Stories" is to make evident that the books will detail the adventures of at least two male protagonists who join forces to solve mysteries; the singularity inherent in Nancy's series title, "The Nancy Drew Mystery Stories," makes clear the presence of a solitary female protagonist who will solve the mysteries alone.

This idea of the male sleuth as needing and/or desiring a community of male help and support is reflected in other mystery stories as well: The Rover Boys, The Motor Boys, The Three Investigators, The X Bar X Boys. Similarly, the solitary female detective is prevalent in other mystery stories: Trixie Belden, Judy Bolton, Vicki Barr, Penny Parker, and Cherry Ames, to name a few. This singularity of the girl sleuth seems to have begun with Nancy Drew; though several book series that preceded Nancy Drew presented communities of females working together (The Motor Girls, Aunt Jane's Nieces, and Girl Aviators), mystery solving was not the primary activity depicted within the novels, and these books certainly did not achieve the popularity that the single-girl detective series enjoys. (In fact, few contemporary readers have likely even heard of these series.) Mason points out that many of these series were quite limiting in terms of their depictions of female protagonists and their ability to work together; she notes the girls "weren't truly independent, for their money came from Daddy and their main interest was boys.... Many of them spent a good deal of time chattering and stuffing themselves with chocolate" rather than working collectively to solve the case(s) at hand (12). Mason also discusses the rise of the solitary girl detective, noting the connection between solitary girl sleuths and commercial success: "With the increasing independence of the heroines, there emerged a strong mystery pattern.... By the 1930s, in girls' fiction, the focus gradually narrowed to a single sleuth on the trail of a gang of crooks" (15). Apparently, female readers in the 1920s and 1930s did not find female sleuthing teams intriguing. Yet, when Nancy Drew drove her blue roadster onto the scene in the early 1930s, "there was a deliberate focus on an unusually strong heroine, far more accomplished and independent than any of her predecessors.... With her success, the amateur girl detective became the staple heroine" (Mason 16). Indeed, Nancy Drew's independence as both a female and a sleuth inspired the creation of several series featuring independent female protagonists (Judy Bolton, Cherry Ames, Penny Parker, and Kay Tracey, to list a few).

This preference of readers for a solitary girl sleuth and a community of male sleuths may be puzzling initially, for it seems to be in direct opposition to the traditional American gender ideals that uphold characteristics of independence, self-reliance, and autonomy as positive for men and submissiveness, fragility, and docility for females. Both series' writers depart from such gender constructions in the portrayal of their protagonists and present instead compellingly different gender depictions.

The portrayal of the Hardy boys as interdependent upon and inherently connected to other men contrasts starkly to the established masculinity ideals of nineteenth and twentieth-century America, since the hegemonic ideal of masculinity in Western culture has, for centuries, been defined as "a man who is independent, risk-taking, aggressive, and rational" (Barrett 79). Indeed, the icon of the cowboy, as embodied in such figures as John Wayne and The Marlboro Man, represents a universally recognized icon of American masculinity. Though these particular icons succeeded the publication of many of the early Hardy Boys books, the ideology they represent does not. In fact, as Michael Kimmel and Amy Aronson point out, the cowboy as a representative icon of rugged, individualistic masculinity is not a twentieth-century invention:

> The cowboy is among the most enduring symbols of American masculinity. The cowboy is emblematic of a strong, hard, ruggedly independent masculinity that settled the West, conquered Indians, tamed a hostile land, and ensured the spread of American democracy from sea to sea. From his origins in the middle of the nineteenth century, through his valorizations in the westerns at the turn of the century, the cowboy ... is America's contribution to the world's stock of mythic heroes [188].

Thus, to see a contrasting depiction of masculinity within a book series as highly successful as the Hardy Boys is indeed noteworthy. This divergence from the standard masculinity ideal within the characterization of Frank and Joe may represent a competing version of masculinity emerging in American culture. The books make clear the strength and importance of male bonding and solidarity — rather than independence and isolation. The males in the Hardy Boys books often depend upon each other for their very survival, and thus the connections formed between and with other men are cast as highly valuable. Whereas the cowboy leads an isolated life on the range, living and working efficiently alone, the Hardy boys have both the desire and need for the help and input of other men. Readers, then, likely come to understand the essence of the Hardy boys' success as the utter reverse of the cowboy's stoic independence and self-reliance. The depiction of Frank and Joe as being not only dependent upon each other but also on other men and boys reveals to readers the power of male unity, not independence.

This male empowerment offered within the text may, perhaps, represent a site of fantasy in which the reader participates in a type of gender opposition in which he escapes the established gender order. Indeed, both the Hardy Boys and Nancy Drew books present protagonists who represent the utter reverse of the standard gender norm. Though the female reader's desire to escape the gender identity of docility, submissiveness, and dependence is immediately understandable, the male reader's desire to escape an identity as a virtually omnipotent single agent is a bit more enigmatic. Yet, perhaps the departure from such an ideal in the depiction of the Hardy boys and their adventures illustrates the reader's disillusionment with the established patriarchal ideal and his corresponding desire to participate in a differing experience and definition of manhood. Such a desire is understandable in that the books allow for an escape from the pressure that such an ideal creates and perpetuates, for such an identity requires him to know all, to solve all, and indeed to be all. The Hardys, however, do not — as individuals — achieve such a feat. Neither Frank nor Joe single-handedly saves the day or the world; rather, their characterization illustrates that these males not only need but also enjoy others' company, help, and support. The Hardys do not act as single agents but rather as a team, and indeed their ability to work with others is clearly the secret to their success, both in mystery solving and in physical survival. Thus perhaps the depiction of the solidarity of the Hardys and their friends may present readers a type of fantasia in which they gain an experience of boy/manhood in which boys are needed by — and in need of — others, where males are designed not as individual constructions but rather as crucial members of a well-functioning clan or team. To experience this differing idea of manhood may represent wish fulfillment, an affirmation to the reader that he is, in fact, a needed, wanted, and integral member of his community rather than an isolated individual who must fend for himself.

The serial nature of the books points to the reader's repeated desire to experience this escape, and the depiction does seem to make clear that such a breaking away offers him (and his community) several benefits. To perceive himself as interdependent upon others (rather than a single agent responsible for and to himself only) would likely increase his responsibility to and investment in his community. As the stories illustrate, this collaboration and investment promote better safety for all — including the individual male. In contrast, the reader may come to understand not only the potential loneliness but also the vulnerability of the isolated male in that he has only himself; he possesses only the resources and power that he alone can attain. Yet a group of men working together can clearly draw on their collective abilities, power, and assets to solve any impending crisis. Thus, the depiction of male community within the books reveals not only a potential fantasy of the reader to experience his gendered opposite, but also illustrates the ways the writers expose the limits — and dangers — of the solitary male ideal. The fantasy of gender opposition thus contains a great deal of wisdom that highlights the ways in which collaboration and cooperation increase a male's ability to survive, and it conversely exposes the ways in which a life of isolation and self-reliance may threaten it.

Though the books may indeed foster communication and cooperation by presenting a fictional world in which boys learn the value of breaking out of the strictures of the autonomous male ideal, the books unfortunately do not encourage such cooperation and community across gender lines. Thus, if the books do represent the site of fantasy for a differing patriarchal order, or indeed a differing gender order, the vision offered is still a quite limited one. Though the books may encourage bonds with other men and boys, the books do not promote meaningful connections with women and girls based on equality and respect. Indeed, in this male unity lies an espousal of traditional gender roles that dictate the separation of male and female domains.

Women must or should remain within their domains (namely the home) and men in theirs (in this case, the ever-expanding terrain and occupation of mystery-solving). Thus, the motivation behind this depiction of male solidarity and bonding may not necessarily be as competing or enlightened a notion of masculinity as it may seem, for upon closer examination, its goal seems strikingly similar to that of the independent male: to represent and defend the patriarchal order. The boy sleuth as epitomized within Frank and Joe may then, sadly, simply represent yet another site of defense for patriarchy as the necessary, true, and right means of governing society and ensuring the advancement of truth, justice, and the "American way." Fred Erisman claims that Stratemeyer's fictional worlds are indeed "overtly and unequivocally American.... His protagonists, one and all, seek to heighten the status of the United States in the eyes of the world, and build national pride in the hearts of American citizens" (21). Thus, the "American way" that Stratemeyer and his ghostwriters seem to advance is still a staunchly patriarchal one in which men have the means and ability to act, to *help* others, while women remain acted upon and *helped by* men. Men and boys gain agency, while women and girls are denied it.

Frank and Joe's status as boys, rather than grown men, proves important as well, for Annette Wannamaker convincingly argues that adults' notions of themselves and their societies, specifically their place(s) within these societies, are often projected onto depictions of children and childhood:

> Childhood is socially constructed within public discourse and often becomes a signifier in larger political battles. Childhood becomes an empty vessel of a word; it is heavy with contradictions that can carry multiple meanings, and within public discourse it can signify our hope for the future, or nostalgia, or innocence, or fear. Therefore, if public discourse about childhood is a blank state onto which we write our cultural anxieties ... what fears and desires are we projecting onto our boys? [Wannamaker 3].

The fears the Hardy Boys books may address in their depiction of the boy sleuth, then, reflect those concerning the disappearance of solely-male domains and the corresponding nostalgia for a world where men and boys engage in traditionally "male" activities and women and girls partake in those cast as "female." To present a textual world in which women are marginalized and men empowered does indeed seem to support a world view in which patriarchy reigns.

The casting of the domain of mystery as a solely male territory in the Hardy Boys series points to the deep-seated anxiety over the changing gender order within twentieth-century America. Although the differing depiction of manhood offered within the pages of the novels may indicate a disillusionment of readers with the autonomous male ideal, the books do not, overall, attempt to debunk or subvert the idea of male supremacy. The stories cast boys and men exclusively as the primary actors, thinkers, and rulers of their communities and societies, and women remain mere secondary accompaniments. The gender segregation and binarism present within the books and their connection to the figure of the boy sleuth may thus reveal him as the embodiment of an anxious reaction to the changes in newly constructed gender identities, and a nostalgic longing for the known, antiquated gender order of the past that defined the male as the ruling head.

When comparing the gender ideology of the Nancy Drew books to that of the Hardy Boys, the equivocal nature of the "proper," and perhaps even possible, roles for men and women in American society becomes clear. The depictions of both the girl and boy sleuth thus point to the utter apprehension inherent in the twentieth century regarding the divergence from the strictures of the patriarchal order. The Nancy Drew books reveal an inherent cynicism about men and women's abilities to work together in solving mysteries, righting wrongs, and indeed in functioning as equals. The Hardy Boys books reflect a similar concern, but also point to the inability of women to match wits and physical strength with men. Thus, we may regard both book series as sites of anxiety over the erosion of traditional gender structures. The books' writers seem particularly interested in the challenges these changes posed to the established credo that men exclusively own the abilities to provide and protect, for the realm of mystery-solving encompasses both. Detectives obviously protect by righting wrongs, returning stolen property, and providing safeguard for citizens against criminals and swindlers. Detectives also play the role of provider, not largely through physical resources, but rather with intellectual ones; they provide the logic and thinking abilities necessary to solve cases, and indeed their cool logic and clear thinking are often regarded as their key assets. Such skills have, however, been largely deemed "male" competencies, and thus the twentieth-century reader may indeed have experienced anxiety over facing the possibility of women's abilities to fill these roles.

If the series book does indeed function as a mirror of ourselves and our culture, as Paul Deane claims, then the Hardy Boys series ultimately reveals that we, as postmodern readers and people, bear a great resemblance to the Hardy boys and their friends; we, too, are attempting to navigate an unknown, sometimes threatening, mysterious new realm: postmodern gender ideology. For even in the twenty-first century, readers likely still seek to understand and solve the mystery of the essential nature of gender and the ways in which our conceptions of it define us — not only in terms of how we see and define ourselves, but also how we see and define each other. The voluminous scholarship on the myriad ways that literature, film, and popular culture attempt to define what it means to be male or female points to the continuing presence of gender coding and questioning. We clearly still seek to understand what it means to be male or female when we strip off the stereotypical gender distinctions that have marked us for centuries. What exactly the essential natures of man and womanhood are remains largely unknown and contested. Thus perhaps herein lies a potential reason for the continued success of each book series: the sleuths' quests for answers are analogous to our own.

Both book series seem to point to both men and women's inadequacy, thus far, in achieving an understanding of how to include each other in our respective worlds. For both the Nancy Drew and Hardy Boys books could certainly benefit from a more enlightened and inclusive view of gender. Nancy seems relatively unwilling (or perhaps unable) to include as her equal both men and women in her domain as sleuth, and though the Hardy boys may achieve solidarity with other boys and men, they have a great deal of work ahead of them in viewing and treating females as their intellectual, political, and professional equals. In spite of their shortcomings in terms of promoting gender equality and understanding, though, both series promote some of the most highly valued ethics of human society: hard work, determination, honesty, and, above all, justice. The books clearly have a timeless ability to engage readers, and thus they likely also help to cultivate another invaluable benefit — the love of reading.

Carol Billman notes yet another positive aspect of the books; she argues they provide a story in which "the young and relatively inexperienced triumph ... the security of the Hardys' existence ... offers comfort from the anxieties brought on by the biological and psychological pressures of growing up in a world that resembles Bayport and its extended universe but little. Readers need to spend quiet hours in such a retreat — in a moratorium, if you will — during which they can amass latent energy for the last stage of growth into adulthood" (96). Perhaps, then, we can be somewhat forgiving for the gender offenses committed within the books and note them more positively as guides that help their readers understand — and face — the many limitations and fears that remain within our society regarding the changing, and indeed mysterious, nature of our conceptions of gender. By viewing the books in this regard, we can perhaps begin to move toward solving one of the most baffling mysteries of humanity: how to achieve true gender equality.

Works Cited

Barrett, Frank J. "The Organizational Construction of Hegemonic Masculinity: The Case of the U.S. Navy." *The Masculinities Reader.* Eds. Stephen M. Whitehead and Frank J. Barrett. Cambridge, UK: Polity, 2001. 77–99.
Billman, Carol. *The Secret of the Stratemeyer Syndicate: Nancy Drew, the Hardy Boys, and the Million Dollar Fiction Factory.* New York: Ungar, 1986.
Connelly, Mark. *The Hardy Boys Mysteries, 1927–1979: A Cultural and Literary History.* Jefferson, NC: McFarland, 2008.
Cornelius, Michael G. "Introduction: The Mystery of the 'Moll Dick.'" *Nancy Drew and Her Sister Sleuths: Essays on the Fiction of Girl Detectives.* Eds. Michael G. Cornelius & Melanie E. Gregg. Jefferson, NC: McFarland, 2008. 1–12.
_____. "'They Blinded Her with Science': Science Fiction and Technology in Nancy Drew." *Nancy Drew and Her Sister Sleuths: Essays on the Fiction of Girl Detectives.* Eds. Michael G. Cornelius & Melanie E. Gregg. Jefferson, NC: McFarland, 2008. 77–95.
Deane, Paul. *Mirrors of American Culture: Children's Fiction Series in the Twentieth Century.* Metuchen, NJ: Scarecrow Press, 1991.
Dixon, Franklin W. *The Great Airport Mystery.* 1930. Rev. ed. New York: Grosset & Dunlap, 1965.
_____. *The House on the Cliff.* 1927. Rev. ed. New York: Grosset & Dunlap, 1959.
_____. *The Jungle Pyramid.* New York: Grosset & Dunlap, 1977.
_____. *The Secret of the Old Mill.* 1927. Rev. ed. New York: Grosset & Dunlap, 1960.
_____. *The Stone Idol.* New York: Wanderer Books, 1981.
_____. *The Tower Treasure.* 1927. Rev. ed. New York: Grosset & Dunlap, 1959.
Erisman, Fred. *Boys' Books, Boys' Dreams and the Mystique of Flight.* Fort Worth: Texas Christian University Press, 2006.
Johnson, Deidre. *Edward Stratemeyer and the Stratemeyer Syndicate.* New York: Twayne, 1993.
Keene, Carolyn. *The Clue in the Diary.* 1930. Rev. ed. New York: Grosset & Dunlap, 1962.
_____. *The Haunted Showboat.* New York: Grosset & Dunlap, 1957.
_____. *The Hidden Staircase.* 1930. Rev. ed. New York: Grosset & Dunlap, 1959.
_____. *The Mystery at Lilac Inn.* 1930. Rev. ed. New York: Grosset & Dunlap, 1961.
_____. *The Secret of the Old Clock.* 1930. Rev. ed. New York: Grosset & Dunlap, 1959.
Kimmel, Michael, and Amy Aronson, eds. *Men & Masculinities: A Social, Cultural, and Historical Encyclopedia.* 3 vols. Santa Barbara: ABC-CLIO, 2004. Vol. 1.
Mason, Bobbie Ann. *The Girl Sleuth: A Feminist Guide.* Old Westbury, NY: Feminist Press, 1975.
Parry, Sally E. "The Secret of the Feminist Heroine: The Search for Values in Nancy Drew and Judy Bolton." *Nancy Drew and Company: Culture, Gender, and Girls' Series.* Ed. Sherrie A. Inness. Bowling Green, OH: Bowling Green State University Popular Press, 1997. 145–158.
Roth, Marty. *Foul & Fair Play: Reading Genre in Classic Detective Fiction.* Athens: University of Georgia Press, 1995.
Wannamaker, Annette. *Boys in Children's Literature and Popular Culture: Masculinity, Abjection, and the Fictional Child.* New York: Routledge, 2008.

3

Terminal Immaterial: The Uncertain Subject of the Hardy Boys Airport Mysteries

Christopher Schaberg

Since their inception, airports have occupied a contested yet tentative spot in the national imagination: these icons of technological progress must be deemed to be secure *and* to be outmoding themselves at every instant. This paradox of progress plays out in cultural representations of airports, such as in Steven Spielberg's 2004 film *The Terminal*, in which the JFK International Terminal stands as a revolving set, at turns utopian and dystopian, open and closed, democratic and fascistic. This revolving action of airports hinges on the logic of the uncertain subject, a logic that appears regularly in the Hardy Boys stories to activate the aura of mystery. At the outset, one might note that this is a series with its own uncertain author-subject, the pseudonym "Franklin W. Dixon" standing in for numerous named and unnamed scribes who have written the Hardy Boys since 1927. Frank and Joe Hardy frequently find themselves at airports on their way to solve mysteries, and three books are staged specifically in and around these sites: *The Great Airport Mystery* from 1930, *Hostages of Hate* from 1987, and *Tagged for Terror* from 1993. In these airport adventures, when one looks for the airport, what one usually finds is empty or generic space; when one looks at the subject within or around the airport, one discovers flexible, indeterminate personae who can hold many subject positions in the action of the stories being unfolded.

In the 1993 Casefiles mystery *Tagged for Terror*, Frank and Joe are dispatched to Atlanta, Georgia, to attend to a rampant baggage theft problem that is plaguing the airline "Eddings Air." En route to Atlanta, in the private jet of the eponymous airline owner Michael Eddings, the Hardy boys are informed of the situation: "The thefts started large-scale about six months ago.... The stolen luggage usually contains valuables like jewelry or cameras. Why we've been hit harder that other airlines, we don't know. Nobody in the industry has reported losses like ours" (4).

The arbitrary targeting of Eddings Air remains a mystery through the end of the story; indeed, *Tagged for Terror* is something of a mystery about a mystery, where the thievery of personal affects transforms, without reason, into an abstract terrorist plot that seems to rely on — yet have no direct connection with — accomplices who are low-wage baggage handlers. To solve this meta-mystery, the Hardy Boys go undercover as baggage handlers for Eddings Air. When Joe meets one of his fellow laborers for the first time, wages are among the first thing Joe learns about: "Welcome aboard. The hours are bad, the pay is low, the work is tedious. Other than that, it's a great place to work" (23).

From this sarcastic introduction to the material reality of airport work, the narrative unravels into a terror plot of undisclosed scope — as if to suggest that there are inherent (if hidden) links between low-wage laborers and evil terrorists. This linkage of terrorists and airport wageworkers is mindful of the speculative ties made between food service caterers and the hijackers shortly after 9/11/2001, which conjectured that airport ramp workers who had apparently no relation to al-Qaeda had helped to plant weapons on the planes (Trento & Trento 47–48). Furthermore, the lead-in for the sequel of *Tagged for Terror* tells us that this is the first of a series of three mysteries entitled "Ring of Evil," involving a longer storyline in which the terror group "the Assassins are preparing to square off against the ultra secret government agency, the Network" (155). It would seem as if the mundane workspace of the airport serves as a concourse for unrelated — yet structurally associated — plots for political power.

On the other hand, the airport in *Tagged for Terror* is hardly even a distinct site. At one point, Frank "glanced around at the fast-food restaurants, magazine stands, and souvenir shops that turned almost every large airport into a shopping mall" (17). Atlanta's Hartsfield Airport is depicted as an utterly generic location in a consumer culture, merely another place for one-stop-shopping. Even when Frank and Joe are involved in a near-death crash landing, Joe's reaction is to compare the airport emergency protocols with processed food:

> A paramedic herded them away from the crippled jet as fire fighters doused the plane with fire-retardant foam that reminded Joe of whipped cream being shot from a spray can. The crash had almost ripped off the right wing. A trail of motor oil and metal fragments led back down the

runway to the jet engine, which had been torn from the underside of the wing [13].

Amidst this scene of a serious, airport-specific accident, consumer culture is conjured as a seemingly natural referent. Thus, while the airport is staged as a high-stakes venue for all sorts of intrigue, it also barely stands out against the broad metonymic landscape of which it is one mere part. The airport is essential material for the mystery plot, and yet the airport is generic and misrecognized as *anyplace*: terminal immaterial.

Tagged for Terror hinges on the Hardy boys' immersion into airport culture. It is accepted as a definite possibility that certain airport laborers are involved with the luggage thefts:

> "Security is pretty tight," Frank pointed out. "Slipping luggage out shouldn't be that easy."
> "It might not be that hard for someone who's worked here long enough to be trusted," Joe replied. "Maybe as long as you're wearing an Eddings uniform, you can blend in so nobody'd notice you" [54].

The trusted working base of the airport is always already suspect. This paranoia threatens to undermine the very logic of the liberal subject, who would seem to hold an inherent trust value when it comes to *work*. In other words, the travelers and workers who comprise the flows of deregulated airports rely on a fundamental logic of trust that glues the personal work ethic to the idea of private property in transit. Yet the Hardy boys, in their immediate skepticism of this baseline trust (those wearing the right uniforms can therefore be *mis*trusted), unravel the very fabric with which free travel is wrapped. Private property leads to theft, and uniforms are ironically deceptive: the worker might be a terrorist *or* an undercover operative (like the Hardy boys). Indeed, in the final chase of the story, Joe mistakes two men wearing "nylon jackets" for common travelers — but *they* end up being gun-packing government operatives (126–127). By the end of *Tagged for Terror*, identities have been flipped and misperceived to the point that the airport is a darkly comic stage where everybody has something to hide and nobody has a clear destination. The problem of missing luggage fades into the background, and ambient fears of terrorism and misleading identities permeate the inconclusive ending. As Frank says about this airport mystery, "It's over — but not for us" (154).

In many ways, the drama of *Tagged for Terror* is both anticipated and undermined by the earlier *Hostages of Hate*, another paperback Casefile published in 1987. This story again eerily forecasts the rhetoric of 9/11/2001 when, at the beginning of the story, what is supposed to be the staged hijacking of a commercial airliner suddenly turns into a real hijacking:

> Frank and Joe stared as if they were watching a movie. The law enforcement officers ran back and forth. Some rushed forward, as if to charge the plane. The Uzi snarled again, stitching a line of broken runway just in front of the police. They stumbled to a stop, falling over themselves in Keystone Kops style [9].

Recall one of the most common responses concerning the World Trade Center strikes of September 11: *It was like watching a movie.* In this passage, the story takes a tonally awkward detour into comic pop culture. The real police officers running from real machine gun fire manage to eclipse the idea of simulation and wind up as anachronisms on the dark side of a comic moon: an actual, clamorous terrorist strike is equated with a silly, silent show. At the outset of *Hostages of Hate*, the airport tarmac is used to simulate a terrorist attack; the novel revolves around a national seminar on counterterrorism. However, the tarmac converts into the site of a *real* hijacking — and this conversion turns full circle throughout the story, where in the penultimate scenes the Hardy Boys go undercover as terrorists in order to board the hijacked plane and confront the "real" terrorists.

As if to emphasize this indeterminacy of genres and allegiances, the shady terrorist contact that the Hardy Boys first meet up with identifies himself as an ex–U.S. Marine:

> "I can still use my old Marine contacts to get guns for the cause," Lonnie said, settling his bulk behind a desk. "Still got some buddies. Even down in the barracks by the Navy Yard. And, of course, there are my detonation skills. I built the bomb that's in the airplane" [45].

In this bold schema, the U.S. soldier easily becomes a terrorist operative, and the exchange of armaments between national and terrorist "causes" is fluid. Now, to lubricate this already slippery slope, as the Hardy boys carry out their mission and infiltrate the terrorist cell, they undergo increasingly violent confrontations with the law. At one point during an altercation, Frank brutally knocks out a lead government agent, handcuffs him, and leaves him in the backseat of a police cruiser as Frank and Joe escape with a terrorist who (they hope) will lead them to the ringleader. After this encounter, the narrative ruminates on the predicament: "If Frank couldn't free the hostages after all this, he'd probably be better off with the hijackers" (92). The threshold of heroism is success; otherwise, a hero is just a terrorist by another name.

At one point, as Frank and Joe are fleeing the law, the usual monotonous prose of the Hardy Boys series heads down a curiously literary path. Frank and Joe are being chased by federal agents, and they are nearly about to be caught; Frank is trying to figure out a plan of escape, when suddenly just ahead of him, Joe turned and waved his arm. "This way!" He plunged through an entrance and down an escalator. Frank followed his brother in a broken-field run down the moving steps. Then he knew where they were heading—*into a station for the Metro*, Washington's subway system [58, my emphasis].

Embedded in this passage are the makings of the classic Modernist poem, Ezra Pound's archetypal experiment in "vorticism":

> IN A STATION OF THE METRO
> The apparition of these faces in the crowd;
> Petals on a wet, black bough [Pound 35].

It is as if the Hardy Boys story offers a subtle gesture to a quite discordant aesthetic: in the midst of an incredibly suspenseful (if utterly trite) chase scene, the narrative diverges (appropriately enough) into a poetic meditation on public transportation. While the Hardy boys do not linger in this space for long, this passage is nonetheless obliquely intertextual in its wording, as though to underscore the *narrative* material at hand: this is a pursuit made of *words*, and the airport continues to exist on the horizon of a *textual* landscape. If *Hostages of Hate* were to be read as a bizarrely protracted experiment in vorticist expression (imagine a witty English major relegated to writing Hardy Boys mysteries), the airport becomes a vaporous funnel through which many unrelated things come rushing.

By the time the Hardy Boys make it back to the airport and sneak their way onto the hijacked plane pretending to be fellow terrorist reinforcements, the story begins to come undone. Not only do the terrorists swerve from being coolly strategic to firing their machine guns recklessly and at random, but the hostages, too, come very close to revolting *against* Frank and Joe as it seems less and less likely that the Hardy boys will actually be able to overcome the hijackers. After a shootout in the main cabin, the hijackers flee to the First Class cabin and eventually into the cockpit, where it turns out that one of the henchmen can fly a plane. As the jet engines roar to life and the airliner begins to taxi toward the runway, the hostages panic and want to jump from the plane; the Hardy boys warn against this, noting that they will likely hurt or kill themselves: "'You can't jump from a moving plane,' Frank told [them]. 'It's like jumping from a second-story window'" (135). At this point, the hostages start to chant: "Throw them off! Throw them out!"—the captives having turned against their liberators (135). Over the course of a hundred and thirty-five pages, Frank and Joe have transformed from high school boys into savvy detectives, then into simulacral terrorists, then into heroic rescuers, and finally into victims of a hostile citizen mob. To silence the shouting crowd, Frank resorts to firing "a quick burst" from his machine gun into the ceiling of the plane — back to terrorist tactics, indeed. This scene shows yet again how the airport functions as an incredibly ambiguous space in which subject positions can transmogrify dynamically to the point of absurdity.

After much protest, the Hardy boys prevail upon the hostages to throw their personal belongings, along with every detachable object in the cabin of the plane, into the air intakes of the jet engines. The engines burnout, and "[t]he airliner coasted along until it came to a stop, about two-thirds of the way down the runway" (139). A hostage looks out a smashed window of the plane and observes "the most unbelievable trail of garbage you ever saw, stretched out behind us" (139). One could almost consider this a 1980s remix of the closing lines of Shelley's "Ozymandias," in which the speaker declares "round the decay / Of that colossal wreck, boundless and bare, / The lone and level sands stretch far away" (Morton 202–203).

In his essay "The Question Concerning Technology," Martin Heidegger describes "an airliner that stands on the runway" as "such an object ... [of] standing-reserve, inasmuch as it is ordered to insure the possibility of transportation" (322). At stake for Heidegger in this essay, finally, is the relation between technology and the revelation of truth. Yet the essence of technology, for Heidegger, remains "in a lofty sense ambiguous" (338). In the Hardy Boys airport mysteries, it would appear that an airliner on the runway insures nothing more and nothing less than the uncertainty of the self, wherein frameworks of identity lose coherence and become utterly "nonautonomous," to use Heidegger's word. These airport-revealed selves oscillate uncontrollably from friend to enemy, from empowered to powerless, from mobile to standing *still*. In both *Hostages of Hate* and *Tagged for Terror*, the only airplanes in these stories end up wrecked. The airport accommodates an *immaterialization* of traveling bodies: everything solid melts into air — or at least ends up as a junk pile at the end of a runway.

In many ways, the earliest Hardy Boys airport mystery represents the archetype of a terminal immaterial. In *The Great Airport Mystery* (1930), which also begins with a colossal plane wreck, Frank and Joe inadvertently stumble upon a get-rich-quick mail-theft ring operating out of their local airport. When Fenton Hardy first tells his sons about the racket, he explains that mail at the airport is both "carefully guarded" but always open to the possibility of being "left unguarded" as well (74). This paradoxical arrangement is consistent with a corollary experience of airports as both incessantly contained yet inherently unbounded. The double imperative is also mindful of Jacques Derrida's late writings on "autoimmunity," wherein Derrida claims that vulnerable spaces such as airports are integral to the existence of democracy, *in their very vulnerability*. To put it crudely: by being always open to the possibility of hijackings and disaster, airports guarantee living democracy — a state based on the principle of negotiation must invite dialectics of opposition, and thus absolute security is not merely unachievable, it is also undesirable. The guarded airport that can be left unguarded is key to the nation. This aporetic sense of space is often reflected in a physical emptying out, such as in the dump of personal belongings strewn on the runway in *Tagged for Terror*. Yet it is also worth recalling that the scene in which Fenton Hardy explains the "great airport mystery" to Frank and Joe *does not occur at the airport*. Indeed, very little of *The Great Airport Mystery* has anything to do with the airport per se. Rather, the airport is something of a blank canvas onto which bold swaths can be painted without much attention to the materiality of the surface or the medium. In fact, halfway through the story, when the Hardy boys are framed and arrested for another airport robbery, they honestly note: "We've never been to the airport, Dad" (110). Here we are in the middle of *The Great Airport Mystery*, and the real mystery seems to be why the story *has not yet arrived at the airport*. The airport remains a mysterious, elliptical, peripheral location for practically the entire story. The airport's space in the story is *spaced out*.

The "spacey" spatiality of airports can be seen in crystallized form in *The Great Airport Mystery*, and it is a form that comes to have a literary futurity of sorts. As Frank and Joe first drive out to the newly built, redundantly named Bayport airport (yet never to actually arrive, keep in mind), they discuss the geographical spread of the site:

> "Wonder why they built the airport so far out," Joe said.
> "They have to have plenty of ground. It was the only place available..." Frank explained.
> The roadster bounced along the rutted road toward the airport. A signpost near by conveyed the information that the flying field was three miles away. A little later, as the car came over the brow of a hill the Hardy Boys could see the great flat field lying in the valley below. In front of a hangar they could see a plane with silver wings [3].

Frank's assertions of "plenty" and "only" introduce a double bind of excess and lack: on the one hand, we are to understand airports as sites of expansive space and sublime vistas, metonymies for a land of "plenty." On the other hand, not "only" is such a suitable spread of land difficult to find, but citizens also accept limitations, restrictions, and routines that they would "only" put up with in airports. Also notable in this passage is the cascade of spatial descriptors by which the Hardy boys' trip to the airport is vertiginously narrated: the boys drive over a hill and see a flat field in a valley, on which a hangar lies behind a plane with silver wings. The description is almost cubistic in its opening up and flattening out of the perceptual field, and this suggests perceptual difficulty: airports are hard to perceive as totalities, because their boundaries are at once material and ethereal, discernible and yet illusive, both virtual and policed.

Such approaches to airport topographies still abound in contemporary popular culture and literature. For instance, Barry Lopez's short story "Light Action in the Caribbean," published in 2000, includes a similar account of how airports can induce a particular spatial perception. Lopez's story opens with the main character embarking on an ill-fated trip: "Driving from Arvada all the way to the new Denver airport, thought Libby, was like driving to another country before you could take off. Miles and miles of these nothing fields, no houses, no mountains, no development, no roads, no trees" (127–128). The emptying out of landforms calls attention to how the airport figures into — and dissolves — the surrounding (narrative) landscape. The airport's borders are not exactly visible, and yet the space is apparent via negative perception: what counts is what Libby *cannot* see.

In her essay "Transcapitalism and the Multiple Ecologies of an Aviopolis," media scholar Gillian Fuller claims:

> Airports are "terraformers." They literally make land. They flatten difference into manageable contours, reconfiguring geography according to the spatio-temporal rhythms and cross-modal standards of global capital.
>
> The airport is a world of looping horizons. It unfurls out over the city and insinuates itself into the daily activities of the dispersing world. In its endless grasping of the environment, old futures are abandoned and new ones appear [105–106].

Here Fuller describes the way in which airports actually create open space, against, yet also with, the hyper-consolidations of urbanism and Modernity. In the Hardy Boys' and in Libby's accounts of airports, we see this "endless grasping of the environment" in which mental awareness of open space — the experience of "looping horizons" — is a prerequisite. This spatial opening is hardly an innocent process, either. Both *The Great Airport Mystery* and "Light Action in the Caribbean" can be read as violent examples of what Fuller calls "cross-modal standards of global capital." The Hardy boys discover that a postal pilot has gone rouge and is stealing mailbags full of cash from airport hangers. The airport "insinuates itself" via the pretense of a mystery into the quaint high school lives of Frank, Joe, Chet, Biff, and the other Hardy Boys stock characters. In Barry Lopez's chilling story, two average American tourists depart on a scuba diving vacation only to be abruptly accosted, robbed, raped, killed, and dropped into the ocean by modern day pirates in a cigarette boat. The geographical emptiness around the airport is proleptic, anticipating the murderous episode with which the story ends. These narratives indicate a paradox at the intersection of vulnerable subjectivities and increased spatial perception: the opening of perceptual space around airports, as it were, also opens up possibilities for *unforeseeable* circumstances.

This particular airport problem is akin to what the critic Patricia Yaeger picks up on in her recent article "The Death of Nature and the Apotheosis of Trash; or, Rubbish Ecology." By way of arguing for a politicized aesthetics of trash, Yaeger discusses a moment in Don DeLillo's *Underworld* where a character drives around New Jersey looking for New York City, and instead finds a garbage dump just past the Newark Airport (331). Where Yaeger, however, focuses on the dump, one might back up and consider the airport that precipitates the dump. In DeLillo's spatial schema, the airport *creates* the perceptual field of empty space required to then *see* a landfill. Here is the passage from *Underworld*:

> When he went past Newark Airport he realized he'd overshot all the turnoffs and their related options. He looked for a friendly exit, untrucked and rural, and found himself sometime later on a two-lane blacktop that wended uncertainly through cattail mires. He felt a bitey edge of brine in the air and the road bent and then ended in gravel and weeds [183].

DeLillo's prose is mindful yet again of Frank and Joe's first trip to the Bayport airport, particularly in the sense of temporal indeterminacy associated with the way to (or around) an airport: "sometime later..." for DeLillo, "a little later..." for the Hardy Boys. This indefinite time pairs with flattened space and a whole host of sensory perceptions. In the opening scenes of *The Great Airport Mystery*, an errant plane swoops down upon Frank and Joe, and they note its proximity by the fact that they can hear the sonic vibrations of the plane's struts; DeLillo's character ends up in a swampy, synaesthetic ecotone, tasting the air and hearing the "gravel and weeds" crunch beneath his tires. The beautiful neologism "untrucked" performs a paralepsis of sorts, making space for the mind's eye by conjuring non-existent broadsided vehicles. DeLillo's opening up of spatiality in the service of scrutiny is, in a strong sense, the same treatment of terminal immaterial that the Hardy boys encounter again and again: airports make space for *sensing*.

By the time Frank and Joe finally arrive at the airport in *The Great Airport Mystery*, "[t]he road entering the grounds was under guard, and the big hangers were closely watched, the authorities evidently taking no chances on a repetition of the robbery"—a peculiar description, since at this point in the story the robbery has *already been repeated*; this scene occurs *after* the *second* robbery (115). This narratological forgetfulness is entirely in line with the Hardy Boys series, which tends to replay themes and tropes across numerous episodes. However, this repetition is doubly apt around the space of the airport, which functions as a kind of architecturally embodied repetition compulsion: in order to operate, users of airports must willingly undergo incredible acts of arguably self-stripping repetition. However, these acts of repetition are precisely what give airports security and stability: the stable subject requires a space of calculable repetition. And yet, amidst all the repetition of themes and schemes, the subject of the Hardy Boys airport stories remains uncertain, for one can never be certain if the mystery is about securing space, stabilizing personae, or some mixture that takes place in the elision between space and self.

In *The Interpretation of Dreams*, Freud suggests that the way to approach the manifest content of dreams is to never think it can be "over-interpreted" (923). Rather, one must precisely linger on interpretive conundrums in order to grasp the fathomless amounts of "condensation" that have taken place within the latent content of dreams. In this analysis, I have borrowed Freud's methodology, albeit to analyze a quite different environment. My subject of analysis is not the nebula of dreams; instead, it is the site of airports in the Hardy Boys mysteries, this rhetorical hub that condenses thematic material from far-reaching destinations. In these stories, and around this *site*, one discovers repressed spatial ambiguities and uncertain subjectivities. To continue traveling with Freud for a moment, we might even go as far to say that the light distractions of airport reading involve not just an uncertain subject, but an *unconscious* subject as well.

It is worth noting, by way of conclusion, that throughout many of the Hardy Boys mysteries, Frank and Joe continually carp about not wanting to go to college; they have no interest at all in higher education. In *The Great Airport Mystery*, which is set around Frank and Joe's high school graduation, Frank rhetorically pleads with his mother, "Do we have to go to college?" (71). Instead, Frank and Joe want to be private detectives like their father, the famous Fenton Hardy. The Hardy Boys series represents a sort of endless deferment of college: these "boys" never grow up, never want to grow up, and the stories keep Frank and Joe in an adventurous — if also routinely infantilized — comportment, decade after decade. This strain recurs in *Hostages of Hate*, when at one point Frank and Joe find themselves searching the Georgetown University campus for a radical student named Pia who has been recruited by international terrorists to advertise their cause on a college campus. When Frank and Joe first encounter Pia in a student union, she is making homemade signs advocating revolution. Finally, in *Tagged for Terror*, one of the baggage handlers suspected to be involved with the luggage theft ring (and therefore inexplicably linked to a terrorist cell) is reasoned to be tight on cash because he is trying to pay for college. Continually, the college campus is alluded to as a place that can breed terrorists and thieves — uncertain subjects, par excellence. For Frank and Joe, college is at the distant end of a theory/practice spectrum, with the Hardy boys representing the practical, hands-on end of street smarts and deductive reasoning. Yet the subject of the airport seems to warp this spectrum in a compelling way, simply by acting as *terminal immaterial*, that open space in which indeterminate scenarios can play out, allegiances can shift, and identities can be swapped. The airport puts pressure on the individual subject, on the very concept of "the subject," and offers itself up as subject for investigation: one might even say that the airport is open to *theory*. Amidst the anti-intellectual impulse of the Hardy Boys series, Frank and Joe find themselves schooled at the airport. In other words, the airport *as subject* becomes a pedagogical space — a space for thinking within and about the uncertain subjects of everyday life.

WORKS CITED

Augé, Marc. *Non-Places: Introduction to an Anthropology of Supermodernity*. New York: Verso, 1995.
DeLillo, Don. *Underworld*. New York: Scribner, 1997.
Derrida, Jacques. "Autoimmunity: Real and Symbolic Suicides — A Dialogue with Jacques Derrida." *Philosophy in a Time of Terror: Dialogues with Jürgen Habermas and Jacques Derrida*. Ed. Giovanna Borradori. Chicago: University of Chicago Press, 2003. 86–136.
Dixon, Franklin W. *The Great Airport Mystery*. New York: Grosset & Dunlap, 1930.
_____. *Hostages of Hate*. New York: Archway Paperbacks, 1987.
_____. *Tagged for Terror*. New York: Archway Paperbacks, 1993.
Freud, Sigmund. *The Interpretation of Dreams*. *The Norton Anthology of Theory and Criticism*. Ed. Vincent Leitch, et al. New York: W.W. Norton, 2001. 919–929.
Fuller, Gillian, and Ross Harley. *Aviopolis: A Book About Airports*. London: Black Dog, 2004.
Heidegger, Martin. "The Question Concerning Technology." *Basic Writings*. Ed. David Farrell Krell, 2d ed. New York: Harper Collins, 1993.
Lopez, Barry. *Light Action in the Caribbean*. New York: Alfred A. Knopf, 2000.
Pound, Ezra. *Selected Poems*. New York: New Directions, 1957.
Shelley, Percy Bysshe. "Ozymandias." *The Cambridge Companion to Shelley*. Ed. Timothy Morton. Cambridge: Cambridge University Press, 2006.
The Terminal. Dir. Steven Spielberg. Perf. Tom Hanks, Stanley Tucci. DreamWorks, 2004.
Trento, Susan, and Joseph Trento. *Unsafe at any Altitude: Exposing the Illusion of Aviation Security*. Hanover: Steerforth, 2006.
Yaeger, Patricia. "The Death of Nature and the Apotheosis of Trash; or, Rubbish Ecology." *PMLA* 123.2 (2008): 321–339.

4

Strategies of Adaptation: The Hardy Boys on Television

BRIAN TAVES

The Hardy Boys, while never appearing in the movies like Nancy Drew, have emerged in five television incarnations beginning in the 1950s, offering each generation since a version of its own. Two of these have secured a place in public memory for different generations: the two *Mickey Mouse Club* serials (1956–57) and *The Hardy Boys/Nancy Drew Mysteries* (1977–79). Major DVD releases of the first of the Walt Disney versions, *The Mystery of the Applegate Treasure* (1956), and the initial two seasons of *The Hardy Boys/Nancy Drew Mysteries*, have amplified their canonical status. However, there were other versions, important in their own right for demonstrating alternative ways to bring the characters to the screen. For young children, *The Hardy Boys* (1969–71) used a cartoon form, while *The Hardy Boys* (1995) sought to place the team in a more adult, live-action context, although the latter achieved little attention during either broadcast or DVD release. The 1967 pilot, *The Mystery of the Chinese Junk*, only available from archival sources today, foreshadowed how the classic characters could be faithfully filmed a decade later in *The Hardy Boys/Nancy Drew Mysteries*. While *The Mystery of the Chinese Junk* and *The Mystery of the Applegate Treasure* are the only dramatizations of specific books on the screen, the various television incarnations have influenced not only perceptions of the Hardy Boys books, but also the revision of the original books from 1959 to 1973 and the plots of some subsequent publications.[1]

Nearly three decades passed from the first Hardy Boys book in 1927 before one visionary perceived that the stories could be brought to the screen. By the time Walt Disney signed a contract with the Stratemeyer Syndicate, he had expanded beyond animation to live action movies, a theme park, and television, all functioning in an unprecedented symbiotic relationship. The arrangement was advantageous to both the Syndicate and Disney; with the 1954–55 Davy Crockett mini-series and feature films, Disney had proven the corporate ability to film an American icon, as well as to carry the subsidiary rights into a myriad of ancillary markets. On February 7, 1956, Disney bought the rights to all Hardy Boys books published to that date (through *The Hooded Hawk Mystery*), with a contract that included not only full authority for dramatizations but to issue every kind of tie-in and novelty item, from games to comic books to coloring books (U.S. Copyright Office). The Stratemeyer Syndicate must have believed that this related activity, and the connection with the nation's premier purveyor of juvenile movies and television, would boost sales far beyond the potential payment for the rights, which was a mere $5,700 (Kismaric and Heiferman 104). There were only three caveats: use of the name Franklin W. Dixon would continue; the Disney publications would not supplant the original book series or its continuation; and in recognition of the juvenile audience, alcohol, tobacco, or firearms (save for hunting) were forbidden (U.S. Copyright Office).

Disney lost no time, delegating Bill Welch to produce the program. A wraparound announcing the show was placed on editions of *The Clue in the Embers* issued in early 1956 (Carpentieri with Mular 364). Beginning in October of that year, the first Hardy Boys novel, *The Tower Treasure*, was broadcast through serial-style segments within the multi-subject daily mix of the children's variety show, *The Mickey Mouse Club*, on ABC. Retitled *The Mystery of the Applegate Treasure*, it ran for nineteen episodes (plus one introductory show hosted by Tim Considine and Tommy Kirk and composed of clips) of about twelve minutes apiece, for a total running time of close to four hours.

This was the second season of *The Mickey Mouse Club*, with the Hardy Boys as the follow-up to the previous year's three serials, most notably *Spin and Marty* (Mallory 53). One of its stars was retained to play Frank Hardy, Disney contract player Tim Considine (son of 1930s and 1940s producer John W. Considine, Jr.). After an open casting call for Joe, Tommy Kirk was selected (and also began a long Disney association). Both actors were in their mid-teens, but behaved for the show as if they were between nine to thirteen years old. This is even younger than the ages given in *The Tower Treasure*, fifteen and sixteen, and slightly younger than the traditional seventeen and eighteen that would become predominate in the later books. There may have been valid reasons for the shift on screen, most notably the desire to more closely approximate the characters to *The Mickey Mouse Club* audience. In a practical sense, too, for ongoing performances, actors must be selected who can "grow" into their roles, since child and young adult actors often mature too quickly and visibly. Nonetheless, making the characters apparently so much younger on screen undercut the viability of the mysteries, rendering their exploits even more improbable than those of the boys of the novels in their late teens.

The plot in Jackson Gillis's teleplay *The Mystery of the Applegate Treasure* drew very loosely from the original 1927 novel, *The Tower Treasure.* Young Perry Robinson (Donald MacDonald) becomes an inadvertent victim of the theft of valuables from the querulous, wealthy Applegate (Florenz Ames). Most of the townsfolk in the book and program believe Applegate's accusation against Perry, with only the Hardy boys retaining their faith in his innocence. The desire to assist him becomes the motivation for their involvement in the case. In *The Tower Treasure*, Perry is a school chum of the Hardys, one of the brightest lads in school, and offspring of the caretaker accused of the theft by Applegate. Perry is forced to quit school to help support his family now that his father has been dismissed. By contrast, in *The Mystery of the Applegate Treasure*, Perry is an orphan, employed and suspected by Applegate, and Perry could be sent from the suburb to the city orphanage unless the Hardy boys can prove his innocence. In both the book and serial, Perry provides a serious undertone, the innocent who has been condemned on circumstantial evidence, with only the Hardy boys trying to save him.

Gillis's adaptation replaces the book's prosaic theft of jewels and bonds with the juvenile dream of discovering pirate treasure in one's own neighborhood. This was further emphasized through the daily repetition of an opening credits montage taken from Disney's *Treasure Island* (1950) and a theme song shifting the focus from detection to the latest in a long line of thefts. At the beginning of the song, the pirate's treasure chest is overflowing with doubloons; at the melody's conclusion it is empty, establishing the task of the narrative — to fill the chest once more, to regain the largesse of the past that has been lost in the present. As Joe assures the audience in the introductory episode, there aren't any real pirates any more. However, the lure that motivated them remains, and to save Perry and find Applegate's booty, the boys will have to bridge past and present in uncovering the mystery, and learn to negotiate the worlds of childhood and adulthood, understanding a range of individuals who at first seem distant and strange. This is particularly true of Applegate, whose delusions about his pirate ancestry became part of this new narrative recipe, with such key support as the plumber (and former Applegate groundskeeper) played by Arthur Shields added as a red herring. Only when they have successfully negotiated these challenges of time and generation are the Hardy boys able to achieve their objective, establishing the case as an analogy for the passage toward adulthood.

The rotund Chet Morton, the most constant companion of the Hardys and a frequent source of amusement, is replaced in the program by his sister. Instead of a regular date for Joe, as in the books, on screen Iola Morton (Carole Ann Campbell) is made even more childish in age and manner than the brothers, negating any question of even the most innocent teenage crush. While presumably intended to ensure a female character with whom female and/or younger viewers of *The Mystery of the Applegate Treasure* might identify with more than the two brothers, the severe alteration of Iola's disposition made her into the neighborhood pest (with predictable shrieks of fright), accentuating the problem caused by under-aging the brothers.

The Disney studio also adopted a frequent patriarchal narrative tactic, emulated by subsequent adaptations of the Hardy Boys on screen, of eliminating mother Laura Hardy, already a marginal figure in the books. The only other woman in the series brought to the screen for *The Mickey Mouse Club* is the polar opposite of the impetuous Iola, Aunt Gertrude (Sarah Selby). Depicted as father Fenton Hardy's maiden sister and an omnipresent scold in the novels, Aunt Gertrude is here portrayed as being more earnest as a steady homemaker and the only maternal presence for the boys. This structure allowed the moral concerns of both Stratemeyer and Disney to be met; although the boys might not quite follow to the letter the instructions of their aunt, this could be viewed as less serious than disobeying an actual parent.

Gertrude even pointedly upbraids typical 1950s crew-cut father Fenton Hardy (Russ Conway) for his frequent absences from home as detrimental to the boy's development. While the issue is dealt with seriously, and is a valid one, its importance also serves to undermine the possibility of the lads' collaboration with their father in the investigation, a motif of the novels. Fenton Hardy's detection is not seen as incarnating the action ideal; rather, he is a standard 1950s father-with-a-briefcase. Instead of the boy's emulation of him as a positive factor, in an unusual twist for Disney family entertainment, his career seems to be a source of tension in the home and a possible bad influence. It was also the opposite of the dynamic at work in the books, wherein the father's career is an inspiration leading to positive behavior by the boys.

While Tommy Kirk recalled a sixteen-week shooting schedule, which would have been lavish for television production at the time, the serial does not reflect the typical Disney quality (Valley 61). Outside of the gloomy Applegate mansion, there is little sense of atmosphere. All of the settings (such as the Hardy house, a local park, and the mansion) were created on a single large stage on the Disney lot, and they are used so repetitively as to become stifling under Charles Haas's direction.

The Mystery of the Applegate Treasure changes Bayport from a town with varied possibilities for intriguing cases into a prosaic 1950s American suburb, distant from the metropolis and ultimately stultifying. In the books, the redundantly-named city, situated on Barmet Bay in the Northeast coast, offers varying locales for the brothers to discover, ranging from the town itself to the surrounding countryside and the harbor, sea lanes, and nearby islands. Increasingly as the books continue, clues lead to more distant regions, sometimes in other countries. However, with the evident change in age and social class of the Hardy boys on screen for *The Mickey Mouse Club*, the possibility for this mobility was lost. Only bicycles were available as a mode of transportation, placing an inherent limitation on the boys' roving. The familiar scenes in the books of the Hardys motorcycling on the Shore Road or boating along the coast in the *Sleuth* were beyond the capacity of the heroes as presented in this television incarnation.

The variation of locales in the Hardy Boys books that had been lost in *The Mystery of the Applegate Treasure* determined that the follow-up, broadcast exactly a year later, should have a contrasting setting. Instead of the suburb and a creepy mansion, *The Mystery of Ghost Farm* presents outdoor thrills, finding menace and uncertainty in the most bucolic of surroundings, actually Morrison Ranch in the San Fernando Valley. At a supposedly abandoned farm, the animals are being fed — but by whom? This premise proves no less durable than the missing "pieces of eight" in *The Mystery of the Applegate Treasure*. The combination of day and night, of indoors and outdoors, becomes stronger in this new setting, as helmed by western director R.G. Springsteen.

The Hardys try to solve the riddle of Ghost Farm while also securing the lives of the animals, aged and slated for destruction. "A man named Fred" (Paul Wexler) in a truck is ready to take them away to their fate, and in the best Disney tradition, the Hardys spoil his plans and uncover a larger case in the process. Nonetheless, following the Disney pattern, a jolt of realism is injected amidst the make-believe, and the deadly fate of surplus animals may have caused consternation among some viewers — as well as insuring that they would return for the next day's installments. Just as Perry's innocence had been proven in *The Mystery of the Applegate Treasure*, at the Ghost Farm the Hardys again offer moral superiority, as well as sagaciousness, as advocates for a burro, a horse, a sheep, and a goat.

In *The Mystery of Ghost Farm* the Hardy home only occasionally reappears, with Fenton Hardy and Aunt Gertrude in smaller roles. Iola becomes a more active player, and, a year older, Considine and Kirk are more appropriate for their roles. Frank is verging on an obsession with girls, rather than detection, causing friction with his brother, as Joe wants nothing to do with the pursuing Iola.

Adding panache is venerable performer Andy Clyde as the "ghost" of the farm, old man Lacey, who faked his death a month earlier in a plan to use his life insurance to keep his animals alive. The scheme was hatched by his cousin Eric (John Baer), but not for a similarly altruistic motive. Instead, Eric wants to keep people away from the farm because he has learned that Lacey's late brother Billy hid his bonds somewhere around the house. A pragmatic lawyer, Mr. Binks (Hugh Sanders), is ready to take almost any side in the resulting dispute, and while not a villain, provides a yardstick against which to measure the selflessness of the Hardys and zookeeper Bray (John Harmon). Eric fails to realize that the note above the fireplace, "Take Care of All God's Creatures, and They Will Take Care of You," is to be taken literally. The Hardys, however, realize this homily has a double meaning, and inside the bell of Billy's goat is the key to a safety deposit box with the bonds.

While *The Mystery of Ghost Farm* has fewer obvious "thrills" than *The Mystery of the Applegate Treasure* with its dark mansion and pirate loot, the new serial maintains suspense and is a worthy successor. *The Mystery of Ghost Farm* offered a number of scenes no less memorable than its predecessor, especially considering the young audience. Before Lacey is revealed as alive, his ghostly voice-overs are heard while the camera observes only Billy's goat, as if the animal has some special insight, but also foreshadowing the goat's pivotal role in the resolution of the case. Lacey himself is finally introduced as alive through a shot that reveals him hanging upside-down, unkempt hair dangling, in a scene parodying the idea of a ghost but one which also offers its own shock value. Toward the conclusion, as Iola is hidden in the truck with the animals on the way to be destroyed, she signals frantically but is unable to get Joe's attention — the expression of every child's nightmare of finding themselves in peril and unheard.

Slightly more compact, at around two and a half hours, *The Mystery of Ghost Farm* ran a mere fourteen chapters, ten minutes apiece, or three weeks of *The Mickey Mouse Club* airtime, as opposed to the month of twelve-minute episodes for *The Mystery of the Applegate Treasure*. (Like its predecessor, *The Mystery of Ghost Farm* begins with an introductory episode of clips that serves as an extended advertisement for the coming segments.) Jackson Gillis again scripts, but as an original rather than an adaptation, *The Mystery of Ghost Farm* flows more smoothly than its predecessor, partly because there are fewer suspects. The cliffhanger climaxes at the conclusion of each episode are less disruptive and repetitive than they had been when inserted into the narrative of *The Mystery of the Applegate Treasure*.

A number of Hardy Boys tie-ins were created during *The Mickey Mouse Club* years, including records, a game, a coloring book, four comic books, and adaptations of the Hardy Boys books in several Disney magazines. Curiously, some of these show an actor who is not Tommy Kirk in the role of Joe, while Tim Considine remains in the shots; Kirk was apparently not participating in all the publicity. This was the last season of new material on *The Mickey Mouse Club*, already only a half-hour show instead of the hour daily presentation of previous seasons, and Disney dropped the Hardy Boys to bring other literary characters to television.

When the Hardy Boys were tackled again, exactly one decade later, in *The Mystery of the Chinese Junk*, it was by 20th Century Fox television, having already successfully transformed venerable heroes into contemporary television with *Batman* (1966–68) and *The Green Hornet* (1966–67). Avoiding the camp of the former and resembling the latter, this color pilot for a Hardy Boys series was a near-miss for the NBC 1967 season ("TV Pilot Reviews").[2] While only a single sixty-minute program, instead of a serial, the choices made in *The Mystery of the Chinese Junk* clearly take into account aspects of its Disney forerunner.

Unlike the children's audience of *The Mickey Mouse Club*, *The Mystery of the Chinese Junk* was aimed at viewers several years older. The reviewer for *Variety* noted the fundamental question as to whether or not the youth of the day would follow the old Stratemeyer formula, and it was probably precisely this uncertainty that kept the pilot from becoming a series ("TV Pilot Reviews"). The Hardys are presented as short-haired and immaculately clean-cut, ideals of the young generation, tinkering with chemistry and gadgets and incarnating a pre–Vietnam innocence.

The Mystery of the Chinese Junk may have been selected since, as one of the later volumes (published in 1960), it appeared after the Disney purchase of the rights to the first thirty-four books. Moreover, filming *The Mystery of the Chinese Junk* required presenting a range of Bayport areas and a considerably more diverse use of outdoor locales than had been the case with *The Mickey Mouse Club* serials.

Similarly, the book's ethnic appeal made it an obvious selection, and the Far Eastern overtones were fully exploited. Such properties as *The King and I* and *South Pacific* were still fashionable entertainment in 1967, on television and with stage revivals, and Bruce Lee's Kato was the most popular element of *The Green Hornet*. Casting a Hardy friend (Brian Fong as Jim Foy) in *The Mystery of the Chinese Junk* who could exhibit martial arts skills would have made him a viable regular, particularly in a racially progressive era that was beginning to demand minorities in television supporting roles.

The choice of *The Mystery of the Chinese Junk* reflected the simultaneous integration of American audiences and youth; just as the Hardy Boys books had offered an ethnically diverse Bayport, the Hardy Boys on screen need not be the bastion of white suburbia that *The Mickey Mouse Club* had offered a decade earlier. (Three of the episodes of the 1970s *The Hardy Boys/Nancy Drew Mysteries* would also use Asian characters and motifs: "Wipe Out," "The Mystery of Jade Kwan Yin," and "Sole Survivor.")

The pilot was not tailored to any existing contract stars or program demographics, as had been the case with the Disney serials. 20th Century Fox, wisely enough, realized that the property itself was sufficient headliner; unlike the holdover of Considine from the previous *Mickey Mouse Club* serial *Spin and Marty*, familiar faces were unnecessary. Richard Gates played Frank, and Tim Matheson was Joe, both nineteen at the time, and thus the boys' ages were appropriate on this screen occasion.

However, writer and producer Richard Murphy follows the Disney precedent regarding the women in the household, with Laura Hardy not figuring at all. Aunt Gertrude (Portia Nelson) is purely a homebody, without the verbal bite so memorable from the books. Unable to keep up with the deductions of her nephews but providing loose adult supervision, she is a comfort to parents, and adolescents as well, knowing a maternal figure is ready — but only if needed, and far less interfering than even her *Mickey Mouse Club* counterpart.

The boys' father only provides remote, general guidance over a shortwave radio until he is captured with them near the end. (Richard Anderson's performance is perhaps Fenton Hardy's best incarnation, effortlessly exuding intellect and paternal caring.) As so often occurs in the Hardy Boys books, father and sons begin working on separate problems that turn out to be two sides of the same case, bringing them together at the end of a narrative in a sequence marked by peril, shared sleuthing ability, and family reunion.

Certainly the adaptation of *The Mystery of the Chinese Junk* was more faithful to the novel than *The Mystery of the Applegate Treasure* had been to *The Tower Treasure*. No incidents were invented for the screen version of *The Mystery of the Chinese Junk*, and only a few were deleted from the middle of the book (those most difficult to stage, such as a cave rescue). The conclusion was slightly rearranged to bring together all the major characters at once. The one addition was harmless: a large hound, "Tiny," ferocious but lovable, fulfilling a convention of youth-directed entertainment.

In the pilot, the Hardy boys and their friends invest in the Chinese junk *Hai Hau* (appropriately translated as "calm sea") as a summer harbor tourist venture. Essentially independent, they are on the cusp of adulthood in the indeterminate, eternal summer vacation at the end of high school and before college. As portrayed in the pilot, the Hardy boys are not unusually intellectual characters; no teenage Sherlock is to be found here. Yet they are diligent, curious, and have a scientific bent, the best of the younger generation, while still capable of enjoying fun at the beach.

For the first and only time on screen, the Hardy schoolmates, male and female, are shown interacting to solve a mystery, particularly chums Chet Morton, Tony Prito, and Biff Hooper. Emphasis is given to the youthful milieu; the soft-rock/jazzy score of *The Mystery of the Chinese Junk* is pervasive, enhancing the teen appeal. The mid–1960s was the era of beach movies, and the *Hai Hau* is even the scene of a teenage dance party. Dominating the plot, fortunately, are not teenage high jinks but rather the uncovering of why so many other individuals are desirous, sometimes violently so, of the seemingly valueless *Hai Hau*. A number of character actors enrich *The Mystery of the Chinese Junk*, from Malcolm Atterbury as a rival ship owner to James Shigeta as an enigmatic Chinese agent, and give the show a capacity to be accepted by older viewers. Edward Andrews is an odd villain for a Hardy Boys mystery, initially appearing in a Dracula-style cape, and seems to be channeling the effeminate yet menacing "Dr. Zachary Smith" from *Lost in Space* (1965–68).

Despite the virtues of *The Mystery of the Chinese Junk*, Gates and Matheson offer little vitality as the brothers, and Larry Peerce's direction fails to achieve the necessary suspense. The pilot's tone doesn't quite capture what made the books memorable, and is a little too redolent of television conventions. Nonetheless, *The Mystery of the Chinese Junk* deserves plaudits for its fidelity, particularly in comparison with other Hardy Boys television adaptations.

"Oh boy, here come the Hardys; oh boy, we're having a party..." (*The Hardy Boys*, Sutherland). So went the theme song of Filmation's *The Hardy Boys*. Directed by Hal Sutherland and produced by Lou Scheimer & Norm Prescott, the series premiered on September 6, 1969, on ABC's Saturday morning cartoon lineup and ran for two years. Whereas *The Mystery of the Chinese Junk* had mirrored an already fading era of youth as epitomized in the Grosset & Dunlap books, this new animated program dismissed this previous conception to launch the Hardys into the mod era.

Each of the seventeen episodes consisted of a pair of perfunctory mysteries, sometimes using elements from the books, but low on narrative credibility and coherence. The Stratemeyer Syndicate's Nancy Axelrad was not pleased, at least aesthetically: "The stories were so action-packed, you couldn't follow them at all. It was not a success" (Herz 67). The Hardys were now a traveling five-piece band, solving cases in between gigs — success as a rock performer becoming a new, more topical ambition for youth, supplementing the appeal of becoming a detective. An influence of the series was recognizable in the revision of one of the books, *The Flickering Torch Mystery*, published in 1971. An added plot thread included the boys having a band that helps solve the case — although it is handled in such a way that it could be modified to fit the musical culture of any era.

The animated portions of the series were bridged by a central live action musical interlude with a Hardy Boys band accompanied by psychedelic colors and designs. In this way the young and unsophisticated viewer accepts the cartoon as not a separate or stylized form, but a faithful rendition of the Hardy's off-stage detecting, the live action serving to validate the characters in animated form. Several records were issued in conjunction with the show, sung by the Hardy Boys band that had been created for it. (Other tie-ins included comic books and a View-Master version of the Hardy Boys book, *The Secret of the Caves*, from the revised text published in 1964.)

Within this new mix, for the first time the many skills of the group come to the fore. They display not only the expected athleticism (apprehending villains without violence), but also pilot a speedboat (the *Sea Sleuth*), go scuba diving, fly a seaplane (the *Sky Sleuth*), and even play the steam calliope at a circus. However, other than Aunt Gertrude and Fenton Hardy, only a fretful Chet, renamed "Chubby," remained of the friends, with a new African American companion, Pete Jones, added along with a decorative female singer, Wanda Kay.

As distant as this concept was from the Grosset & Dunlap books, it did reinforce the link between the Hardys and contemporary music that was prefigured by *The Mystery of the Chinese Junk* and would blossom in the 1970s *Hardy Boys/Nancy Drew Mysteries*, and still find echoes in the rock background score of the 1995 version. Whereas readers may have absorbed the books in the relative vacuum of the individual experience, television partook of the larger entertainment and pop culture of the late 1960s and 1970s. Hence, Filmation's desire was less to attract readers of the books to a television show, than to create an expanded television experience that would appeal beyond those who knew the books. Nonetheless, the show rebounded to the benefit of the volumes, and sales steadily improved during the years of the Filmation broadcasts (Kismaric and Heiferman 120).

Although the Hardy Boys and Nancy Drew are often thought of together because of their reputation as the premier characters of juvenile detective fiction, previously they had divergent screen interpretations, with Nancy not visualized since her flighty 1930s motion picture impersonation by Bonita Granville. By the mid–1970s, classical detective programs were popular once more on the small screen as cop shows faded and a demand grew for family entertainment. Universal brought to fruition a combined Nancy Drew/Hardy Boys series that would alternate every week, following the lead of *The Bold Ones* and the *NBC Mystery Movie* that offered *Columbo*, *McMillan and Wife*, and *McCloud* in rotation. In one respect, *The Hardy Boys/Nancy Drew Mysteries* returned to the primacy of the thriller elements that had been subsumed by Filmation and even failed to fully register in *The Mystery of the Chinese Junk*. Quickly, however, under the guidance of executive producer Glen Larson, supervising producer Michael Sloan and producer Joe Boston, this new version also became a live action successor to Filmation.

As a mid-season replacement, casting for *The Hardy Boys/Nancy Drew Mysteries* took place in November 1976 and production did not begin until January 2, 1977, shooting about twelve hours a day (Herz 24, 44; Turner 30–31). *The Hardy Boys/Nancy Drew Mysteries* premiered Sunday, January 31 at 7 P.M. on ABC, opposite *60 Minutes* on CBS and *World of Disney* on NBC. *The Hardy Boys/Nancy Drew Mysteries* became the first ABC show to best Disney for family ratings in this time slot (Turner 32). The new program seemed to have the potential for a long-running, straightforward mystery series similar to the books, geared towards early teens but also acceptable to adults. Even though episodes entitled "The Disappearing Floor" and "The Flickering Torch Mystery" had little relation to the novels, the fact that even some of the book titles were used was a comfort to those who came to the show as readers of the books. ("The Flickering Torch Mystery" was even issued as *Flight to Nowhere*, one of three 1978 novelizations of the series published by Grosset & Dunlap but credited to the Stratemeyer Syndicate itself, rather than Franklin W. Dixon, establishing the tie-ins as a separate commodity.)

Apparently Harriet Adams demanded, and received, a level of script approval, perhaps on the basis of the Filmation experience. Axelrad noted the adherence was to a basic formula: "Good mystery and lots of action, with some educational material" (Herz 8). As in *The Mickey Mouse Club* versions, the Hardys of the 1970s are untouched by alcohol and tobacco, and do not use guns; they rely on their brains, and occasionally their brawn. Tension had to be created without violence, although by the end of the second season, this was being circumvented, partially, through psychological elements, such as the eerie schizophrenia of the episode "Campus Terror."

Initially, by retaining relative fidelity to the conception of both the Franklin W. Dixon and Carolyn Keene books, the program started out well.

Arlene Sidaris and Joyce Brotman, novices who had spent several years guiding the Hardy Boys and Nancy Drew to television form, brought affection for the original premises as the show's co-producers. Parker Stevenson played Frank, and Shaun Cassidy portrayed Joe in credible, late-teens manner. Both stars had read some of the books, and Stevenson re-read them while shooting (Herz 33, 46). The hour format allowed time for sufficient development of the mystery plot. There, too, was Fenton Hardy (Edmund Gilbert) and Aunt Gertrude (Edith Atwater), and even Lisa Eilbacher as Callie Shaw — although here replacing the book's Sam Radley as Fenton's assistant, rather than acting as Frank's girlfriend. She did not last beyond the first season.

The Nancy Drew segments were of better quality than the Hardy Boys, which perhaps more easily fell into the formulas, sets, and supporting players on the Universal lot (a proclivity amusingly chided in the two-part episode "The Mystery of the Hollywood Phantom," using the undisguised backlot and studio tour area). In an age of feminism and set against a slew of male television crime solvers, Nancy was inherently a contrast. As enacted by Pamela Sue Martin, Nancy conveyed a serious, cerebral quality, and the necessary earnestness for a mystery heroine. Her embodiment of girl power, as well as incidental sex appeal, gave her a charisma for viewers in both genders. At the time, Nancy Drew books had actually outsold the Hardy Boys by millions of books, yet as *The Hardy Boys/Nancy Drew Mysteries* progressed, not only did Nancy lose her preeminent position on screen, but the Hardy Boys supplanted her (Herz 17).[3]

The Hardy Boys had finally transcended previous screen limitations, partly as a result of casting. Shaun Cassidy as Joe was the first of the duo to be selected, although he was then an acting novice, age eighteen, who had had some musical releases in Europe but not the United States. Surely more important was that he was best known as the younger brother of David Cassidy, star of *The Partridge Family* (1970–74). Stevenson was the more experienced, and visibly older at twenty-four, bland but still appropriate as Frank. As in the books, there are abundant local mysteries and scenic landmarks to provide arresting settings, but the Hardy Boys quickly left Bayport for travels as distant as Africa and South America.

Unfortunately, *The Hardy Boys/Nancy Drew Mysteries* had no time to develop the characters intrinsically. Cassidy's burgeoning teeny-bopper popularity as a pop singer overwhelmed his character and began to invade the show. Cassidy's Joe became romantic and impulsive, given all the scenes demanding sensitivity and emotion, although his acting skills were less consistent than Stevenson's. Stevenson took on the role of the more believable, dependable older brother, as reflected in his providing the narration. Episodes frequently had to make time for Cassidy's songs, interrupting the narrative for musical interludes that began to compete for narrative supremacy. Many episodes were placed in settings to make the singing likely, although not advantageous for a mystery, Joe often seeming to care as much about resolving the mystery in time to sing a song as bringing criminals to justice. Most improbable were the occasions when performing became a method of going undercover. Cassidy also lacked the essential attributes for the male portion of the audience; while his elastic gyrations were part of his singing persona, he was too slight for an action role. Frank became Joe's foil, the masculine side of the duo, with a running gag that whenever Joe performed, Frank was away solving the case.

With Cassidy's soaring popularity, the Nancy Drew episodes almost inevitably failed to garner the same ratings (Herz 50–51). To resolve the problem, Nancy was no longer left alone, but absorbed within the Hardy orbit during the second (full) season, becoming Frank's love interest. The merger was undertaken with Harriet Adams's permission; she had been pleased with the development of *The Hardy Boys/Nancy Drew Mysteries* (Herz 25–26). Unfortunately, Nancy thereby became recessive in a program that was otherwise overwhelmed by patriarchy, with the Hardy Boys themselves and the parallel widowed parents, Carson Drew and (apparently) Fenton Hardy. Perhaps had Nancy been allowed to remain a rival and spirited sometime adversary, rather than linked romantically, the concept of some shared exploits might have functioned. Larson was apparently unaware that endless deferral is possible in such series, and the most memorable romantic partnerships are based on immediate and ongoing sparring, sparks that leave the viewers eager for the next installment — rather than seeing Nancy melt at Frank's first kiss.

The Universal Hardy Boys programs more frequently used horror themes than the books, and placed Bayport firmly in Massachusetts. Occasionally there was a standout episode, such as "The House on Possessed Hill" (novelized as *The Haunted House*) where director Daniel Haller composed a minor television masterpiece fit to rank with his work in the 1960s American International Pictures horror cycle. The *Psycho* house exterior, still standing on the Universal lot from 1960, itself such a cliché that it might have overwhelmed many a lesser talent, is converted into a gothic chiller through décor, shadows, and camera angles. The score and sound effects were often asynchronous and had a tenuous relation to the diegesis, leaving the audience uncertain as to the portions which were heard only subjectively by one of the characters, or might even be supernatural. By editing around ellipses, Haller was able to minimize the standard manners of Stevenson and especially Cassidy, and guest star Melanie Griffith's childish voice embodies a woman trapped in the trauma of a murder she saw when she was four years old. Numerous throwaway shots that other directors would have missed enhance the atmosphere; Griffith's pursuers are photographed to resemble specters, and a fight between Frank and a suspect is played out in silence. By contrast, the highly touted two-part second season opener (heavily advertised and published as a novelization) that introduced the merging of the two previously separate shows, "The Hardy Boys and Nancy Drew Meet Dracula," is filled with cringing absurdities. Frank and Joe attend a rock concert in Vlad the Impaler's ancestral castle, and while supposedly broadcast around the world, the few extras in director Joseph Pevney's "crowd" constantly reveal the modest television budget. Paul Williams as a rock star and Cassidy offer contrasting tunes, and casting against type is carried to the ultimate degree with Lorne Greene (late of *Bonanza*) as the age-old vampire masquerading as a foreign agent. (Curiously, in the novelization he is not an actual vampire, while on-screen, that is the inescapable conclusion.) Only in returning such horror veterans as Carl Esmond, Martin Kosleck, and Fritz Feld to supporting roles is any resonance achieved with the genre.

Guest stars became a standout feature by the second season, with such names as Craig Stevens, Dennis Weaver, Stuart Whitman, Ray Milland, Howard Duff, Joseph Cotton, and Lloyd Nolan lending gravitas. Increasingly, two-part episodes were used. However, between a star who became the idol of the *Tiger Beat* generation, and the merging of two separate sets of characters into one, *The Hardy Boys/Nancy Drew Mysteries* inherently lost the viewers who were readers of the books. The emphasis on Joe-becoming-Cassidy also alienated the male audience that enjoyed the original premise of the books. Moreover, the ratings had been shaky from the start, and never reached the plateau for producers to resist juggling with the formula. *The Hardy Boys/ Nancy Drew Mysteries* made the mistake of trying to expand its potential audience, rather than secure the one it had, moving steadily away from the conventions of the source. It thereby lost both its own dramatic validity and alienated its base.

Janet Louise Johnston took over as Nancy in the second season, and the character was dropped entirely by the third. Now simply called *The Hardy Boys Mysteries*, the brothers were recruited by the government, in order to allow stories that displayed more adult emotions. Bayport was abandoned for a California base, with the FBI or CIA assisting in cases that increasingly revolved around national security (Turner 6). However, this only confused younger viewers who could no longer identify with the Hardy's new milieu, and for a show pegged to Cassidy's personal popularity, this induced a decline that led to its mid-season cancellation.

For the studio, however, what might seem like a series of illogical decisions, tampering with and ultimately sabotaging a proven formula in favor of experimenting with new ones, was a decision based on economics. Cassidy's musical franchise was regarded as at least as profitable at the moment as *The Hardy Boys/Nancy Drew Mysteries* might prove to be over time, so transforming it into a showcase for a singer was a source of quick and obvious profit. His first two albums had gone platinum, selling more than a million copies (Turner 8). When Joe performs his trademark "Da Doo Run Run" for the second time in "The Mystery of the Flying Courier," the fifth of the Hardy episodes in the first season, the show has clearly become a promotion for a star and song which ascended to a top slot on pop-records charts, with Cassidy's record released only two days prior to the episode (Turner 23–24). Similarly, removing Nancy Drew demonstrated the abrupt lack of importance of the source novels, allowing full focus and promotion in press coverage on Cassidy.

This was also reflected in the credits sequences. Seasons one and two opened with book covers of Hardy Boys and Nancy Drew novels, emphasizing the more recent and stylized Rudy Nappi cover designs, before flowing into the stars incarnating the literary heroes, emphasizing their derivation from the printed page. By the third season, the book tie-in opening is removed completely; the Hardy Boys have morphed into television action heroes, aimed at a slightly older audience of maybe sixteen instead of fourteen, according to *Variety* ("Returning Network TV Program"). Curiously, shots of action and explosions involving both stars are followed by romantic lead Cassidy kissing a woman, while Stevenson is kissing someone of distinctly androgynous appearance. This is followed by an older man asking the Hardy boys to work for the Justice Department. Clearly the basis of the Grosset & Dunlap novels has been visibly abandoned, although one episode took its title from a recent Hardy book, *The Sting of the Scorpion* (1978).

In all, forty-six hour-long Hardy Boys episodes were produced, with another ten solo outings for Nancy Drew. While beginning as a reasonable facsimile of the books, Universal's version was equally notable for taking the Hardys in new directions, some of which impacted the subsequent books, partly because of the Stratemeyer Syndicate's nearly simultaneous switch from Grosset & Dunlap to Simon & Schuster. The idea for the third season premier, the two-part "The Last Kiss of Summer," in which Joe's fiancée is killed just before their wedding, would reappear a decade later when the first of the Hardy Boys Casefiles was published, *Dead on Target*. Similarly, the concept of joint exploits shared by the Hardys and Nancy was emulated, beginning in 1984, in the Nancy Drew and the Hardy Boys Be-a-Detective Mystery Stories and in 1988 with the Nancy Drew and the Hardy Boys Super Mysteries. Hence, Universal could be said to have mapped out some of the directions for the books to go.

In 1995, the television careers of the Hardy Boys and Nancy Drew were revived in a pattern similar to the original *Hardy Boys/Nancy Drew Mysteries* concept, before the characters joined forces. Each episode was a brisk half hour (actually only about twenty minutes of narrative after commercials and credits). Although both *Nancy Drew* and *The Hardy Boys* emerged through New Line from the same Canada-France coproduction, Nelvana and Marathon Productions in association with Westcom Entertainment Group and France 2, the results of the two series could not have been more different.

Nancy Drew and *The Hardy Boys* were intended to be shown back-to-back, occupying the traditional hour block of syndicated air time, with thirteen hours produced. However, in many cases *Nancy Drew* was the only offering widely seen, with *The Hardy Boys* relegated outside of prime air times, because of the wide recognition of its lower quality. Perhaps as a result, the character of Nancy Drew was brought in to enhance the final two *Hardy Boys* episodes. However, after *The Hardy Boys/Nancy Drew Mysteries* and subsequent books, the combination was now almost a cliché rather than an innovation. Nancy is presented as their intellectual superior, going so far as to tell these new television Hardy boys that meeting them has made her glad to be an only child. Their relationships are strictly platonic, and clearly Nancy would not desire more, perhaps creating a more believable trio than *The Hardy Boys/Nancy Drew Mysteries*.

In both *Nancy Drew* and *The Hardy Boys*, Nancy and her friends, and the Hardys, are advanced from their original teen ages to the college years and slightly beyond. Computer hacker Joe is still taking classes, while Frank is a cub reporter, frequently at odds with his editor, played by *Hardy Boys* regular Fiona Highet. The brothers share their home now that their father has left (leaving neither mother nor Aunt Gertrude) and "hang out" at a 1950s style diner, impishly named "F.W. Dixon's." The cast of both shows were pictured on their respective Case Files book series, indicating the inflection from the original novels toward slightly older viewers in their teens. Credits for both *Nancy Drew* and *The Hardy Boys* specifically reference them as a Simon & Schuster imprint.

The update in ages is not disruptive in the case of the twenty-ish Nancy Drew. While brimming with self-confidence and pluck, Tracy Ryan also portrays Nancy with quiet, unassuming caring. Ryan herself exuded charm, as did Nancy's friends Bess (Jhene Erwin), red-haired, feminine and flirtatious, and George (Joy Tanner), brunette, able to fend for of herself, yet easily the most seductive of the trio. *Nancy Drew* even succeeded in the screen's only persuasive portrayal of her romance with Ned Nickerson (Scott Speedman) as a modern, intelligent and sensitive male.

Unlike the believable quartet of *Nancy Drew*, the casting of Colin Gray as Frank and Paul Popowich as Joe lacks the brotherly chemistry of *The Mickey Mouse Club* serials and *The Hardy Boys/Nancy Drew Mysteries*. Nor do Gray and Popowich share the necessary facial similarity essential to audience acceptance of their sibling status, a resemblance managed by all the previous acting combinations. Even worse is Ken Samuels as Fenton Hardy, resembling a dried-up Latin gigolo in his sole appearance, the episode "The Last Laugh." For the most part *The Hardy Boys* dispenses with the surrounding characters, thereby losing the warm friendships that *Nancy Drew* exudes. In a single episode, "The Curse," Mark Lutz enacts Chet Morton as ravenous and amusing as always, but the performer's physiognomy is entirely wrong—athletic rather than rotund.

This modernization of *The Hardy Boys*, as developed by David Cole and produced by Patrick Loubert and Michael Klein, lost all the advantages of the original Stratemeyer concept. In its place is a car with a license plate that reads "Bayport—Land of Mystery" and an alternative hard rock score with heavy metal and grunge elements. From the skewed angles, hand-held camera, black and white photography, and jump cuts of the disruptive credits, everything seems off-key, perhaps deliberately eschewing previous screen models of the Hardy Boys.

Nancy Drew managed uniformly convincing and arresting stories that made the best use of locations around Toronto, doubling on occasion for European locales, while *The Hardy Boys* fails to build on these same environs, offering nothing more than drab repetition. The initial *Hardy Boys* cases were trite and poorly plotted, and the show barely reached a passable standard in its best episodes, whereas the Drew segments had the proper flavor from the outset. In a reverse of the outcome of *The Hardy Boys/Nancy Drew Mysteries* almost two decades earlier, not even introducing Nancy could save these dismal Hardy Boys from cancellation.

Over forty years of adaptations, the Hardy Boys have been brought to television in a variety of forms and against different historical backdrops. Children's serials for *The Mickey Mouse Club*, and a Filmation animated series, offered distinct styles from the more standard television norms of *The Hardy Boys/Nancy Drew Mysteries* and *The Hardy Boys* in the live action hour and half-hour form respectively. Despite this variety of incarnations, several motifs have been evident throughout these many versions, in characterization, in the Hardy Boys' companions, in mobility, in attitudes toward authority, and in intended audience.

In *The Tower Treasure*, Frank had been described as "dark, with straight, black hair and brown eyes," while Joe "was pink-cheeked, with fair, curly-hair and blue eyes" (Dixon 1927, 2). This process allowed a boy of almost any appearance to identify with one or the other of the brothers. However, with the casting of Considine and Kirk for *The Mickey Mouse Club* serials, these established physical differences nearly vanished. The same was true in *The Mystery of the Chinese Junk*, with the brothers almost indistinguishable and their hair colors reversed, with Joe brown and Frank a blond. Only subsequently would the brothers both look, and behave, in a distinct manner.

Over the years the most obvious evolution in the depiction of the Hardy Boys has been in fashion, visibly reflecting the varying periods of production. Considine and Kirk have typical 1950s butch haircuts and wear striped short-sleeved shirts, and even just t-shirts, which may have been a subliminal way of suggesting working class roots. They are certainly no higher on the economic scale, which may have resonated with the intended *Mickey Mouse Club* audience. By contrast, *The Mystery of the Chinese Junk* hints at an upper middle class setting, with a two-story home, the boy's lab, and the savings to spend on a summer business. Yet their plain white shirts and close-cropped hair indicate their appeal to an audience as yet untouched by the cultural changes that were so evident in the hairstyle and clothing of the Filmation series.

Although this animated version began only two years after *The Mystery of the Chinese Junk*, the contrast is striking, with the animated Hardy Boys and their friends now having long hair and wearing bell bottoms, vests, and turtlenecks. Almost ten years later, high fashion still dominates in *The Hardy Boys/Nancy Drew Mysteries*, with form-fitting clothes and partially unbuttoned shirts. Seemingly no danger could pluck a strand of Stevenson or Cassidy's blow-dried and perfectly coiffed hair from its designated place. The Universal program reflected its intended youthful audience with the discretionary spending for the latest clothes and musical records. In the 1995 television series, the format returned to the working class roots etched by *The Mickey Mouse Club* serials, with Frank in an entry level job and Joe still in school. In all of these are reflected different methods of presenting the Hardys as all–American boys of their time, their own characterization and style reflecting the context of the moment of production.

Almost as obvious, at least to audiences familiar with the volumes, is the presence — or more often the absence — of the boys' friends and the books' adult figures. Fenton Hardy and Aunt Gertrude appear in all the television incarnations through the 1970s, but Laura Hardy is repeatedly eliminated. The small screen, unlike the books, creates a new, single-parent household. This is a concession to television's patriarchal dominance, ranging from the comedic *My Three Sons* (1960–72), which costarred Tim Considine from *The Mickey Mouse Club* serials, to the western *Bonanza* (1959–73) and even the Supermarionation science fiction of *Thunderbirds* (1965–66). A single paternal figure is all the family requires, with the maternal side anchored by a relative, in the manner of Gertrude, or a feminized male, such as Uncle Charley of *My Three Sons* or the cook Hop Sing in *Bonanza*.

The standard plot device in the novels, of Frank and Joe's case proving to be tied in with one their father is investigating, offers rich possibilities for exploring professional and familial bonds. This tension reveals how Fenton and his sons sometimes work as rivals, sometimes at cross purposes, or even as unwitting allies, eventually concluding in a team effort. Through dramatizing this relationship, situations are analyzed that reveal a contrast of attitudes to clues and the suspects they encounter. This format intrigues, through varying approaches to similar subjects, and simultaneously reassures, reconciling any divisions that may arise during the case. This dynamic between the father and his sons opens a Hardy screen adaptation to a broader range of family viewers than strictly children. However, only *The Mystery of the Chinese Junk* and *The Hardy Boys/Nancy Drew Mysteries* have realized this potential, which was a major element of the latter's success.

As a joint hero, the brother's thoughts can easily be externalized by a screenwriter in their dialogue with each other. Aged between fifteen to eighteen years old in the books, the brothers offer ready appeal to audiences of that age and younger, and if presented effectively, may attract older viewers as well. The books offer a strong framework of characterizations, with family and chums to join the sleuths as necessary.

Yet surprisingly little use has been made of their peers on the screen. Only Chet Morton (renamed "Chubby") appears as a regular in the cartoon, and only three episodes in the entire run of both *The Hardy Boys/Nancy Drew Mysteries* and the 1995 *Hardy Boys*. Such other regulars as Tony Prito, Biff Hooper, and Phil Cohen are never seen outside of *The Mystery of the Chinese Junk*. Of the girlfriends, only Iola Morton appeared in *The Mickey Mouse Club* serials, more of an annoyance than a companion, probably a concession to the expected juvenile gender attitudes among boys in its young audience. When Callie Shaw was included in the first season of *The Hardy Boys/Nancy Drew Mysteries*, it was as Fenton's assistant, not Frank's girlfriend.

The only regular characters television added were Filmation's creation of Pete Jones and Wanda Kay, and the merger of Nancy Drew engineered by Universal; otherwise, companions are for a single story only. The interest "in girls" becomes key in not only *The Hardy Boys/Nancy Drew Mysteries*, but as early as Frank's incipient female interests in *The Mystery of Ghost Farm*. In this way, dramatic interaction on screen has tended to be more skewed toward the brothers with one another, in the manner of the "buddy" genre, and even with adults, than was the case with the books, with their emphasis on the chums. In this way, the Hardys on screen have less of their own universe of self-sufficient young people than was found in the novels.

Much of the friendship in the books was based on shared enthusiasm for motorcycles, automobiles, boats and even airplanes, nearly always away from adult supervision. Frank and Joe, and to a lesser degree Chet Morton and Tony Prito, could operate these with efficiency, at a time when access to such relative novelties was an unusual and exciting prospect for most readers of the books. Not until the 1950s might older brothers be able to commonly use a car or motorbike, so that the books for decades served as a type of wish-fulfillment for access to such vehicles that imply speed and navigation. In this way the books also kept up-to-date, and not only mobility but increasingly travel became a component of the later Grosset & Dunlap books. The basic physical movement also facilitates the minimizing of actual physical violence, placing the Hardy Boys at odds with adult, hardboiled detectives; thrills come from vehicles rather than gunplay.

However, use of such transportation necessitated an older age than implied by *The Mickey Mouse Club* serials. Filmation, in portraying the boys as part of a band, was the first to take the Hardy Boys to a variety of locales, such as the Canadian northwest of *The Viking Symbol Mystery* (1969). By the second season of *The Hardy Boys/Nancy Drew Mysteries*, the Hardys were literally on the road in an orange van, whether in Nevada, Transylvania, Egypt, Africa, or Mexico. Frank is even a small plane pilot who can handle a jetliner in an emergency over the Caribbean in "The Strange Fate of Flight 608." Following their father's cases or traveling to musical engagements are given as the reasons for their peregrinations, and the studio's library of stock shots substitutes for sending the cast beyond the environs of Southern California. In this respect Universal, like the books, followed the pattern established by many other detective series that sent the hero to different places to vary the setting and antagonists.

Despite their youth, the Hardy boys take on the mantle of law enforcement, no matter where they may be. In Bayport, while Chief Collig, Con Riley, or Detective Smuff may make the arrests, it is the Hardy boys who solve the cases, no less than Sherlock Holmes did for Inspector Lestrade. In the early Hardy Boys books, before the revisions, youth could enjoy the fallibility of authority around them. Similarly, it was in *The Mickey Mouse Club* serials more than any other incarnation that the Hardy boys take an adversarial stance, whether toward the police or even their father. While Disney product is often regarded as a conformist force, in this version the Hardy boys follow clues despite a relative lack of parental encouragement. Finding they are treated as inferiors in the social structure, they struggle to be accepted as equals, ultimately triumphing in their efforts to save Perry Robinson and the farm animals. Some of this spirit endures in *The Mystery of the Chinese Junk*, with Fenton Hardy at a distance and the boys tracking the case with only the help of their friends, all the while dodging adult antagonists. By 1977 and *The Hardy Boys/Nancy Drew Mysteries*, this attitude has shifted completely. The Hardys accept the veracity of authority figures, even becoming government agents in the third season, somewhat surprising in the wake of Vietnam and Watergate and the cynicism these events engendered. This may be a result both of the entrenched formulas of Universal television, as well as the completion of the revision of the Grosset & Dunlap books to eliminate, among other elements, any disrespect for police.

Ironically, before the revisions, when the books were geared toward a slightly older readership than the prime *Mickey Mouse Club* demographic, the boys in it were cast at a reduced age. Subsequently, even as the Stratemeyer Syndicate's rewrites of the Grosset & Dunlap books took place, making them more accessible for younger readers, television presented the characters as older. Only *The Mystery of the Chinese Junk* was fully compatible with the original, classical Stratemeyer conception. *The Hardy Boys/Nancy Drew Mysteries* began by following the books, but gradually presented the Hardy Boys as slightly more advanced in age, and undertaking the musical career that Filmation had pioneered.

Most important is the interaction between the television programs and the Hardy Boys books themselves. *The Mystery of the Applegate Treasure* had been based on the original 1927 text of *The Tower Treasure*. While Disney's intervention in the evolution of the Hardy Boys was not the sole reason for the Stratemeyer Syndicate to rewrite the books, it was one of the motivations, with the revisions beginning two years afterward. *The Mickey Mouse Club* serials pointed to the television-weaned generation whose readership the Syndicate wanted to secure, through shortening the books and heightening the action. This was reinforced by the success of the Filmation series and the failure of *The Mystery of the Chinese Junk* during the years the revisions were composed. There are also some direct reflections of television's innovations in the revised volumes, with not only the Filmation style-rock band in *The Flickering Torch Mystery*, but also added emphases in the 1959 revision of

The Tower Treasure; digging up the grounds in the search for the gold and the boys nearly trapped in the water tower are both clearly derived from *The Mystery of the Applegate Treasure*.

By the time of *The Hardy Boys/Nancy Drew Mysteries*, the revisions of the Grosset & Dunlap books were complete, and by the end of the Universal program, the Hardy Boys books expanded to new Simon & Schuster series for various ages. These not only incorporated the program's combination with Nancy Drew, but also the death of Joe's girlfriend, and were compatible with the twenty-something stars offered in the 1995 *Hardy Boys* program. Similarly, *The Hardy Boys/Nancy Drew Mysteries* had spawned three new novelizations; no longer, as had been the case with the Disney tie-ins, were readers directed toward the original source material. The changes television wrought in the source material had facilitated aging the brothers into early adulthood, suggesting new directions in expanding and revising the oeuvre of Hardy Boys books. Not only are the screen adaptations important in and of themselves for creating preconceptions readers bring to the stories, but they have also played a role in reshaping the source material itself.

A special thanks to James Keeline for generously assisting my research.

Notes

1. There is one other version, independently made, which has proven impossible to view. The Hardy Boys were included in *Clue??*, a parody of Neil Simon's *Murder by Death* by way of Agatha Christie's *And Then There Were None / Ten Little Indians*. *Clue??* was a half-hour 1988 video by Chris Brainerd for BBS Productions that featured television crime solvers Columbo and Ironside joining figures from page and screen such as Mike Hammer and James Bond. Jamie Jorgenson as Nancy Drew joins Philip Kelley as Frank Hardy and Robert Warnock as Joe. Gathered together mysteriously in a country mansion, one murder is followed by another. The actors each had thirty seconds at the close to offer multiple explanations for what had occurred.

2. A 16 mm color print exists in the American Film Institute collection at the Library of Congress.

3. According to Peggy Herz, at the time, the figures were about 60 million Nancy Drew books to 50 million Hardy Boys.

Works Cited and Consulted

Axe, John. *All About Collecting Boys' Series Books*. Grantsville, MD: Hobby House Press, 2002.
Billman, Carol. *The Secret of the Stratemeyer Syndicate: Nancy Drew, the Hardy Boys, and the Million Dollar Fiction Factory*. New York: Ungar, 1986.
"Boys in Peril: The Hardy Boys Episode Guide." 7 Mar. 2005. <http://www.geocities.com/me_richter/hardy.htm?20057>.

Cain, Chelsea. *Confessions of a Teen Sleuth*. New York: Bloomsbury, 2005.
Caprio, Betsy. *The Mystery of Nancy Drew: Girl Sleuth on the Couch*. Trabuco Canyon, CA: Source Books, 1992.
Carpentieri, Tony, with Paul Mular. *Hardy and Hardy Investigations*. 4th ed. Rheem Valley, CA: SynSine Press, 2001.
Connelly, Mark. *The Hardy Boys Mysteries, 1927–1979: A Cultural and Literary History*. Jefferson, NC: McFarland, 2008.
Cornelius, Michael G., and Melanie E. Gregg, eds. *Nancy Drew and Her Sister Sleuths: Essays on the Fiction of Girl Detectives*. Jefferson, NC: McFarland, 2008.
Cotter, Bill. *The Wonderful World of Disney Television*. New York: Hyperion, 1997.
Crawford, Robert L. *The Lost Hardys: A Concordance*. Thomasville, GA: R.L. Crawford, 1993.
Dixon, Franklin W. *Dead on Target*. New York: Pocket Books, 1987.
_____. *The Disappearing Floor*. New York: Grosset & Dunlap, 1940.
_____. *The Disappearing Floor*. New York: Grosset & Dunlap, 1964.
_____. *The Flickering Torch Mystery*. New York: Grosset & Dunlap, 1943.
_____. *The Flickering Torch Mystery*. New York: Grosset & Dunlap, 1971.
_____. *The Mystery of the Chinese Junk*. New York: Grosset & Dunlap, 1960.
_____. *The Sting of the Scorpion*. New York: Grosset & Dunlap, 1979.
_____. *The Tower Treasure*. New York: Grosset & Dunlap, 1959.
_____. *The Tower Treasure*. 1927. Bedford, MA: Applewood Books, 1991.
Dyer, Carolyn Stewart, and Nancy Tillman Romalov, eds. *Rediscovering Nancy Drew*. Iowa City: University of Iowa Press, 1995.
Erickson, Hal. *Television Cartoon Shows*. Jefferson, NC: McFarland, 1995.
Erisman, Fred. *Boys' Books, Boys' Dreams, and the Mystique of Flight*. Fort Worth: Texas Christian University Press, 2006.
Finnan, Bob. "The Hardy Boys Unofficial Home Page." 9 Jul. 2009. <http://hardyboys.bobfinnan.com/>.
Gianakos, Larry James. *Television Drama Series Programming: A Comprehensive Chronicle, 1975–1980*. Metuchen, NJ: Scarecrow Press, 1981.
Goldberg, Lee. *Unsold Television Pilots*. Jefferson, NC: McFarland, 1990.
Greenwald, Marilyn S. *The Secret of the Hardy Boys: Leslie McFarlane and the Stratemeyer Syndicate*. Athens: Ohio University Press, 2004.
Grover, Tim. "My Adventures with the Hardy Boys and Nancy Drew." 7 Mar. 2005. <http://www.bayportgazette.com/bg/12/bg_12_5.html>.
"The Hardy Boys." 26 Oct 2009. <http://hardyboysgame.com/>.
The Hardy Boys. Dir. Hal Sutherland. Animated. Perf: Byron Kane, Dal McKennon, Jane Webb. ABC-TV, 1969–71.
"The Hardy Boys / Nancy Drew Mysteries." 7 Mar. 2005. <http://yesterdayland.web-daemon.com/primetime/ptl178.php>.
"The Hardy Boys / Nancy Drew Mysteries." 7 Mar. 2005. <http://jumptheshark.com/h/hardyboys.htm>.
Hardy Boys / Nancy Drew Mysteries Annual. London: Grandreams, 1979.
Hardy Boys / Nancy Drew Mysteries Annual. London: Grandreams, 1980.
The Hardy Boys/Nancy Drew Mysteries—Season One. Universal City, CA: Universal Studios, 2005.
The Hardy Boys/Nancy Drew Mysteries—Season Two. Universal City, CA: Universal Studios, 2007.
The Hardy Boys—The Complete First Season. Nelvana Limited/Marathon Productions S.A. Toronto: kaBOOM! Entertainment Inc., 2006. DVD.
The Hardy Boys—The Mickey Mouse Club, 1956–1957. Dir. R.G. Springsteen. Perf. Tim Considine, Tommy Kirk. Walt Disney Treasures. Burbank: Buena Vista Home Entertainment, 2006. DVD.
Henerson, James. *Flight to Nowhere*. New York: Grosset & Dunlap, 1978.
Herz, Peggy. *The Hardy Boys and Nancy Drew*. New York: Scholastic, 1978.

Hoff, Benjamin. *The House on the Point*. New York: St. Martin's Minotaur, 2002.
Johnson, Deidre. *Edward Stratemeyer and the Stratemeyer Syndicate*. New York: Twayne, 1993.
Keeline, James. "Stratemeyer Syndicate." 16 Jun. 2008. <http://stratemeyer.org/>.
Kismaric, Carole, and Marvin Heiferman. *The Strange Case of Nancy Drew & The Hardy Boys*. New York: Simon & Schuster, 1998.
Larson, Glen A., and Michael Sloan. *The Hardy Boys and Nancy Drew Meet Dracula*. New York: Grosset & Dunlap, 1978.
Mallory, Michael. "Mystery in Mouseland." *Scarlet Street* 10 (Spring 1993): 53–58, 97.
_____. "Still Frank After All These Years: An Interview with Tim Considine." *Scarlet Street* 10 (Spring 1993): 70–74, 98.
Mann, Thomas. *Horror and Mystery Photoplay Editions and Magazine Fictionizations*. Jefferson, NC: McFarland, 2004.
Martindale, David. *Television Detective Shows of the 1970s*. Jefferson, NC: McFarland, 1991.
McAlpine, Gordon. *Mystery Box*. Chicago: Cricket Books, 2003.
McFarlane, Leslie. *Ghost of the Hardy Boys*. New York: Two Continents, 1976.
McMahan, Ian. "Today's Hardy Boys Adventures: A Social-Developmental Analysis." *Dime Novel Round-Up* 63 (October 1994): 83–89.
Meyers, Richard. *TV Detectives*. San Diego: A.S. Barnes, 1981.
The Mystery of the Chinese Junk. Dir. Larry Peerce. Perf. Richard Gates, Tim Matheson, Richard Anderson. 20th Century Fox, 1967.
Nancy Drew—The Complete First Season. Nelvana Limited/Marathon Productions S.A. Toronto: kaBOOM! Entertainment Inc., 2006. DVD.
Nash, Ilana. *American Sweethearts: Teenage Girls in Twentieth-Century Popular Culture*. Bloomington: Indiana University Press, 2006.
"Old Stories, New Heartthrobs." 7 Mar. 2005. <http://1forparker.tripod.com/parkerstevenson/id4.html>.
Phillips, Louis. "Me and the Hardy Boys." *The Armchair Detective* 15 (1982): 174–177.
Pickrell, Alan. "Frank, Joe, and Nancy: Machiavelli for Minors?" *Dime Novel Round-Up* 69 (August 2000): 126–233.
Pioneers, Passionate Ladies, and Private Eyes: The Library of Congress Symposium on Dime Novels, Series Books, and Paperbacks. Library of Congress, Washington, D.C. June 9–10, 1995. Conference.
Plunkett-Powell, Karen. *The Nancy Drew Scrapbook*. New York: St. Martin's Press, 1993.
Rehak, Melanie. *Girl Sleuth: Nancy Drew and the Women Who Created Her*. Orlando: Harcourt, 2005.
"Returning Network TV Programs: The Hardy Boys." *Variety* 12 Oct. 1978.
Sloan, Michael. *The Haunted House*. New York: Grosset & Dunlap, 1978.
Stratemeyer, Edward. *The Tower Treasure*. Undated manuscript outline. 16 Jun. 2008 <http://keeline.com/Strat/outlines/>.
Turner, Mark. *Hardy Boys*. Mankato, MN: Creative Education, 1979.
"TV Pilot Reviews." *Variety* 13 Sep. 1967.
U.S. Copyright Office. Copyright transfers, Assignor/Assignee. 379–386. Vol. 950.
Valley, Richard. "Just an Average Joe (Hardy): An Interview with Tommy Kirk." *Scarlet Street* 10 (Spring 1993): 60–69, 97.
Watson, Bruce. "Tom Swift, Nancy Drew and Pals All Had the Same Dad." *Smithsonian* 22 (October 1991): 50–61.

5

Natural Detective Work: Ideas About Nature in the Early Tom Swift Books

ELIZABETH D. BLUM

In the early twenty-first century, a flurry of children's pop culture sources emphasized environmental values explicitly. *Hoot* (2004), a Newbery award–winning book and later feature film, extolled the virtues of protecting animal life from corporate greed. Through the story of a young penguin, *Happy Feet* (2006), an Oscar winner, warned of danger to wildlife in the depletion of fish resources. *Wall-E* (2008), another Academy Award–winning film, critiqued the "throw-away" culture of the United States. This emphasis on environmental themes was hardly surprising. With increased interest in global climate change, pollution, and environmental degradation, environmental issues have stood as some of the most important of the time. Clearly, with these films and books, adults hoped to inculcate youngsters with a consistent message of the importance of caring for the earth and all its inhabitants.

Some upcoming projects aimed at children have similar environmental themes. In 2007, Albie Hecht, an executive at Nickelodeon, acquired the rights to the popular and long-running Tom Swift series of books. Centered around a teenaged boy from New York, the original Tom Swift stories began in 1910 and combined technological innovations with crime solving. Hecht reported to *Variety* magazine that "the initial concept is to posit that Swift Industries is now a leading 'green technology' company, giving the 20th century series a modern twist" (Hayes). In 2009, Hecht brought well-known director Barry Sonnenfeld on board, with Sony Pictures supporting the project scheduled for a 2011 release date (McNary and Siegel; White). At least one blogger expressed considerable dismay at the "reinvention" of the series. Josh Tyler at CinemaBlend.com lamented angrily, "This isn't a movie. It's another opportunity for Hollywood to shove more 'green' propaganda down our throats.... I have no interest in a heavy handed movie where we watch Tom Swift fight loggers" (Tyler). Blogger reservations aside, Hecht's vision for the new film emerges as all the more striking with the decidedly different views about nature and the environment expressed in the early books of the original Tom Swift series.[1]

Certainly, pop culture directed toward young people in the early twenty-first century reflected concern and awareness over the changes of attitudes about the environment. An examination of children's popular culture sources during the early twentieth century might be expected to yield similar results, since that period saw similar changes in attitudes. Boys' detective series books, particularly the early Tom Swift novels, provide an interesting venue to examine attitudes about the natural world in the early twentieth century. First, the books span a long period of time with relatively consistent authorship. Second, the books were also intensely popular among young men as forms of leisure reading. Yet despite the fact that environmental concerns filled the Progressive Era, the early Tom Swift novels reflect a striking lack of consistency of values about nature and the environment. Earlier Gilded Age ideals dominate in some areas, while other areas mix Progressive Era and Gilded Age influences uneasily. Importantly, nature values in the Swift books shift decidedly into the Progressive Era only when dealing with connections between non-whites and nature.

Scholars describe the Progressive Era as a period when values about the environment changed considerably, giving birth to the modern environmental movement. The Tom Swift books, however, indicate a period with far more cultural conflict over attitudes about the natural world, with the Gilded Age's heavy hand present throughout. Interestingly, the exception to the rule — the connection of nature with non-whites — provides an explanation as to why the series seems to demonstrate such inconsistencies in values about nature.

Gilded Age and Progressive Era Attitudes About Nature

The late 1800s saw huge changes in American society and culture.[2] During the "Gilded Age" from 1875 to 1900, Americans witnessed increased industrialization and urbanization as the United States began its transformation into a world power. Technology was an important component of this growth, allowing American factories to produce large quantities for growing markets. At this time, "factories pumped out mass-produced commodities in an atmosphere of fierce competition" and very little government regulation (Kline 38). In addition,

> building on the traditional belief that nature existed for the benefit of humanity, the mechanized period glorified tools as a means to further exploit the riches of nature. Use of the nation's natural resources during the Industrial Revolution followed a persistent theme — a resource was exploited until it ran out, was no longer economically attractive, was replaced by technological advancement, or was made obsolete by an alternative invention [Kline 38].

The growth of cities added to demands for food, mass produced and packaged. With the monotonous, indoor reality of factory work, "the workings of nature steadily became more myth than reality" (Kline 39). Because of these factors, Americans proudly drained wetlands, intensively farmed the Great Plains, enthusiastically mined coal and oil, generously poured smoke into the air and other waste into the water, and ably hunted the passenger pigeon to extinction (Kline 40–46). During this period, Congress even founded the first national parks with these principles firmly in mind. Yellowstone, and other early national parks, according to Congress, contained only "worthless" land — no gold, coal, or iron deposits, for example — and therefore could be set aside without risk of losing economic assets (Runte 48–64).

As the late nineteenth century fed into the early twentieth, ideas about the role of government in American life shifted, as did many ideas about the relationship between man and nature. The Progressive Era (1890–1920) in general witnessed a dramatic amount of reform across urban areas in the United States. Whether focusing on reforming city government, expanding the vote, ensuring garbage pickup, developing compulsory attendance for schools, or calling for safer and healthier working conditions, many Progressive Era reformers responded to the problems of the unbridled urban and industrial growth during the Gilded Age. These reformers pressed for a more active role for government in protecting its citizens and the American landscape in a variety of ways.

Some groups turned away from urban areas to protect and defend "wilderness" or to "conserve" nature as a response to problems in the city.[3] President Teddy Roosevelt and Gifford Pinchot, first chief of the U.S. Forest Service, led the conservation movement, pressing for efficient use of resources in the nation, rather than wasteful overuse and elimination (Hays). Roosevelt, an ardent and enthusiastic hunter, also advocated efforts to conserve animals through proper hunting ethics. The president oversaw a huge expansion of the national park system, as well as an increase in the number of national monuments (Opie 379–380; Kline 49). John Muir arose as a prominent spokesperson for the preservation movement, stressing keeping "wilderness" intact for its spiritual, restorative, and aesthetic value (Muir). Others certainly agreed with these philosophies. Some, concerned for the mental and physical health of children in corrupting urban environments, founded groups to get them back into nature through camping and hiking. The Boy Scouts, Girl Scouts, and Campfire Girls formed a part of this legacy. Summer camps also became increasingly institutionalized as a form of recreation for children (Paris 17–60; M. Smith).[4]

Rather than trying to escape the cities, other reformers attempted to reduce pollution and improve environmental conditions within urban landscapes. Women often dominated Progressive Era environmental reform within cities. Seeing threats to their families' health, women worked against smoke and noise pollution and for neighborhood parks as play spaces for children, as well as for increased city services like garbage pickup. These women frequently formed a potent political force, even as men denied them basic suffrage rights. The women fought against entrenched attitudes, since many saw this pollution not as a negative for their cities, but a sign of progress. If a city had smoke, it had productive industry, and therefore wealth. In Houston, the *Daily Post* triumphantly declared, "Smoke stacks are a splendid sign of a city's prosperity. Smoke stacks are multiplying in Houston. Ergo: the signs of prosperity are multiplying in Houston" (*Houston Daily Post* 1). Yet women attained notable successes. By 1915, every major city in the nation had some form of smoke pollution control legislation (Stradling; Gugliotta, Hoy).

Although activists argued for a different relationship with nature during the Progressive Era, scientific racism popularized and reinforced notions about the relationship between non-whites and nature. Scientific racism gained significant ground among the general public during the Progressive Era, with major scholars and thinkers developing significant treatises on the subject. Generally, scientific racists used biological, anthropological, and anecdotal information to classify non-whites, particularly blacks, as lower on the evolutionary scale. Race also led to certain innate, unchangeable characteristics being designated to groups of people: blacks were lazy, unintelligent, and slow, while whites were clever, inventive, and hard working. Scientific racists tended to believe that nature played a key role in these differences. Groups of people from colder climates, like Europeans, had to adapt and become more creative to overcome the difficulties presented by their environments. People in warmer climates lacked that outside pressure, and remained "primitive" and without "civilization" and the technological advances of whites. Too much civilization, however, could "soften" whites. Many preservationists and conservationists, including Roosevelt, used elements of scientific racism to argue for protecting wild, natural spaces as a place to keep whites, and especially white boys, vigorous and powerful (Smith 105–113).

Overall, the Progressive Era saw some significant changes in attitudes about the environment. Rather than simply seeing nature as a tool for economic and technological growth, many worked to conserve resources, preserve wild spaces, and reduce pollution. Yet nature could also be a tool of oppression. A group's relationship with and closeness to nature might dictate their place on an evolutionary, cultural, and social scale.

The Subjugation of Nature

During the later stages of the Progressive Era, the Stratemeyer Syndicate, later responsible for the Hardy Boys and Nancy Drew series, began churning out Tom Swift novels under the pseudonym Victor Appleton (Keeline 19–23). From 1910 to 1941, Edward Stratemeyer and Howard Garis wrote most of the volumes in the original series. Both men came of age during the Gilded Age, and their attitudes about the natural world expressed in the series clearly reflect that association rather than the time in which the books were written.

The novels themselves served as a staple of many boys' libraries beginning in 1910 (Molson; Von der Osten 268). The Stratemeyer/Garis creations revolved around Tom Swift, a Shopton, New York teenager who follows in the footsteps of his father, the illustrious inventor Barton Swift. Decidedly upper middle class, Tom's life revolves around perfecting machinery and solving various mysteries that come his way. The very image of the perfect son, Tom is honest, respectful, industrious, athletic, well-mannered, devoted to his father, and (through sporadic appearances by Mary Nestor) heterosexual. He is also extremely intelligent, but in a practical sort of way, rather than simply book-smart. Technology holds his attention, and it also serves as the main way through which he experiences and interacts with the natural world.[5]

Nature serves a variety of purposes for Tom and other characters. First and foremost, nature serves as something to be conquered and dominated by whatever technology Tom develops. In each of the early books, Tom's inventions (or improvements to existing machines) serve to dominate specific spaces in nature in an orderly pattern. Tom's improvement of a used motor-cycle allows him to conquer land at a greater speed and with more efficiency than his bicycle. The second book moves to the water, where Tom improves a modest boat into one that outraces machines with larger engines. The third focuses on conquering the sky when Tom designs and constructs his own airship. For the fourth book, the author notes, "Not satisfied with having conquered the air, Tom and his father set to work to gain a victory over the ocean" (*Diamond Makers* 6). At one point, Tom's friend Ned makes the connection explicit, stating "it seems that you are never going to stop doing things. You've conquered the air, the earth and the water" (*Submarine* 78). Basically, the subordination of nature to man's needs and desires remains a prominent theme in the early books.

During the Gilded Age, the domination of nature mainly served the purpose of sustaining and developing capitalism and private property. The early Tom Swift books repeatedly stress the extreme importance of capitalism and property, to the exclusion of other values. Indeed, the Swifts rarely complete any task without the motivating factor of money — the more substantial the reward the better. Even patriotism and benefiting the government take a secondary place to increased payoff. In *Tom Swift and His Submarine Boat*, Barton Swift had originally intended his new submarine to compete as part of a competition offered to benefit the American government. Yet in response to his son's desire to go after $300,000 worth of sunken treasure off the coast of Uruguay, the elder Swift quickly abandons the government contest (5–6). Tom and his friends later travel to Africa on a hunting expedition. Although they discover that two American missionaries have been kidnapped and are in dire straits, the group decides to focus on their primary goal, hunting for ivory. Only later, "it was agreed now, when they had made such a good start in collecting ivory, that they would spend the next few days in trying to get on the trail [of the missionaries]" (*Electric Rifle* 51).

Nature connects these two themes of dominating nature and the importance of capitalism by serving primarily as a way to advance material gains. Nature, for the Swifts, produces commodities to enhance their wealth. During a voyage for sunken treasure, the Swift's submarine moves along the ocean floor, where "great crabs walked around on their long, jointed legs, and Tom saw some lobsters that would have brought joy to the heart of a fisherman" (*Submarine* 40). When Tom journeys to the Rocky Mountains, his main object is to find an enterprise "where diamonds could be made, partly in a scientific manner, and partly by the forces of nature" (*Diamond Makers* 10). In Alaska, the author speaks for Tom by stating his excitement upon arriving at their destination: "To be in a place where gold could be picked up! Where they might all become fabulously wealthy!" (*Caves of Ice*

65). This philosophy of nature's worth stands out most prominently during Swift's trip to Africa. The entire purpose of the expedition rested on excitement for Tom and a professional hunter's "order for a pair of big elephant tusks ... I could get a pair of them, and live easy the rest of my life" (*Electric Rifle* 16). After the party kills a large number of stampeding elephants, the professional hunter "gave instructions about saving the ivory tusks, and the valuable teeth, each pair worth about $1,000" (*Electric Rifle* 48). Thus, the ocean, mountains, Alaska, and Africa are a focus of interest only because of the commodities and wealth Tom hopes to extract from them.

In addition to conquering spaces, Tom competes against and dominates nature in other ways as well, particularly regarding his interaction with storms and other natural phenomenon. While traveling in his airship, Tom and his companions encounter a roaring forest fire. The ship's motor fails, and the fire begins sucking the aircraft closer, "right toward the heart of the mass of black vapor, which ... was streaked with bright tongues of flame" (*Airship* 58). Keeping his head, Tom lightens the craft by throwing stores of food overboard, saving the day (*Airship* 60). Tom encounters more natural troubles when he crash lands an aircraft on a deserted tropical island. The castaways learn that "Earthquake Island" is literally tearing itself apart. The island knocks the party off their feet "by a swaying motion, and not far off a great crack opened in the earth ... [later,] the whole cliff toward which they had been walking appeared to shake itself loose. In another instant, it was flung outward and into the sea" (*Wireless Message* 47, 53). In the heat of all this activity, Tom patiently repairs a radio and focuses on contacting their rescuers.

Nature comes after Tom again in the Rocky Mountains. His group watches, terrified, as "great forked tongues of lightning leaped from the clouds.... Then, once more, came a terrific clap! [and] the whole side of the mountain slip[ped] away, and [went] crashing into the valley below" (*Diamond Makers* 50). Tom again keeps his head and notices that the landslide revealed a trail leading to the diamond caves for which they had been searching (*Diamond Makers* 52–54). Throughout the books, whenever nature challenges Tom, he remains cool, rational, and thoughtful, putting faith in his expertise and technology to rise over the challenge. Nature, even with the strongest and most intimidating of forces, proves unable to derail Tom's goals.

Views of urban areas in the books also match those of the Gilded Age, rather than the Progressive Era. Attitudes about cities certainly suffered at the hands of Progressive Era reformers. Muckrakers like Upton Sinclair and Jacob Riis exposed horrible, unsanitary conditions for the working class at both work and home. Pollution became a central concern as settlement house and middle class women exposed the filth of accumulated garbage and the health problems of industrial smoke and soot. Above all, many worried about the mental and physical health of children: middle class women saw cities as immoral corruptors of both body and mind (Hoy; Platt).

The Tom Swift novels, however, portray none of these negative attitudes about cities so prevalent during the Progressive Era. Instead, cities are neutral places of commerce. Tom travels to nearby Mansburg to mail a letter or purchase parts for inventions, to Albany to deliver papers, to Lanton for a motor boat auction, to Chester to have diamonds appraised, and stops at various towns and villages for supplies, gasoline, and other necessities on his trips. The author mentions in passing various industries or economic ventures within urban areas, but without negative comment. Mill whistles serve useful purposes, helping keep track of the lunch hour, rather than note a point about working conditions (*Motor-Boat* 56). "Church spires and towering factory chimneys" in Chester welcome Tom to the city rather than provide a way to discuss the evils of smoke pollution (*Diamond Makers* 17). In all, the early books evidence no concern with pollution or with cities as corrupting influences. In fact, urban areas seem to have positive connotations as places of commerce and business for the Swifts.[6]

As with nature in general and urban spaces more specifically, ideas about "wilderness" rest squarely within a Gilded Age conception of the world as well. For American whites, ideas about wilderness trace back to Europe and generally demonstrate two threads.[7] These threads occur concurrently, and are often conflicting. Under one strand of thought, Americans saw wilderness as places of danger, physical testing, and the absence of civilization. Under the other, wilderness reflected a place of beauty, spirituality, and restfulness. During the transcendental movement in the mid 1800s, a minority led by Ralph Waldo Emerson and Henry David Thoreau emphasized the inherent value of wilderness as a healthy, restful, spiritual place which provided an antidote to the corruption of urban spaces (Nash 8–20, 84–95). The early Tom Swift books emphasize wilderness as the antithesis of civilization, places of danger, and spaces where societal norms and laws run amuck.

The characters in the novels repeatedly notice a dichotomy between "civilization," generally meaning a human-constructed, more urban, world, and "wild and desolate" spaces, generally with sparse or no white human settlements. The author describes the Rocky Mountains as "a wild and desolate country," with "at best but small settlements" (*Diamond Makers* 39). Earthquake Island, a remote Caribbean island, "suddenly loomed up in the wild and desolate waste of the ocean" (*Wireless Message* 44). They discover the island to be uninhabited and "practically unknown" (*Wireless Message* 30). As Tom moved north to Alaska, he quickly encountered another "wild and desolate country," this one of snow and ice with "scarcely any signs of habitation" (*Caves of Ice* 55). The elephants Tom seeks are in "the very deepest wilds" of Africa, where only "now and then" does the group locate native villages (*Electric Rifle* 26, 36).

In addition to linking wilderness with a lack of population centers, Swift characters link "civilization" to the antithesis of "wilderness." When off the coast of South America in the submarine, the hired captain hopes to "get back to civilization" (*Submarine* 78). On their way to the Rocky Mountains, Tom abandons a violent stowaway "near the Nebraska National Forest," where, one of the party states, "I guess you'll be some time getting back to civilization" (*Diamond Makers* 37). In addition, where wilderness means a lack of human occupation, "civilization" means urban centers, comforts, and services. For example, prior to landing in "the wildest part of the Rocky Mountains," the crew stocks up on gasoline, since it "is difficult to procure there" (*Diamond Makers* 37). In Africa, one character asks if they "have to go back to civilization soon" for supplies (*Electric Rifle* 56). Alexander Durban, a professional hunter in Africa, "had very little chance to see the wonders and progress of civilization" since he had been "in the wilds of the jungle so much" (*Electric Rifle* 17).

Tom encounters wilderness much closer to home through other natural spaces, particularly in densely forested areas. Heavily wooded areas provide a safe space for criminals and unsavory elements, because, as wilderness, they lack the norms of law and society. In the first book, a gang of criminals responsible for stealing Barton Swift's plans hides in a house Tom finds "looming up in the forest" (*Motor-Cycle* 70). Although Tom cleverly recovers his father's plans, the men quickly "disappeared into the dense woods" (*Motor-Cycle* 79). One of the clearest examples of lawlessness in the woods occurs in *Tom Swift and His Electric Runabout*. On his way home from purchasing some chemicals, a dozen masked figures surround Tom and force him "off into the woods" (28). The group, called the "Deep Forest Throng," includes several boys Tom's age. They tie Tom securely to "the sacrificial tree" near a large campfire, and proceed with a bogus "trial" against him. Found guilty of being a "snob," "too fresh," and "uppish," the Deep Forest Throng decides to tar and feather him, a punishment the young inventor only narrowly escapes (*Electric Runabout* 29–30).

Other conventions of society, including gender norms, are also lost or overthrown temporarily in the wilderness. While home in Shopton, only the housekeeper, Mrs. Baggert, cooks for the Swift men. However, the wilderness overturns strict adherence to gender roles. On his all-male forays, Tom or one of his companions, usually Mr. Damon, assumes cooking duties. On their way to the Rockies, for example, Tom, with Mr. Damon's help, "served a fine meal in the dining room" (*Diamond Makers* 32). On Earthquake Island, the men assume all roles as the distraught, nervous women "get some much needed rest" (*Wireless Message* 58). Only after several days of the men constructing a mini-village in the wilderness does civilization return to normal with appropriate gender roles. At that time, the two women "assumed charge of the 'housekeeping' arrangement, and also the cooking, which relieved Tom of those duties. The two ladies even instituted 'wash-day,' and when a number of garments were hung out on lines to dry, the camp looked like some summer colony of pleasure seekers" (*Wireless Message* 61).[8] According to the novels, natural "wild" areas, unpopulated by humans, lack qualities of "civilization," providing infrequent access to trade, hiding spaces for criminals and lawlessness, and a reversal of some cultural conventions.

As in the Gilded Age, the notion of nature as something to conquer, dominate, and even fear resonates loudly throughout the early series. The alliance between Swift and the earlier era is not monolithic, however. With other aspects of natural values, the Swift novels indicate some tentative, uneasy efforts at change toward more Progressive Era-type ideas and concepts.

Ideas About Nature in Transition

During the Progressive Era, environmental activists began to comment more frequently and loudly about the beauty and positive aesthetic and spiritual qualities of nature. Led by John Muir, this served as a rationale for preserving large areas as national parks (Runte 58–66, 78–81; Nash 122–140). Characters in the Swift novels occasionally comment on nature's beauty or positive aesthetic characteristics. While riding along on his motorcycle, Tom "turned from the main thoroughfare, and was soon spinning along the sandy stretch, which was shaded with trees that in some places met overhead, forming a leafy arch. It was cool and pleasant, and Tom liked it" (*Motor-Cycle* 36). Later, in one of Tom's initial trips in his airship the Red Cloud, he peers down on a "lake spread out ... like some mirror of silver in a setting of green fields ... [with] a winding river, that flowed into the lake, and ... towns, villages, and even distant cities, interspersed here and there with broad farms or patches of woodland, like a bird's-eye view of a stretch of country." Tom sees the landscape below and shouts, "This is great ... I wouldn't miss this for the world" (*Airship* 21). Most interestingly, the author describes the view from a summit peak in the Rockies as "a magnificent scene. A great valley lay at their feet, and they could look off to many distant peaks" (*Diamond Makers* 62). With the exception of the Rockies, each of the areas that Tom appreciates for its beauty involves a fairly significant level of human presence and intervention. Roads and populated areas form an integral part of places described as beautiful.

Describing the "wild and remote" Rockies as "a magnificent scene" comes close to something John Muir might have approved. Yet again, however, the authors indicate older values of nature in other instances. "Wild and remote" Africa yields none of the aesthetic pleasures of the Rocky Mountains or the human-manipulated land near Tom's home. While in Africa, "scudding over the wilderness" and looking down on "the almost impenetrable forest," Mr. Damon notes, "I don't call that much to look at." Another character agrees with him, stating, "No, it isn't much of a view" (*Electric Rifle* 35). Alaska's landscape elicits similar statements. The author describes a "seemingly endless waste of snow and ice" (*Caves of Ice* 55). Looking down, Ned actually shudders and notes, "I wouldn't want to be wrecked here" (*Caves of Ice* 51). Certainly, the author steps toward an aesthetic appreciation of wild areas through the comments about the Rockies, yet the "wilder" areas of Africa and Alaska reveal very different responses. Beauty in nature can generally only be found in familiar, ordered, and human landscapes for Tom.

Various groups during the Progressive Era stressed the outdoors as beneficial to mental and physical health: indeed, the Boy Scouts and summer camp movement centered around these two philosophies (Paris). Through the character of Mr. Damon, and the elder Swift to a lesser extent, characters comment on fresh air and nature as healthy. Mr. Damon obtained a motorcycle on the advice of his doctor, who "thought riding around the country would benefit my health" (*Motor-Cycle* 15). After an accident with the motorcycle, Mr. Damon obtains a car because "my doctor insisted that I must get out in the open air. I'm too stout to walk, and I can't run" (*Motor-Cycle* 77). Other, more physical activity in nature revives spirits as well. Shipwrecked on Earthquake Island, Tom decides to go "for a dip in old Briney ... I think it will make me feel better." Others join in and "They came up from the waves, tingling with health, and their bruises and bumps, including Tom's cut leg, felt much better" (*Wireless Message* 51). Other health benefits accrue from nature as well. The authors make reference to Tom and others using nature for relaxation and bonding purposes. Tom and the elder Swift "used to spend many pleasant days boating [on Lake Carlopa], for Tom and the inventor were better chums than many boys are, and they were often seen together in a craft rowing about, or fishing" (*Motor-Cycle* 5). When his father seemed especially worried, Tom takes the elder Swift and his friend Ned on a camping trip. The vacation outdoors immediately improves the elderly man's appetite and outlook as well (*Motor-Boat* 32).

Nature, however, can also be an unhealthy influence. In Africa, Ned brings along quinine to combat malaria, and one member of the party looks forward to returning to America, since Africa is "not healthy in the first place" (*Electric Rifle* 25,78). In addition, Tom's jaunt in Alaska's cold environment saps his "spirits and strength" (*Caves of Ice* 78). As with ideas about nature's beauty, the author's ideas about nature and health are also mixed.

One Progressive Era value particularly espoused by President Teddy Roosevelt appears in conflicting ways in the stories. Roosevelt, an ardent big game hunter who made trips to Africa, saw hunting as a sport with certain ethical rules. He also advocated careful hunting to help protect species for later generations. At one point, Roosevelt stated forcefully, "When I hear of the destruction of a species, I feel just as if all the works of some great writer have perished" (Kline 54; Testi 1517–1518; Cutright).

Tom has considerable hunting skills, and these come in handy during his adventures. Spying on a lair of criminals in the woods at night, Tom "made his way forward, taking care not to make too much disturbance in the bushes. He had been on hunting trips, and knew the value of silence in the woods" (*Motor-Cycle* 71). Despite his experience hunting, the values and ethics of hunting in the stories reflect a mixed and incomplete reaction to Roosevelt's message. The Tom Swift books show some appreciation of these rules, yet monetary concerns continue to be paramount when dealing with hunting.

While planning a hunting trip to Africa, Tom soon learns that overhunting for ivory has led to a scarcity of elephants. Rather than stop the trip or hunt another animal, the scarcity only provokes greater urgency among the group. Scarcity of the elephants has caused the price of ivory to rise, and therefore the hunters must take advantage of economic conditions (*Electric Rifle* 25). As another example, when an approaching herd of elephants threatens them, Durban instructs the group to "kill all you can." Tom, "who was not needlessly cruel, even in hunting," initially balks, until Durban reminds him of the "necessity" of getting ivory and protecting adjacent grain fields (*Electric Rifle* 44–45).

In other places in the story a hunting ethic appears. Although "game was plentiful" in Africa, the group "only shot what they needed" when hunting for food (*Electric Rifle* 37). During the elephant hunt, Durban approaches a conservation ethic when he advises the group to "aim for the bulls, every one, [but] don't kill the mothers or little ones" (*Electric Rifle* 45). Later, when a herd of buffalo stampede, the hunting party again takes down a large number of animals. The narrator interjects, "It seemed like a needless slaughter, but it was not"; the native village had been protected (*Electric Rifle* 55). As one of their last acts in Africa, Durban shoots a rogue elephant, who was "instantly killed, and was out of his misery, for often it is great pain which makes an otherwise peaceable elephant become a 'rogue'" (*Electric Rifle* 77). Not incidentally, the elephant also had "an enormous pair of tusks" (*Electric Rifle* 77). Although the hunting party often wantonly kills large numbers of animals, they do abide by some rules, including which ones to kill or not. In addition, the author feels compelled to justify explicitly the killings as either mercy killings (in the case of the rogue elephant) or to protect the native villages. This conflict and the narrator's explicit statements indicate hesitant steps to include some Progressive Era values alongside the Gilded Age ones.

Non-Whites and Nature

Throughout the early series, values about nature either clearly reflect the Gilded Age, or, in some instances, reflect a transition period toward Progressive Era values. Only with their descriptions of non-whites and nature, however, do the books rest squarely within their Progressive Era origins. Racism and nativism stood as prominent, accepted values of American society in the early twentieth century, and certainly played a large role in the period's popular culture. In 1915, for example, shortly after the debut of the Tom Swift novels, MGM released *The Birth of a Nation*, a movie so successful it saved the company from bankruptcy. The film portrayed African Americans as violent, lazy, corrupt usurpers of Southern power.

Racism moved into academics as well, with the popularization of scientific racism, especially in biology, anthropology, and history. Madison Grant wrote probably the most well-known of these tracts, *The Passing of the Great Race* (1916), although other works codified similar reasoning. Scientific racism linked perceived relationships or closeness to nature with ethnicity: non-whites were closer to nature, less civilized, and therefore lower on the evolutionary scale. Grant summed up this relationship when he stated "where the environment is too soft and luxurious and no strife is required for survival [i.e., Africa], not only are some weak strains and individuals allowed to survive and encouraged to breed but the strong types also grow fat mentally and physically" (Grant 39). Men like Grant also acted on their philosophies. As a leader of the New York Zoological Society, Grant encouraged the Bronx Zoo to display human "specimens" of indigenous populations in cages alongside apes and monkeys, making the explicit connection between these groups and animals.[9]

The series closely follows these basic tenets of scientific racism, using nature as a tool of oppression for people of color. Non-whites serve as foils to middle-class white values about nature idealized through Tom. Groups of people who fail to use nature in accordance with these accepted values are subject to denigration and subordination. Uses of nature become a litmus test for appropriate attributes of civilization and middle class values. Tom and other major characters tend to use rural or wilderness areas by proscribed middle class ideals, as sources of commodities, as something to tame and civilize, or for sport or leisure. Those who use these areas for necessity, or are linked too closely to these spaces or other natural objects, defy these conventions of appropriate behavior in nature and are subject to derision, suspicion, fear, and subjugation.

Eradicate "Rad" Sampson, the Swifts' handyman, serves as the most prevalent recurring example of the connection between nature and non-whites. Where Tom's world consists of motorcycles, motorboats, and aircraft, Rad's labor is qualitatively different. Rad consistently works outdoors, in low-level, menial tasks like whitewashing, mowing, and milling lumber. His status and duties as a laborer keep him consistently closer to nature and dirt in particular. His name instantly solidifies his status. Given the name "Eradicate" for his ability to, as he puts it, "eradicates de dirt," the black man continues to be linked to the most lowly in the stories (*Motor-Cycle* 27).

Perhaps the most prominent example of the nature/non-white connection rests with Rad's continued close association with his mule, Boomerang. The two share characteristics stereotypically allotted to African Americans under racist ideology. The authors depict both Rad and the mule as slow, lazy, and unreliable. For example, Tom describes the mule and his owner as moving "slow as molasses." Boomerang "waggled his ears lazily" and "peered lazily around" (*Motor-Cycle* 25, 26, 27). The author describes the elderly black man in similar ways. Rad returns to work in the Swift garden at one point "with slow and lagging steps" (*Wireless Message* 16). Both need appropriate incentives to work more efficiently. The mule only moves quickly when promised a "stable full ob oats" (*Airship* 16). In the same way, Rad often brightens up when offered a job or compensation for some work (*Motor-Boat* 16, *Wireless Message* 4). For example, when Tom hits Rad with his motor-cycle and then believes he is exaggerating his injuries, Rad validates Tom's assumptions when "now that there seemed to be a prospect of earning money,

[Rad] rose quickly and easily" (*Motor-Cycle* 27). Rad regularly eats his meals like the mule. While finalizing work on the Black Hawk, Rad and Boomerang "were the only ones who ate regularly" while the other men worked feverishly to finish the project (*Electric Rifle* 20).

Both Rad and the mule experience fear around much of Tom's technology. For example, when Rad first sees the Red Cloud, he "edged away, as if the airship might suddenly put out a pair of hands and grab him," and refuses to come for a ride (*Airship* 42). Boomerang reacts in a similar way when the ship lifts off: "The mule was so frightened that he started off on a dead run" (*Airship* 43). Again emphasizing his closeness to the animal, Rad communicates directly with the mule from time to time. When Tom faced off against a criminal, Rad comes to his rescue, stating that "I yelled t' Boomerang t' hurry up ... dish year time he knowed he were comin' t'help yo,' an' he certainly did leg it" (*Airship* 16). Mr. Damon asks Rad at one point how the mule understands him, and Rad replies, "I doan't know how he know, Mistah Damon ... but he do know" (*Electric Runabout* 44). Indeed, the two are never physically separated in the books for very long. Rad even refuses a trip to Africa when Tom flatly denies the mule a place on his airship (*Electric Rifle* 26).

As he is closer to nature and therefore farther from civilized man, Rad lacks knowledge and understanding of technology, and he frequently serves as a foil to demonstrate Tom's superior scientific understanding. Tom offers to help Rad repair the brake on his wagon by improving the leverage on the handle. Rad immediately misunderstands the scientific term, stating, "I ain't never had no liverage on dis yeah wagon. It ain't dat kind ob a wagon" (*Motor-Cycle* 28). Rad greets Tom's knowledge and skill with appropriate submissiveness and awe: he watches the repair job with "open-mouthed amazement" and applauds Tom's work by stating, "Yo' am suttinly a conjure-man when it comes t'fixin' wagons!" (*Motor-Cycle* 27, 28). Rad further indicates that he does not approve of leaps in technology. In *Tom Swift and His Motor Boat*, Tom enters a boat race. Rad reacts to this by stating, "Dat's all de risin' generation t'inks about now ... racing an' goin' fast. Mah ole mule Boomerang am good enough fo' me" (*Motor-Boat* 83). Overall, Rad's closeness to nature through his labor and his relationship with his mule violate white norms. This deviation serves to separate Rad further from Tom and the other whites in the books, and to make him an appropriate subject for domination.

The stories associate other non-whites with nature as well, most noticeably to native Africans, when Tom journeys to "the dark continent" in *Tom Swift and His Electric Rifle*. Although Appleton insinuates associations between Rad with Boomerang, he wastes no such subtleties on connections with Africans or Native Americans and animals. Fleeing from stampeding elephants, the black natives move faster than Tom's group, "for they could travel through the jungle, ignoring the trail, at high speed. They were almost like snakes or animals in this respect" (*Electric Rifle* 47). Later, during another elephant hunt, the natives "were like snakes, unseen but ever present, wriggling along on their hands and knees" (*Electric Rifle* 52). Tomba, an African who helps the whites rescue the missionaries, "can see in the dark like a cat," according to Tom (*Electric Rifle* 68). In Alaska, when the group frightens a Native American, Mr. Damon immediately mistakes him for a bear (*Caves of Ice* 45).

The author describes the fictional "red pygmies" of Africa in such a way as to almost negate their humanity altogether. Described variously as "creatures" or "men," the pygmies stand at "about three feet high, covered with thick reddish hair.... They are wild, savage and ferocious.... They're like little red apes" (*Electric Rifle* 20). Rather than a comparison to snakes, the red pygmies sink one level further: "They were so small, and so wild, capable of living in tiny huts or caves, and so primitive ... [that] they were as hard to locate as the proverbial flea" (*Electric Rifle* 51). Their prolific numbers yield other comparisons to insects. The pygmies swarm during attacks "with such singleness of purpose" that when one falls to Tom's gun, "scores of others sprang up to take their places" (*Electric Rifle* 64). Rather than human, the pygmies seem more like ants, bees, or other hive insects. These very direct comparisons to animals place these non-white groups much closer to nature.

Like Rad, though again to a greater degree, the non-whites in the stories also react with fear and superstition to white technology. As the Black Hawk rises in the air in Africa, "several superstitious blacks, who saw the airship for the first time, ran away in terror" (*Electric Rifle* 35). Going over a village, "the whole population, including women and children, were running about like mad." Durban, the hunter, explains their reaction: "The natives are very superstitious, and likely took us for an evil spirit" (*Electric Rifle* 36). Members of the Brazilian military briefly hold Tom and his party hostage on their way to find sunken treasure. Upon seeing the Swift submarine, the "brown-skinned" Brazilians "uttered cries of fright" (*Submarine* 65, 59). In Alaska, a rival airship appears before a tribe of Native Americans threatening Tom and "with howls of fear, the Indians turned and fled" (*Caves of Ice* 49).

African Americans, native black Africans, "red pygmies," Brazilians, and Alaskan natives provide examples of groups who use nature differently than Tom and other elite whites. Each of these groups depends on nature more closely than Tom. The Africans and Alaskans depend on nature for living spaces and sustenance. Rad looks to nature for his livelihood. Each of the non-white groups suffers from stereotypical associations of not only using nature differently, but also from comparisons to animals. Just as Madison Grant and other white New Yorkers viewed Africans as possible zoo exhibits, the Tom Swift novels see non-whites as like mules, snakes, bears, insects, and other animals. In contrast to many views of nature in the books which rest with Gilded Age values, the connection of nature and non-whites through the tenets of scientific racism places this aspect of the works squarely within the racist ethic of the Progressive Era when making connections about nature.

Conclusions

The dating of the early Tom Swift novels places them squarely within the Progressive Era in American history. Certainly, this was a time of prominent events and changes within thinking about nature and the environment. Politicians argued for conservation policies when dealing with natural resources. Activists promoted the protection of some land as national parks. Women changed conceptions of smoke and pressed for reduced pollution in urban areas. None of these themes, however, appear prominent in the Tom Swift novels, which instead promote a Gilded Age-ethic of domination and subordination regarding nature. Tom conquers the land, air, and water. He battles nature in the form of storms, and, most prominently, effectively uses nature for personal monetary gain. The stories develop a concept of wilderness in opposition to civilization, and as places of danger, testing, and lawlessness. Even some Progressive Era values that creep in have contradictory examples to balance them. Glorifying the beauty of the Rockies contrasts with decrying the scenery of Africa. Praise for the health benefits of the outdoors fails to extend to the African landscape. Hunting ethics fall prey to unmitigated capitalism when killing elephants. Overall, and quite clearly, Tom emerges as a Gilded Age hero when examining the views of nature and the environment. One notable exception exists: the books repeatedly argue for a close association with non-whites and nature, something popularized during the Progressive Era.

Evidence of this mish-mash of ideas about the natural world leads to several possible conclusions. First, it may simply reflect the background of the authors involved in the series. Although they wrote for younger boys, the two men who formulated much of the original series grew up during the Gilded Age and must have been influenced by that period's values. The delay may also reflect simply reflect the time necessary for events and causes to percolate down into a common understanding. Although the literature in environmental history shows various events occurring, or people taking up various causes, perhaps this is far less widespread in the national consciousness than would be expected. Such sea changes in how nature is perceived may simply take longer to occur because of the gulf between the two systems of thought.[10]

The lag can also be explained, however, simply through linking the dominant themes in the books with the lone Progressive Era nature value. The Tom Swift books took great pride in keeping the series at, or even beyond, the height of technological and scientific achievement. Tom rides motorcycles, drives cars, builds and flies various aircraft, travels in submarines and motorboats, and communicates by radio, all well before these items became commonplace. Science in the stories had to be up-to-date, and this included the latest theories about race and nature. When scientific racists expounded theories justifying the supremacy of white Europeans and asserting that warm climates yielded lazy, animal-like people, the authors wove those ideas into their stories. The remainder of the breadth of nature value changes during the Progressive Era were largely ignored. Ecology as a science would not come into the popular lexicon until the 1940s (Worster 256–7). Without a "science" of nature, Swift's creators perhaps saw the changes in views about nature as economic or bureaucratic or spiritual, rather than something for their science- and engineering-minded hero.

The adherence to the tenets of scientific racism would certainly have made any of the other shifts to regard nature differently more difficult. Certainly, if popular scientific thought linked nature and "lesser" peoples, then altering conceptions about nature for whites would be a challenging issue. Linking whites more closely to nature in any way might, therefore, challenge the very basis of white supremacy as detailed in the theories of scientific racism. Ultimately, the racism inherent in the early Tom Swift novels is less of an anomaly than it may seem. The novels express the latest ideas about science and technology during the Progressive Era, and the ideas of scientific racism, connecting non-whites to nature, are no exception.

If Albie Hecht intends to "reenvision" Tom Swift into a motion picture that situates the hero as leading an environmentally responsible company, he will definitely be moving the series far from its origins. Strongly grounded in its authors' Gilded Age roots, the early Tom Swift books stressed domination over nature and the importance of nature's subordination to capitalistic enterprise and technology. Whites stereotyped groups as "closer to nature" through racism or classism to justify their continued subordination in society as well. Although values about the natural world were beginning to change during the Progressive Era, the Tom Swift books reflect little of these attitudes. Blogger Josh Tyler may have had a point; the original Tom Swift would not have been interested in chaining himself to a tree to stop the loggers, as we might expect an environmentalist to do today. He would not even have been interested in a Progressive Era idea of managing the forests for future use. In fact, if Tom saw profit in it, the early stories instead point to Tom inventing a new technology to aid the loggers in more efficiently felling trees and slicing the trunks into planks, and then more quickly moving on to clear cut other, more dense and profitable forests. Tom's actions would have won the approval of Gilded Age whites, but not early twenty-first century teenagers.

Notes

1. For purposes of this chapter, by the "early books of the original Tom Swift series," I mean the first ten novels of the 1910–1941 series (listed under "Works Cited"), which generally set the tone for the rest of the original series.

2. The literature surrounding the Gilded Age and the natural world is far too extensive to be cited here in detail. The literature contains significant material on various regions of the United States, notably the West. In addition, sources highlight various industries and resources, including lumber, water power, gold and silver mining, fishing, the development of the Great Plains into agriculture and grazing land, and the effects on Native Americans. For a solid, brief overview, see Kline, 37–50. John Opie's *Nature's Nation* provides a useful textbook overview of these periods as well.

3. Again, it would be almost impossible to cover the scope and breadth of the literature regarding Progressive Era environmentalism and attitudes toward nature. Kline again provides a useful overview (51–69). The standard work on the Progressive Era is Hays, *Conservation and the Gospel of Efficiency*. In this period, the literature has focused on the development of the federal bureaucracy for environmental issues, the ideas and events of the conservation, preservation, and anti-pollution movements as well as minority and women's participation in environmental issues. Roosevelt, Pinchot, and Muir each have multiple useful biographies as do other prominent figures during the period. Some of the more useful material regarding gender and environmental activism during this time include Stradling, Gugliotta, Flanagan, and Hoy.

4. The literature about children and nature in environmental history is most well-developed for the Progressive Era. For an overview, see Mergen. In addition to Paris, Howard Chudacoff provides a look at children's playtime from 1600 to the present in *Children at Play*.

5. Robert Von der Osten briefly discusses the consequences of technological innovation on nature in the entire Tom Swift series. Von der Osten notes "the environmental and ecological insensitivity" of the first series, where "nature is either viewed as a hostile environment to be overcome ... or a resource" (275). In addition, he points out that "by the final series, [Tom] reverts to a desire to transcend nature itself by overcoming gravity" (272). I find that desire strongly situated within the original series, and add to Von der Osten by expanding on some of these ideas, and placing them in the appropriate historical context.

6. This lack of any type of pollution concern is not surprising considering the feminized nature of the anti-pollution movement and the very masculine centered nature of the books. For a discussion of how men responded to what they perceived as a feminized reform space during the Progressive Era, see Rome.

7. The debate over the cultural construction of the idea of "wilderness" is one of the most

well-developed in environmental history. William Cronon's article "The Trouble with Wilderness" is a useful starting place in this area, although the standard canon is Roderick Nash, *Wilderness and the American Mind.* For an updated look at the historiography, see Lewis's edited collection, *American Wilderness.*

    8. Interestingly, the wilderness of Earthquake Island fails to overthrow the boundaries of class relations in any way. The captain and mate of the other shipwrecked vessel are continuously under the orders of their employers (*Wireless Message* 60).

    9. The domination of nature also clearly links to gendered themes of male domination throughout the series (something I have consciously omitted from this chapter). For example, the author explicitly refers to nature as feminine. In Alaska, after an ice cave collapses and destroys Tom's airship, the narrator pauses to state, "Nature, as if satisfied at the mischief *she* had wrought, called a halt to the movement of ice" (emphasis added, *Caves of Ice* 76). Certainly, equating women and nature far predates the Gilded Age (see Merchant), yet the fact that males dominate a female nature is important. As with non-whites, women's close association with nature justifies their obvious subordination to male control and manipulation. The authors portray women as weak, frail, helpless, unintelligent, and certainly untechnological. Tom's world certainly is an explicitly homosocial one, and by their absence, women are rendered almost insignificant. This is an aspect of the Gilded Age that was being challenged during the Progressive Era. This challenge, in fact, led some scholars to describe this period as a "crisis in masculinity." Repairs to this crisis, as suggested by Teddy Roosevelt, including efforts to get young men into same-sex groups and have them participate in outdoor activities (Testi; Bedermen).

    10. The finding that popular culture lags behind environmental events within the literature is not entirely surprising. I have also found this same trend within the *Star Trek* series, which can lag as much as a generation behind environmental events and the adoption of values. See Blum.

WORKS CITED

Appleton, Victor. *Tom Swift Among the Diamond Makers; or, The Secret of Phantom Mountain.* 1911. *Project Gutenberg.* Ed. Michael S. Hart. 17 Jul. 2008. Project Gutenberg Literary Archive Foundation. 3 Aug. 2009. http://www.gutenberg.org/files/128*Motor-Boat* 1282-h/1282-h.htm.

_____. *Tom Swift and His Airship; or, The Stirring Cruise of the Red Cloud.* 1910. *Project Gutenberg.* Ed. Michael S. Hart. 13 Jul. 2008. Project Gutenberg Literary Archive Foundation. 19 Aug. 2009. http://www.gutenberg.org/files/300*Electric Runabout* 3005-h/3005-h.htm.

_____. *Tom Swift and His Electric Rifle; or, Daring Adventures in Elephant Land.* 1911. *Project Gutenberg.* Ed. Michael S. Hart. 16 Jan. 2009. Project Gutenberg Literary Archive Foundation. 14 Aug. 2009. http://www.gutenberg.org/files/377*Diamond Makers* 3777-h/3777-h.htm.

_____. *Tom Swift and His Electric Runabout; or, The Speediest Car on the Road.* 1910. *Project Gutenberg.* Ed. Michael S. Hart. 13 Jul. 2008. Project Gutenberg Literary Archive Foundation. 3 Aug. 2009. http://www.gutenberg.org/files/950/950-h/950-h.htm.

_____. *Tom Swift and His Motor-Boat; or, The Rivals of Lake Carlopa.* 1910. *Project Gutenberg.* Ed. Michael S. Hart. 13 Jul. 2008. Project Gutenberg Literary Archive Foundation. 3 Aug. 2009. http://www.gutenberg.org/files/227*Airship* 2273-h/2273-h.htm.

_____. *Tom Swift and His Motor-Cycle; or, Fun and Adventures on the Road.* 1910. *Project Gutenberg.* Ed. Michael S. Hart. 11 Mar. 2002. Project Gutenberg Literary Archive Foundation. 24 Aug. 2008. http://www.gutenberg.org/dirs/etext0*Airship* 01tom11h.htm.

_____. *Tom Swift and His Sky Racer; or, The Quickest Flight on Record.* 1911. *Project Gutenberg.* Ed. Michael S. Hart. 13 Jul. 2008. Project Gutenberg Literary Archive Foundation. 14

Aug. 2009. http://www.gutenberg.org/files/95*Motor-Cycle* 951-h/951-h.htm.
_____. *Tom Swift and His Submarine Boat; or, Under the Ocean for Sunken Treasure.* 1910. *Project Gutenberg.* Ed. Michael S. Hart. 13 Jul. 2008. Project Gutenberg Literary Archive Foundation. 19 Aug. 2009. http://www.gutenberg.org/files/949/949-h/949-h.htm.
_____. *Tom Swift and His Wireless Message; or, The Castaways of Earthquake Island.* 1911. *Project Gutenberg.* Ed. Michael S. Hart. 16 Jan. 2009. Project Gutenberg Literary Archive Foundation. 3 Aug. 2009. http://www.gutenberg.org/files/422*Diamond Makers* 42*Motor-Boat* -h/4227-h.htm.
_____. *Tom Swift in The Caves of Ice; or, The Wreck of the Airship.* 1911. *Project Gutenberg.* Ed. Michael S. Hart. 16 Jan. 2009. Project Gutenberg Literary Archive Foundation. 3 Aug. 2009. http://www.gutenberg.org/files/3734*Electric Runabout* 3734-h/3734-h.htm.
Birth of a Nation. Dir. D.W. Griffith. MGM, 1915.
Blum, Elizabeth D. "Save the Whales and Beware Wilderness: Star Trek and Reflections of the Modern Environmental Movement." In *The Influence of Star Trek on Television, Film and Culture (Critical Explorations in Science Fiction and Fantasy).* Ed. Lincoln Geraghty. Jefferson, NC: McFarland, 2007.
Chudacoff, Howard P. *Children at Play: An American History.* New York: New York University Press, 2007.
Cronon, William. "The Trouble with Wilderness; or, Getting Back to the Wrong Nature." *Environmental History* 1 (1996): 47–55.
Cutright, Paul Russell. *Theodore Roosevelt: The Making of a Conservationist.* Urbana: University of Illinois Press, 1985.
Flanagan, Maureen A. "Gender and Urban Political Reform: The City Club and the Woman's Club of Chicago in the Progressive Era." *American History Review* 95 (1990): 1032–50.
Grant, Madison. *The Passing of the Great Race, or The Racial Basis of European History.* 4th Rev. ed. New York: Charles Scribner's Sons, 1921.
Gugliotta, Angela. "Class, Gender, and Coal Smoke: Gender Ideology and Environmental Justice in Pittsburgh, 1868–1914." *Environmental History* 5 (2000): 165–93.
Happy Feet. Dir. George Miller. Kingdom Feature Productions, 2006.
Hayes, Dade. "Worldwide Scoops Up 'Tom Swift.'" 26 Nov. 2007. *Variety.* www.variety.com/article/VR1117976545.html?categoryid=13&cs=1
Hays, Samuel P. *Conservation and the Gospel of Efficiency: The Progressive Conservation Movement, 1890–1920.* Cambridge: Harvard University Press, 1959.
Hiaasen, Carl. *Hoot.* New York: Knopf Books for Young Readers, 2004.
Houston Daily Post. 8 Jul. 1881. 1.
Hoy, Suellen M. "'Municipal Housekeeping': The Role of Women in Improving Urban Sanitation Practices, 1880–1917." In *Pollution and Reform in American Cities, 1870–1930.* Ed. Martin V. Melosi. Austin: University of Texas Press, 1980. 173–198.
Keeline, James D. "The Nancy Drew *Myth*tery Stories." In *Nancy Drew and Her Sister Sleuths: Essays on the Fiction of Girl Detectives.* Eds. Michael G. Cornelius and Melanie E. Gregg. Jefferson, NC: McFarland, 2008. 13–32.
Kline, Benjamin. *First Along the River: A Brief History of the U.S. Environmental Movement.* 2d ed. San Francisco: Acada Books, 2000.
Lewis, Michael. "American Wilderness: An Introduction." In *American Wilderness: A New History.* Ed. Michael Lewis. Oxford: Oxford University Press, 2007. 3–14.
McNary, Dave and Tatiana Siegel. "Columbia Slow to Nab 'Swift.'" *Variety.* 31 May 2009. www.variety.com/article/VR1118004356.html?categoryid=13&cs=1
Merchant, Carolyn. *Death of Nature: Women, Ecology, and the Scientific Revolution.* New York: Harper One, 1990.
Mergen, Bernard. "Children and Nature in History." *Environmental History* 8.4 (2003): 643–669.
Molson, Francis. "Three Generations of Tom Swift." *Children's Literature Association Quarterly* 10.2 (1985): 60–63.
Muir, John. *John Muir: Nature Writings.* New York: Literary Classics of America, 1997.

Paris, Leslie. *Children's Nature: The Rise of the American Summer Camp.* New York: New York University Press, 2008.
Platt, Harold. "Jane Addams and the Ward Boss Revisited: Class, Politics, and Public Health in Chicago, 1890–1930." *Environmental History* 5 (2000): 194–222.
Rome, Adam. "'Political Hermaphrodites': Gender and Environmental Reform in Progressive America." *Environmental History* 11 (2006): 440–463.
Runte, Alfred. *National Parks: The American Experience.* 3d ed. Lincoln: University of Nebraska Press, 1997.
Smith, Kimberly K. *African American Environmental Thought: Foundations.* Lawrence: University Press of Kansas, 2007.
Smith, Michael B. "'The Ego Ideal of the Good Camper' and the Nature of Summer Camp." *Environmental History* 11 (2006): 70–101.
Stradling, David. *Smokestacks and Progressives: Environmentalists, Engineers, and Air Quality in America, 1881–1951.* Baltimore: Johns Hopkins University Press, 1999.
Testi, Arnaldo. "The Gender of Reform Politics: Theodore Roosevelt and the Culture of Masculinity." *Journal of American History* 81 (1995): 1509–33.
Tyler, Josh. "Tom Swift Turned Into Green Propaganda Movie." Nov. 28, 2007. Cinema Blend.com.
Von der Osten, Robert. "Four Generations of Tom Swift: Ideology in Juvenile Science Fiction." *The Lion and the Unicorn* 28.2 (2004): 268–283.
Wall-E. Dr. Andrew Stanton. Pixar Animation Studios, 2008.
White, Nicholas. "'Tom Swift' Producer Talks 'Invention' Adventure Plot." 16 Nov. 2009. Moviefone.com.
Worster, Donald. *Nature's Economy: A History of Ecological Ideas.* 2d ed. New York: Cambridge University Press, 1994.

6

Tim Murphy: Superhero Without a Cape

Fred Erisman

The dust jacket of *The Sky Trail* (1932) says it all. An orange, single-engined monoplane cruises above a busy, 1930s-era airport. Along the runway of the airport stand three hangars. Two carry identification numbers on their roofs; the third bears the cryptic legend "S.P." At the controls of the monoplane sits a young man in conventional flying attire — helmet, goggles, perhaps gloves and a leather coat. He is calm, watchful, dedicated. Who can he be? Markings on his airplane reveal his identity. The words "Sky Patrol No. 1" appear below the cockpit, a clear reference to the hangar below and a hint of the far-ranging mission of the monoplane and its pilot. Above them is the clincher: the letters *T* and *M* superimposed on a green background and contained within a circle. All is well. It is the mark of *Tim Murphy*!

Tim is the young protagonist of four novels by Graham M. Dean, published between 1931 and 1934: *Daring Wings* (1931), *The Sky Trail* (1932), *Circle 4 Patrol* (1933), and *The Treasure Hunt of the S-18* (1934). In these books, Dean drew heavily upon his own experience and interests. He was, at the time of his writing the series, editor of *The Iowa City Press-Citizen* and an aviation enthusiast (*Who Was Who in America* 107; Ward and Marquardt 152). In his four books he offers what at first appears to be a cluster of career stories, similar to and contemporaneous with those produced by the Stratemeyer Syndicate and other sources, relating Tim's rise in the journalistic world (Johnson 54–62). On closer reading, though, one finds that Dean goes far beyond simple careerism. Tim does indeed excel in his profession, but the stories also reveal his role as a dedicated agent of principle and justice, anticipating the traits of superheroes to come. In Tim's case, his special powers come from sources man-made and progressive, and his greatest mission, along with the pursuit of truth and justice, is helping to create a progressive, modern America through the agency of aviation.

Daring Wings, the first of the series, introduces twenty-one-year-old Tim Murphy, a reporter for *The Atkinson News* in an unnamed Midwestern state. At the newspaper's insistence, he takes flying lessons and begins to cover aviation affairs for the paper. With sidekick Ralph Parsons, he battles the mysterious Sky Hawk, bane of the United States Air Mail; flies food and medications to flood victims; takes part in a state-wide good-will flying tour; makes a record-setting Arctic flight; and covers a revolution in Mexico. After being named aviation editor of the *News*, Tim continues his exploits in *The Sky Trail*. He and Ralph — in one day — take daredevil photographs of an oil refinery fire and break an ice jam threatening a small town by using army-issue high explosive bombs. The duo then join the search for two downed air mail pilots and are commissioned special undercover deputies of the state police. Tim rides a record-setting run of a mail train, and, with Ralph's help, rounds up the last surviving members of the Sky Hawk's gang.

Circle 4 Patrol, the third volume of the series, finds the *News* being threatened by a rival paper, *The Atkinson Advance*. The *Advance* is sponsored by the deep-pocketed Barnes Syndicate, a tough, even unscrupulous competitor. Like the *News*, it features airborne reporters, boasting a fleet of aircraft against the *News*'s solitary ship, and is known to pay informants for story leads. Tim does his part for the *News*'s victory, filing stories of air-borne drama and civil conflict; then, taking a much-needed vacation at the Circle 4 ranch, he uncovers widespread cattle rustling being masterminded by a local banker. The final volume, *The Treasure Hunt of the S-18*, finds Tim acting in concert with federal authorities to break up a drug-smuggling ring, then teaming with the adventurer Grenville Ford to search for a fortune in gold aboard a sunken freighter. Using a decommissioned submarine (the S-18 of the title), Ford and his crew fight off soldier of fortune Jack Sladek's efforts to scuttle their expedition, then retrieve the gold, allowing Tim to turn in yet another front-page story.

Although Tim's stories are nominally career tales tracking his rise in his profession, they simultaneously cast him in the role of the citizen-avenger. Entirely human in all his (or her) attributes, this legendary individual anticipates the role played in later American popular culture by The Phantom (1936) and Batman (1940) among the wholly human heroes, and Superman (1938), Captain Marvel (1940), and Wonder Woman (1942) among the super folk. Tim is a transitional figure within the group, physically human but figuratively super-human, and carries his responsibilities honorably and capably (Coogan 147, 154–158). Like the mythic superheroes he anticipates, Tim faces a variety of challenges. All are imposing, all in one way or another imperil the larger society, and all are events against which the constituted authorities are powerless. Whatever their nature and origin, all of the challenges require the intervention of a superhero if society is to be saved.

The challenges fall into two categories: benign and malignant. Benign threats occur naturally, the result of human society's coming into contact with abstract forces larger than itself. Though the forces pose a genuine threat to life and property, there is no evil intent behind them. Instead, like the indifferent nature operating in Stephen Crane's "The Open Boat" (1898) or Frank Norris's *McTeague* (1899), they simply *are*, their menace to humanity coming from their immensity and indifference. The forces do not *care*, and humanity's goals and dreams mean nothing to them. Malignant threats, on the other hand, are uniformly man-made. As Peter Coogan points out, they are the work of a human mind that seeks "to bring the normal activities of a society to a halt" (61). They are engineered by a person with "a selfish, antisocial mission," who seeks ends "that will serve his interest and not those of ... the larger culture. He works at cross purposes to contemporary society" (Coogan 77). The minds behind these threats may be weak, they may be evil, or they may even be the mass-will of a group. All, however, operate in ways that thwart the ordinary processes of justice.

Some of Tim's earliest challenges arise from naturally occurring events. In *Daring Wings*, the isolated village of Auburn is cut off by a flood and threatened with starvation and a typhoid epidemic; the authorities are helpless in the face of Auburn's need (*DW* 86–87). The villagers are endangered again in *The Sky Trail* when a wintertime ice dam creates a dangerous buildup of water; should the dam break uncontrollably, the torrent would wipe out the little town. In both instances, Tim does what no one else can do. In the former he flies in food and serum, risking his life by deliberately crash-landing his plane in the river, and in the latter he diverts the ice dam's backed-up water into harmless channels by pelting it with aerial bombs. In neither situation is the society able to rescue itself. It lacks the ingenuity and means; its salvation requires external intervention, and Tim rises to the occasion (*ST* 60–65; White 10–13).

Formidable as the forces of nature are, human evil forms an even greater challenge for Tim, and it occurs in varied incarnations. A familiar one is the simple criminal, who turns to crime in lieu of honest work; another is the outwardly law-abiding individual who violates a social trust for personal gain; a third is the group that sets itself against the common welfare; and the last is the master criminal — the equal of any that the later comic books might offer. Ace McDowell typifies the first. Although a pilot like Tim, he is weak-willed, and chooses drug smuggling over barnstorming. Drugs, clearly, are a social menace (McDowell's "cruel, hard, merciless" eyes and "cold and limp" hands suggest the depth of his villainy), and Tim, as a clean-living individual as well as an officer of the law, wants to stop their distribution (*THS-18* 36, 38). His pursuit of Ace ends when McDowell's parachute collapses as he jumps from his disabled airplane, his death "a just vengeance but a merciless one" (*THS-18* 68). Federal authorities have been hot on McDowell's trail, but it is Tim who does what they cannot and brings him down.

Hiram Escott's offense is of a different sort. As president of the only bank in Yellow River, Wyoming, the setting of *Circle 4 Patrol*, Escott is an agent of his depositors, pledged above all to protect their interests in return for their trust. Tim's first encounter with the banker shows him violating that trust, and his crimes grow in magnitude as his story unfolds. At the outset, waiting to cash a check in the bank, Tim witnesses Escott telling his assistant to call in the interest on the loan of Tim's host Hank Cummins while extending the loan of Kirk Neal, a discharged Cummins employee. Alerted by this incident, Tim looks into the persistent rustling of Cummins's cattle, and discovers that Escott is masterminding the activity. If Cummins cannot pay off his note at the bank, Escott will foreclose on the ranch and gain control of the rich coal deposits in its western range (*C4P* 199–200, 246–250). Escott has blatantly violated bankers' ethics, using his knowledge of Cummins's finances to help Neal and arranging for the theft of Cummins's cattle to expedite foreclosure on the Circle 4. His actions are more than criminal; they are unethical and the violation of a necessary personal trust, and Tim is the agent who brings him to justice.

Hiram Escott is an individual. Tim's third notable antagonist, the farmers of the village of Bennett, is a mob. The issue in Bennett is government-mandated tuberculin testing of local dairy herds, and the farmers are violently resisting. At stake is the general good: "It's a health protective measure," the state editor tells Tim, "and so far, the state veterinarians doing the testing have encountered only slight opposition." In Bennett, however, there's a different situation: "They're a wild, lawless bunch down around Bennett.... They're against everything that will benefit anyone else" (*C4P* 70–72). When Tim goes to cover the story, he discovers an even more complex situation. On the one hand, the farmers are mounting "armed resistance of officers of the law; civil rebellion if you cared to call it that." On the other, the officials sit paralyzed, taking no action. "The sheriff says he is afraid of bloodshed," Tim tells Ralph. "My own private opinion is that he doesn't want to do anything that will lose votes" (*C4P* 80–83). With public health and public peace teetering on the brink, Tim intervenes to help maintain order. What he does is publicize the mobilizing of the state national guard to unsettle the farmers. Using shrewd journalistic tactics, he learns that the guard is on its way and alerts the *News*'s readers of the potential conflict. With the story out, the troops arrive in Bennett, move in on the rebellious farmers, and break their resistance without bloodshed. It is a triumph for the law, and Tim has been a part of it.

The final class of antagonist Tim faces is the master criminal, here represented by the malevolent Sky Hawk of *Daring Wings*. Like the super-criminals of the comic books to come, the Sky Hawk is armed with advanced technology: an engine-stopping electric ray and a reservoir of poison gas. With these weapons he easily downs the airplanes of the United States Air Mail and pillages their cargoes while the authorities watch impotently. As a colleague of Tim's remarks, "The airways aren't patrolled like the highways and some mighty valuable cargoes are carried by planes these days" (*DW* 32–33). Tim, however, fights technology with technology. With the help of "the head of the engineering school of the university, an international authority on electricity," he learns the nature of the electric ray, builds a protective shroud of lead and zinc around the engine of his own airplane, and fends off the Sky Hawk's fearsome weapon (*DW* 17, 22; Coogan 95).

When the Sky Hawk is at last captured, he proves to have a classic attribute of the super-criminal, a scornful disdain for the conventions of normal society and a burning desire to flout those conventions for his own benefit (Coogan 77). Initial accounts of the Sky Hawk speculated that "he was a super-flyer, a famous [First] World War ace who had gone wrong; others had him leading a desperate band of aerial gunmen" (*DW* 56). He proves to be Kurt Blandin, the outwardly respectable owner of a flying circus, who is in actuality Max Reuter, "a former German ace, a great flyer, but obsessed with the idea that by plundering the air lines he can amass a great fortune and eventually attack America from the air" (*DW* 226). In his single-minded quest, Reuter seeks wealth, vengeance, *and* notoriety, flaunting his self-proclaimed superiority before the citizens of the United States.

Notable problems require a notable hero, and Tim Murphy, human though he is, qualifies nicely. The classic superhero is defined by three dominant traits. Whereas the villains are uniformly anti-social types, the superhero has "a selfless, pro-social mission," a determination to work for the larger good to support "the existing, professed mores of society" in ways that do not "benefit or further his own agenda." A second trait is a "dual identity," one part of which is "usually a closely guarded secret." Finally, he or she has superpowers, abilities often deriving from "advanced technology, or highly developed ... mental ... skills." Thus, the three elements of "mission, powers, and identity" characterize the superhero whatever his or her nature or origin (Coogan 30, 31, 39). Though Tim lacks the dark charisma of a Batman or the invulnerability of a Superman, he nevertheless matches them in his support of good.

As a reporter, Tim is charged with giving the public an unbiased summary of the facts. This he does, recording events great and small for the benefit of the *News*'s readers and suppressing his own views as he does so. He has, however, strong opinions about what he sees, and sets himself the personal mission of correcting the evils he discovers. His first reaction to the Sky Hawk, for example, is one of indignation, prompting a friend to remark: "Kind of riles up your Irish pride at the thought of them getting away, doesn't it?" From this indignant beginning comes Tim's explicit statement of his mission: "You know how I feel about crime. Anything I can do to stop it or, after it is committed, to bring the criminals to justice, I'll do." He is, in his own mind and in reality, a crusader against crime, one who sees himself destined to take up the role: "Tim felt that the gods who hold the threads of fate were weaving a new pattern and that he was being drawn deeper and deeper into it" (*DW* 32–33, 59). That destiny leads to a still greater commitment. As a mentor reminds him, Tim is not out "for personal gain or glory.... You do what you think is right" (*ST* 65–66). He may be a reporter, but he recognizes evil when he sees it and is compelled to deal with it.

As a reporter, Tim also has a secret identity. He is known far and wide as the flying representative of the *News*, garnering respect wherever he goes for the accuracy, vividness, and thoroughness of his dispatches. Behind Tim Murphy, Reporter, however, exists Tim Murphy, Secret Agent — an undercover member of the state police. Ironically, his commission comes about in great part because of the inability of the police to deal with a new kind of crime. As Colonel Robert Searle, head of the state police, tells him, "The airplane has placed an entirely new means of escape in the hands of criminals and we must be ready to combat this. With the present economy ... it would be impossible for us to secure funds for the training of our troopers." Tim and his editor agree immediately, whereupon Tim is sworn in as a "special and secret [member] of the state police" and steps in to bolster the inadequacy of the official defenders (*ST* 114–115, 72, 74).

Tim's mission of justice gains new dimensions from his commission, for he now has official status when he chooses to reveal it. His efforts to cash a check at Hiram Escott's bank are frustrated until he produces his badge: "'State police,'" Escott mumbles, "his whole attitude changing with what Tim thought was a cringe of fear." Later, after Escott's gang has been rounded up, the chief henchman asks Tim: "Are you a reporter or a secret agent of the state police?" Tim's smiling answer is "Both" (*C4P* 200, 248). His undercover status is useful to federal agents, who recruit him to provide "a little official help" when they close in on a drug smuggler, while Tim's casual production of a revolver nonpluses a shipmate aboard the *S-18*. "What are you," he asks. "A reporter or a policeman?" Tim's reply clears the air: "I'm a reporter first of all, but once or twice I've had to serve as a policeman" (*THS-18* 169). He fully understands — and accepts — the divided nature of his identity, and willingly embraces the responsibilities of both manifestations.

Finally, Tim, as a reporter, has certain powers not readily available to the ordinary citizen. One of these is speed, gained through his ready access to aircraft — in this instance, "one of those new Larks with a Wasp motor that will take her along at 150 miles per hour" (*DW* 8). With the *News*'s airplane at his disposal he joins the most advanced newspapers in the country in being able to outstrip all competitors: "If it ever comes to a race between us on a big story or picture scoop, we'll be able to pull away from them [the *Advance*]" (*C4P* 62; Piersol 35–37). A second power is the law, for as an officer of the police he wields the authority of officialdom. He is no simple citizen. A third is that of the press, for Tim is well aware his writings help shape public opinion. When he has second thoughts about taking the Aviation Editor's job, a copyreader friend sets him straight: "The newspaper man who knows aviation from the ground up will be in an enviable position — a position to command real power and respect" (*DW* 62). His editor praises him for the capture of the last members of the Sky Hawk's gang, telling him: "We're going on the street with an extra now with the *News* taking full credit for the capture of those men" (*C4P* 106–108). The power of his role as a reporter enables him to cut through red tape and get to the heart of the story during the dairy farmers' revolt, while the larger power of the press influences even the highest levels of government. Seeking bombs from the Army Air Force to break up the ice dam, Tim depends upon his managing editor, saying, "I'll need his political pull to get the material I need at the Fort" (*ST* 250, 44). Whatever his identity, Tim is a person able to wield power, and he wields it judiciously and effectively.

Impressive though the power of the state and the power of the press may be, Tim's ultimate source of power is his mastery of aviation and his fervent support of its modernity. In the Tim Murphy books, aviation is both the conduit of news and the creator of news. Tim's editor sets the scene in the opening pages of *Daring Wings*: "Some of our biggest news stories will break above the clouds.... We must have those stories" (*DW* 7). The *News*'s publisher reinforces this belief, saying later that "Newspaper readers eat up the romance and adventure of the skyways. The more we can give them, the better" (*C4P* 19–20). Tim's superiors acknowledge aviation's potential for good, and their support for aviation empowers Tim to advance that good. His actions, in their turn, show the larger public what aviation can do for all, empowering the American people as much as it does himself. By cultivating public air-mindedness, the airplane will stimulate a national awareness of the world. The more fully citizens come to understand that world, the more effectively they will deal with its problems.

In promoting aviation, Tim takes up the last of his missions: the "selling" of aviation to the American public. The theme of aviation-as-progress pervades the series. *Daring Wings* is barely started when Tim's editor tells him that "the skyways are going to unfold great tales of romance, of daring, possibly of banditry." Shortly afterward, an associate observes that "aviation [is] in its swaddling clothes. Within ten years it will be a giant among giants" (*DW* 7, 62). The publisher of the *News* picks up the theme, asserting that "Aviation is the coming thing and we must keep at the front" (*C4P* 19). He is speaking, of course, of keeping the *News* at the forefront of reporting aviation, but his statement has a double meaning. The American public, too, must "keep at the front," lest it be left behind in the steadily advancing culture of aviation. The nation's status is a function of its assimilation of flight, and the more fully the country embraces aviation, the more advanced it will become. Dean links the power of the press with the power of aviation to make his case. "The growth of aviation is going to be like the growth of the newspapers," Tim's copyreader mentor tells him.

> The young fellows who had plenty of foresight back in 1890 and 1900 are the big men of today.... The aviation game is like a newspaper.... The newspaper went through its baby days and has emerged into one of the greatest institutions of our modern times. So it will be with aviation [*DW* 64–65].

Progress, power, and responsibility go hand-in-hand as aviation shapes society.

That progress, however, is anything but dull, for with it comes a heightening of the drama of flight — thrills that can extend to all existence. Early on, a veteran of the air mails tells Tim that the excitement began when "Lindbergh flew the Atlantic and focused popular interest on aviation." From this conversation comes "a column that was fairly alive with the romance of the air mail and of the flyer who was the master of all birdmen." Tim adds to his chronicle of romance as his story proceeds: he "interviewed all the famous pilots who landed at the field, wrote sketches of the flyers on the regular air mail runs, and described flights over the city and the surrounding towns"

(*DW* 128, 131–132, 133). When Tim sits down to report the rescue of a downed air mail pilot, he relives

> the events of the day, transferring the story of what had happened in the clouds into words and sentences that would thrill the readers of the *News* the next day.... It was a story high in human interest — a story every subscriber of the *News* would read and remember [*ST* 114–115].

Romance and excitement can be found in more than the colorful air mail pilots and the flying celebrities who are in the public eye; they are present in *any* undertaking that involves flight.

The public has no access to the cockpits of the air mail, to be sure. It does, however, have access to an even more progressive instance of aviation's modernity and romance. This is the burgeoning system of air commerce that is swiftly unifying the nation. Dean parallels Tim's adventures with a portrait of emerging commercial air travel, showing its progress from lumbering biplanes to the Boeing 247 all-metal transport, the first truly modern airliner. The first mention of commercial air transport occurs in *The Sky Trail*, when Tim learns that the Transcontinental Air Mail Company is adding "giant tri-motored biplanes, capable of carrying 18 passengers and half a ton of mail or express" and increasing their service to Atkinson. This, in turn, will bring about "the inauguration of the most auspicious air transport program in the country" and Atkinson will "have the best transcontinental air service in the country. The story was news, big news." Excitement, progress, and modernity are melded in air transport, and the world of flight becomes accessible to any and all (*ST* 55, 76–77).

Young readers of the time may have recognized Transcontinental's tri-motored biplanes as Boeing Model 80A airliners, which replaced the single-engined Boeing Model 40B-4 ships being used by Boeing Air Transport. Boeing Air Transport, a precursor of United Air Lines, began flying mail routes throughout the Pacific Northwest and West Coast as early as 1927. Its 40B-4s could carry four passengers in addition to the pilot and the mail — a capability Tim makes use of in *The Sky Trail*, carrying his cowboy helpers in "the mail hole" of one of Transcontinental's original aircraft (*ST* 97). However, when Boeing enlarged the airline to offer trans-continental service in 1928, the expansion required a larger machine. This was the 80A, designed specifically for passenger service and offering passengers greater comfort and space. The craft seated ten passengers, cruised at 115 mph, and after 1930 carried a nursing-trained stewardess to comfort airsick passengers — the origin of the flight attendant (van der Linden 6–17; Bowers 109–114, 122–124).

For all its modernity, however, the Model 80A was quickly supplanted by a still more advanced Boeing product, the Model 247 airliner. Based on the technology used in the twin-engined Boeing B-9 bomber and the single-engined, six-passenger Boeing Model 221 Monomail, the Model 247 made all other airliners obsolete. A streamlined, all-metal, twin-engined transport equipped with retractable landing gear, it offered a significant increase in cruising speed and unprecedented passenger comfort: extensive soundproofing, adjustable seats, and individually adjustable ventilator outlets, not to mention facilities for food service more appealing than the box lunches previously available. When it entered service in 1933, the 247, with the Douglas DC-1/2/3 family of airliners that followed it, marked the beginning of the technological evolution that has led to the jet-propelled airlines of the twenty-first century (van der Linden 65–66, 68, 75–82).

Dean is fully aware of the significance of the Model 247, and quickly writes it into his books. It first appears in *Circle 4 Patrol*, published in the same year as its introduction. Dubbed the "60-B monoplane," the aircraft is described in terms that undeniably refer to the Model 247. It is, Dean writes, an all-metal craft capable of carrying ten passengers, a stewardess, and a pilot. It possesses retractable landing gear, and is spoken of as "a powerful looking, stream-lined, low-wing monoplane with motors set in each wing with the pilot perched in a cabin, projecting out over the leading edge of the wing." Its advances carry over to its interior. Once settled in his comfortable seat, Tim casts an appreciative eye over the stewardess, "an attractive girl of about [his] age," marvels at the well-insulated cabin, and enjoys an apple from the lavish fruit basket the stewardess circulates. "This was traveling de luxe, he told himself, as he stretched luxuriously in his seat" (*C4P* 23–24, 31). "De luxe" travel it was, and entirely worthy of a nation dedicated to the furthering of aviation progress.

In a subtle reference to the 247's ancestry, Dean remarks that the "60-B" is "very similar to the latest type of Army bombers," and later contrasts its size and luxury with that of the Model 221 Monomail. After disembarking from the "60-B" in Chicago, Tim boards the *Grand Rapids Express*, "a single motor monoplane, carrying a pilot and six passengers," for the final leg of his flight (*C4P* 24, 51). The description of the *Express* matches the specifications of the Monomail, a sleek, all-metal craft with retractable landing gear and an enclosed passenger compartment separate from the open cockpit. Only two of the models were built, both briefly serving Boeing Air Transport on short routes (Bowers 175–176, 179). Here, as elsewhere throughout the series, Dean makes use of the latest developments in aviation to stress the progressive nature of aviation.

What, then, do the Tim Murphy books ultimately give their readers? Despite the cover of *The Sky Trail*, the omnipresent Sky Patrol, with its cryptic emblem and secret existence, never materializes. Presumably meant to be a paramilitary band of principled fliers ready to take on the injustices of the world, it anticipates such groups as George L. Eaton's "Bill Barnes's" flying crime-fighters of *Air Trails* magazine in the later 1930s or Will Eisner's comic-book "Blackhawk" troupe of 1941, but remains a figment of an illustrator's imagination (Eaton 8–14; White 40–41). The Patrol does, however, suggest the public appeal of such a cadre of dedicated, principled defenders, striking out at evil whenever and wherever the official forces of law and order prove inadequate. This is where Tim fits in. He may work alone, but is a conscientious, intelligent, and principled citizen with an admirable distaste for injustice, employing the particular powers of the press and technology to serve the public good. He supports a vigorous and important fantasy outlet — the public belief that a single, dedicated person can indeed make a difference for good.

Had his history stopped here, Tim would still be assured of a place, however minor, among the fledgling superheroes of American popular culture. But he offers more, and therein is the significance of the Tim Murphy books. As a *flying* crime-fighter, Tim brings together the vicarious satisfactions of preserving the civic peace and those of aviation itself. His adventures take place at the height of the so-called "Golden Age" of aviation, a time when the prospect of an airplane as an adjunct to every home seemed possible, a time when being air-minded "meant having enthusiasm for airplanes, believing in their potential to better human life, and supporting aviation development." As he writes his stories of the emerging air age, Graham Dean has Tim cast his lot firmly with the air-minded and urges the public to follow. As he goes about his reportorial and crime-fighting duties, Tim looks to the coming of "a great new day in human affairs once airplanes brought about a true air age" (Corn 12, 27). Tim's own anticipation shows the way: "I love the flying game," he says; "it's becoming life itself to me" (*DW* 63). Other Americans can share in that life as well. The new day of the aviation age will be a glorious one, Dean asserts; progress and goodness will prevail, and aviation will make superheroes of us all.

Works Cited

Bowers, Peter M. *Boeing Aircraft Since 1916.* 2d ed. New York: Funk & Wagnalls, 1968.
Coogan, Peter. *Superhero: The Secret Origin of a Genre.* Austin: MonkeyBrain Books, 2006.
Corn, Joseph J. *The Winged Gospel: America's Romance with Aviation, 1900–1950.* New York: Oxford University Press, 1983.
Dean, Graham M. *Circle 4 Patrol.* Chicago: Goldsmith, 1933. Cited as *C4P.*
_____. *Daring Wings.* Chicago: Goldsmith, 1931. Cited as *DW.*

_____. *The Sky Trail.* Chicago: Goldsmith, 1932. Cited as *ST.*
_____. *The Treasure Hunt of the S-18.* Chicago: Goldsmith, 1934. Cited as *THS-18.*
"Dean, Graham M." *Who Was Who in America.* Vol. VI: 1974–1976. Chicago: Marquis Who's Who, 1976, 107.
Eaton, George L. "Death Rides the Sky." *Air Trails* 8 (April 1937): 8–14, 63–80.
Feiffer, Jules, ed. *The Great Comic Book Heroes.* New York: Dial Press, 1965.
Johnson, Deidre. *Edward Stratemeyer and the Stratemeyer Syndicate.* TUSAS 627. New York: Twayne, 1993.
Piersol, James V. "Adapting the Airplane to the Newspaper." *Aero Digest* 18 (January 1931): 35–39, 122.
van der Linden, F. Robert. *The Boeing 247: The First Modern Airliner.* Seattle: University of Washington Press, 1991.
Ward, Martha E., and Dorothy A. Marquardt. "Dean, Graham M." *Authors of Books for Young People.* 2d ed. Metuchen, NJ: Scarecrow Press, 1971, 152.
White, Bradford W. *Comic Book Nation: The Transformation of Youth Culture in America.* Baltimore: Johns Hopkins University Press, 2001.

7

Adventures and Affect: The Character of the Boy Detective and Orphan in Astrid Lindgren's *Rasmus and the Tramp*

CHARLOTTE BEYER

Swedish author Astrid Lindgren's children's book *Rasmus and the Tramp* (1961)[1] tells the story of Rasmus, a nine-year-old boy living in an orphanage in 1910s provincial Sweden. Deprived of love and losing hope of ever being adopted, he decides to run away to find a family. On the road Rasmus meets the scruffy, loveable tramp Oscar, and the two become firm friends as Oscar teaches Rasmus the survival strategies a tramp needs. However, their carefree life is brutally interrupted, as Rasmus accidentally witnesses the lead-up to a robbery of an elderly lady in her home by two dastardly villains, Lif and Liander. Predictably, suspicion falls on our two heroes, who find themselves on the run from both the local Keystone cops and the robbers who have sinister plans to frame the friends or, failing that, kill them. However, with the combined forces of Rasmus's detective skills and courage, and Oscar's strength and experience, our heroes manage to convince the police of their innocence and ensure the real culprits are punished. The happy ending is ensured when Rasmus finds his longed-for home, not with a local rich farmer, but with Oscar. Ultimately, *Rasmus and the Tramp* mixes a conventional quest story with a detective plot and features a dual focus on adventure and affect which adds nuance to the boy sleuth character and invites a complex and diverse range of reader responses.[2]

Genre and the Boy Detective

In *Rasmus and the Tramp*, Lindgren's dual narrative strategy of adventure and affect reflects opposing dynamics inherent in the novel's generic mix. Adventure provides an alternative space away from figures of authority. Temporarily removing characters and readers from mundane and repressive gender and social structures, adventure promises mobility, excitement, and danger. Affect encourages the reader's identification with the boy sleuth and his need for a family and a home, and creates an interesting tension with the novel's hard-boiled detective discourse. Adventure and affect thereby produce a synergy which contributes to negotiating the reader's response to the boy sleuth, providing depth as well as thrill. The boy sleuth, whether a detective on a one-off basis like Lindgren's Rasmus, or appearing in a series of books, is a complex character deserving of further scholarly attention than has hitherto been the case, for the character affords an opportunity to explore the evolution of representations of masculinity alongside generic and textual conventions within children's fiction in various cultural and historical contexts.

Lindgren wrote extensively for children, and several of her books employ generic conventions from detective fiction, primarily featuring boy detective Bill Bergson (originally Kalle Blomkvist) and his friends. Maeve Visser Knoth says of Lindgren's use of the detective genre: "*Bill Bergson, Master Detective* (1952) and the subsequent adventures of Bill Bergson bridge the distance between Lindgren's impossible fantasies and her concrete family stories" (407). Knoth further notes about the Bill Bergson character: "Bill hopes to be a detective and finds himself solving crimes and becoming involved with bandits and thieves. The satisfying mysteries appeal to the reader's sense of adventure while remaining firmly planted in reality" (407). The three Bill Bergson boy detective novels have received attention from critics (see Edström 40); however, elsewhere Lindgren's oeuvre more broadly reflects her interest in the detective fiction genre and the boy sleuth. Knoth reads *Rasmus and the Tramp* as "another mystery complete with thieves, stolen jewels, and a chase through an abandoned town, but it is also the story of an orphan, Rasmus, who runs away from an orphanage to find himself a family" (407). Reading Lindgren in translation involves a re-writing of the text, a process which has consequences for constructions of the boy detective, and also for the way we read the genre,[3] a point highlighted by Vivi Edström: "[Lindgren's] intertextual relation to tradition is particularly noticeable in her choice of genre" (20). Lindgren's mixing of genres echoes postmodern concerns with form: "Genres today operate as open models; they are interactive 'modes' within variegated, plurivocal texts ... genre is intricately elaborated within novels that can be classified, beyond being historical, as pulp, romance, adventure, allegorical, political or philosophical" (Earnshaw 223–4). By mixing genres, *Rasmus and the Tramp* becomes a vehicle for both social commentary and suspense, thereby situating the boy detective character in a specific cultural and literary context.

Lindgren's experimentation with genre reflects postmodern reappraisal of so-called pulp fiction, and a willingness to embrace generic diversity, for *Rasmus and the Tramp* attempts to bridge the divides between the *bildungsroman* (high art) and the detective novel (popular art), as well as the divide between adult literature and children's genre writing. On the surface, adventure and affect appear to be two opposing impulses belonging to separate and distinct narrative genres, with differing linguistic and emotional registers. However, "Astrid Lindgren is a writer of contradictions," and in *Rasmus and the Tramp* she "work[s] with sharp contrasts between good and evil, black and white, sorrow and joy" (Edström 27). The significance of narrative depth is also apparent in Christopher Routledge's evaluation of children's detective fiction: "The formal investigation of 'whodunit' in children's detective fiction allows the investigation of other kinds of mystery — mysteries that become apparent during childhood itself and concerning issues such as identity, economic power, and social status" (64).

Rasmus and Oscar: Heroes Against the Odds

Rasmus and Oscar are heroes against the odds, whose predicament reflects Routledge's assertion that "detectives are marginal figures, whose status as 'outsiders' in relation to the society in which the crime takes place, assists them in their detecting" (68). Rasmus and Oscar echo the motif of detective and sidekick which, according to Frederick Joseph Svoboda, has "been present in detective fiction since its beginning." Svoboda further argues that "the formulaic sidekick has evolved with detective fiction into more fully developed variety of characters [for example] as friends of the detective" (230). However, the partnership between Rasmus and Oscar exposes the tension between the traditional pairing of detective and his trusted sidekick and the team built on individual strengths and skills which acknowledges the adult/child dynamics of that partnership.

In *Rasmus and the Tramp*, the boy detective, although not a conventional boy sleuth like Lindgren's Bill Bergson character, is in pursuit of justice and, on a personal level, traces the "clues" he needs to gain self-knowledge. The tramp Oscar becomes the trusted sidekick and father figure to Rasmus's boy sleuth, as seen through "Oscar's sensibility and his truly fatherly understanding of and respect for the boy who attaches himself to him" (Edström 55). Lindgren's novel depicts a poverty-stricken but free road lifestyle for boys and men: "On the road there were no thieves and bandits. Everything was peaceful.... Lonely and empty the road stretched out before them as far as the eyes could see, and at the horizon, where earth and sky met, it seemed to continue on straight into heaven" (106). In her essay "I Remember...," Lindgren describes her childhood memories of vagabonds roaming the countryside: "They came in the evening and bought a little milk and bread, and we stared at them, standing inside the kitchen door. Fancy there being people who didn't live anywhere, just walked and walked! With the tramps a breath of adventure blew into our rural world. There was something attractive and a little bit dangerous about them" (159–60).[4] Rasmus and Oscar occupy a marginalized position within conventional bourgeois society, as well as embody a sense of mobility, mirrored in Lindgren's fast-moving literary language that adds dramatic suspense to her sleuths on the run plot. Their quest together echoes nineteen-sixties American road writing, such as Jack Kerouac's *On the Road* and "The Vanishing American Hobo," which advocates masculine mobility as a lifestyle and a protest against nineteen fifties' social conformism.

The motif of "boys' own" adventures echoes Mark Twain, an influence Lindgren has acknowledged, providing the narrative framework for her characters to cut loose: "[Lindgren] carries us away to the uncertain and irrational, to risktaking and danger" (Edström 28). *Rasmus and the Tramp* contains further references to literary and cultural links between Sweden and America which reflect the inspiration Lindgren took from classic American children's books, and form part of her social critique, through allusions to nineteenth-century Swedish migration to America to escape rural poverty at home and seek new horizons abroad (Lindgren 107–8). Rasmus and Oscar represent a challenge to middle-class bourgeois masculinity, with its expectations of cultural conformity, domesticity and employment, and a predictable life style, as they refuse fixity and remain on the move. This gentle rebelliousness encourages a sense of recognition and identification in any reader, child and adult, who may struggle to conform and find themselves on the margins of social acceptability.

Lindgren employs a subversive doubling strategy in her portrayal of the boy detective and his sidekick which foregrounds the instability of these positions and of good-evil categories. This doubling is most obvious in Lindgren's boy detective and sidekick character, cast as the good guys the reader roots for but whose marginal social position means they are equally conceivable as the bad guys. The character of the homeless man, a person of no fixed abode, is a description which Oscar superficially appears to match and is surrounded by negative associations. Likewise, the figure of a boy runaway from a children's home may conjure up negative imagery of streetwise feral youths. Lindgren's portrayal of the positive and negative potential of her boy sleuth and his sidekick adds suspense and depth, as their wicked alter egos are projected on to the book's minor characters, with the good guys Rasmus and Oscar versus Lif and Liander the crooks, and Martina the virtuous working-class woman versus Mrs. Hedberg's dishonest maid Anastina, in cahoots with Lif and Liander. This doubling reflects a typical dynamic in detective writing, according to Heta Pyrhönen: "Ever since Poe, doubling between detective and criminal has become a recurrent pattern in the genre. Their positional constellation makes them each other's doubles if only because they represent the two fundamental terms of the conflict which characterizes the genre" (32). In his identification with the wrongly imprisoned Oscar, Rasmus imagines himself as a prisoner during a sugar rush afternoon spent hiding behind a woodpile, thereby acknowledging the existence of his own lawless alter ego (Lindgren 151–2). Laura Marcus sees the blurred "distinction between pursuer and pursued, detective and criminal" as an aspect of "postmodernist crime fiction exploits," exposing social hierarchies and double standards (247).[5]

In *Rasmus and the Tramp*, Lindgren exploits this doubleness, thereby creating suspense and adding psychological complexity to her characters. She ensures that the reader's identification is firmly on the side of Rasmus and Oscar, through the evocation of affect, and by challenging the reader's negative perceptions of feral youths and vagrant males. Lindgren's novel confronts readers with their unconscious fears and prejudices by exploring those characters' humanity. Portrayals of characters who are noble but impoverished, and of outsider figures performing heroic acts, are of course quite commonplace in literature. However, by positioning Rasmus and Oscar at the novel's cynosure, reversing notions of center and periphery, Lindgren adds an innovative and unique dimension to the portrayal of the boy sleuth. By bringing a marginalized character into the center, by making him the hero, Lindgren rescues such characters from falling into the trap of predictability, a potential pitfall in detective fiction, redeeming them from the stereotypes they might otherwise have become.

Discourses of Affect

"To have parents was the greatest joy the children at the orphanage could imagine. Not all of them would admit their hopeless longing openly.

But Rasmus was only nine and too young to hide his heart" (Lindgren 15). The quest for origins in narratives featuring adoptive children and orphans is complicated by a lack of knowledge about who they are: "[Rasmus] had been at Vaesterhaga ever since he was a baby. He didn't remember any other home or any other mother than Miss Hawk" (Lindgren 35). Marianne Novy points out that "most of the adoptees in canonical literature, fairytales and folklore find their identity by meeting their birth parents" (1). *Rasmus and the Tramp* exposes the tension between the notion of the ideal family and the crime/detective plot which reflects the wider, external world of violence and crime, thereby interrogating the family as an ideological construct, as noted by Esther Saraga (194). Rasmus' quest for a family draws attention to the centrality of human relations and family in literature. Edström sees Rasmus as "a lonely, excluded boy in search of a father" (53). However, the reader is well aware from both crime fiction and media reporting that frequently the family constitutes the source of crime, rather than security. Saraga argues that family is seen "as the cornerstone of society, its natural building block. Strong families are seen as essential for the maintenance of social order," but that the family can also be the site where abuse and violence are perpetrated against the vulnerable and the powerless (195). This paradox is illustrated in *Rasmus and the Tramp* when the callous criminals invade a family home, infiltrating it through a member of the household, the maid Anastina, and subject an elderly lady to a terrifying ordeal. Lindgren's fiction thus maintains the balancing act between the security of the family for the boy detective and the compulsion for adventure and detection. Knoth's comments concur with this, as she argues, "Lindgren recognizes and writes about the needs, dreams, and fantasies of children" (407).

Rasmus is portrayed as a child marginalized in society by his classless and orphaned status, but also importantly through his gender, as he knows he is unwanted, due to the prospective adopters visiting the orphanage having a preference for pretty girls with blue eyes and blonde ringlets: "'Just think,' he said eagerly, 'if they should pick me! Oh how I wish that they would want me.' 'Bah! Don't get any ideas,' said Gunnar. 'They always pick girls with curly hair'" (Lindgren 15–6). As Edström notes: "[Rasmus] knows he does not stand a chance of becoming the foster child of any couple who occasionally visit the orphanage; bitter experience has taught him that they only want little girls with curly hair" (52). The discursive contrast between the boy sleuth's assertiveness and the orphan's position of powerlessness is reflected in Rasmus's strategic awareness of the way he is required to use his voice to project powerlessness and humility, for the benefit of adults with authority: "It was the special orphanage voice they had to use when talking to the directress, or to the parson ... the orphanage children had to put all the gentleness and obedience they could muster into their voices because that is what was expected" (Lindgren 8). By representing Rasmus's point of view, Lindgren encourages a reader response of affect and identification, thereby adding emotional complexity to her portrayal of a boy detective who is also an outsider: "Some of the other Lindgren characters can also be seen as metaphors for different life-styles, however real and alive they may appear. The child stands for play, freedom, ease, creativity — but also for exposure and powerlessness" (Edström 25). Rasmus's negotiation of masculinity bears out Annette Wannamaker's point that "in more than a few contemporary texts written for boys, masculinity is ... portrayed in complicated, contradictory, often paradoxical ways that highlight the difficult negotiations boys are making as they develop gendered identities within, against, or on the margins of current cultural constructions of masculinity" (10).

However, Rasmus' orphanage background has equipped him with the survival skills and presence of mind needed in crime fiction for the sleuth to prevail and ensure the right outcome. The orphan detective figure, with a question mark over his background that renders him vulnerable, presents a challenge to the dominant order, but also enables him to re-invent himself. This motif can be seen elsewhere within children's detective fiction, particularly in portrayals of girl sleuths such as in the Nancy Drew or Dana Girls books, and is described by Maria Nikolajeva as a "convenient removal of parents" which enables "the hero's freedom of action" (192). In both cases, the "orphan" detective protagonist embarks on a journey of self-discovery in order to gain a deeper sense of self-knowledge as part of his quest for justice. Rasmus's determination to actively search for a family illustrates that, rather than feeling sorry for himself, the orphan boy sleuth possesses a healthy desire to self-invent, through the construction of a self and family where before there were none, via the "happy families" ending which sits alongside the resolution of the juvenile detective plot. The *bildungsroman* quest for self and meaning thus sits successfully with the detective plot in *Rasmus and the Tramp*, and the violence and suspense of its adventure narrative is greatly enhanced by the enrichment of the character of the boy sleuth through affect and a healthy dose of humor.

Adventure, Danger, and Risk

Lindgren's appealing boy sleuth, and her use of detective conventions in *Rasmus and the Tramp*, ensures that pace and suspense are never lacking from the boy detective's quest for self. Newspaper reporting of the crime first draws Rasmus in:

> He has stumbled on something really exciting. Eagerly, he spelled his way through the article, which read: "ROBBERY AT SANDOE FACTORY. A daring hold-up took place yesterday at Sandoe factory. Two masked bandits forced their way in to the office and with pointed guns escaped with the week's payroll for the entire factory, without leaving any traces." Rasmus saw those masked men before his eyes and he shivered with excitement [Lindgren 31].

The suspense-filled popular appeal of the journalistic discourse signals a change of register and pace as the crime plot is introduced into the story, adding the all-important elements of adventure and violence which characterize boy sleuth fictions. Rasmus is courageous, willing to take risks, and adventurous to extents that sometimes causes his adult companion Oscar to hesitate. Rasmus' physical courage is a hallmark of the boy detective. His prowess, which is belied by his skinny frame, is combined with speed and intelligence: "Rasmus was afraid of many things ... but he had amazing physical courage. If it was a question of climbing or diving, it didn't make any difference how risky it looked—his skinny little frame had exaggerated confidence in its own ability and there wasn't a speck of fear in him" (Lindgren 84). He shows bravery in situations of danger, such as during a chase (Lindgren 122–4), or when he physically disarms and knocks out one of the crooks (Lindgren 131), thereby gaining Oscar's approval: "Oscar looked at him with a broad grin. 'The king of the fighters,' he said. 'You're not scared of anything, are you?'" (Lindgren 133). The change of discursive pace in the detective sections encourages a range of reader responses, such as anticipation, suspense, dread, and relief—conflicting impulses and sensory elements which are echoed in Rasmus's perceptions: "Rasmus is so afraid his heart is pounding, but in the midst of danger he also senses 'the wildest desire for adventure'" (Edström 55).

Violence, adventure, and aggression inevitably play a crucial part in detection plots and are an important aspect of what makes Lindgren's text a boy sleuth book. Lindgren's use of setting foregrounds this aspect: "Crime is something Lindgren tends to locate in ghastly outposts, and here in the deserted village one of her most hair-raising cat-and-mouse chases takes place between the child and the armed thieves" (Edström 55). However, Lindgren did hold complex views of violence, which did not sit easily with the generic requirement for action-driven plots and physically aggressive boy sleuths, as expressed in her 1978 essay "Never Violence." In the book, Rasmus experiences violent behavior within the context of the orphanage as a negative stratagem used by adults and children in order to subdue or belittle others.

Hence, Lindgren's self-conscious portrayal of violence foregrounds the generic codes of crime fiction and boy sleuth characters and their function in the book.

Rasmus and the Tramp draws on hard-boiled crime fiction conventions of physical and direct engagement, a common feature in children's fiction according to Routledge, who argues that, whilst some detective figures in adult crime fiction may rely on scientific methods, the preference for "hard-boiled" detective methods in children's detective stories is typically "more to do with following the thief, watching, and finally apprehending him than it is with interpreting clues" (77). Lindgren deals with this tension through representations of affect, and through the use of humor and wit. The representation of (mostly) slapstick violence, such as running and chasing, hiding in barrels, tripping up, and trapping crooks in cellars forms part of the creation and build-up of suspense in the story, and is effective in creating excitement. Physical aggression in *Rasmus and the Tramp* is mostly comedic violence, as in the episode where the gangster Lif chases Rasmus:

> The landing creaks ominously as Lif comes running. Now at last that tough youngster will get what he deserves. Lif dashes after him round the corner of the boathouse. Suddenly the pounding footsteps are no longer heard. Instead there is a big splash. Mr. Lif doesn't even have time to shout before the salt waves wash over him. He tries, but only a little "blup" comes out [Lindgren 126–7].

While Rasmus is fearless and courageous, the reader is never permitted to forget that he is a vulnerable and sensitive child. Likewise, Lindgren is mindful of her readership, ensuring that her balancing act of adventure and affect gives readers enjoyable thrills and frights, but not nightmares. However, the presence of a gun, combined with the criminals' willingness to make use of it, adds a darker, hard-boiled edginess to the narrative. Apart from adding suspense, this also reminds us of the vulnerability of the boy detective when confronted with the threats posed by malevolent adults. Rasmus's fear and hatred of the terrifying black gun reflects his aversion to the masculine, phallic power to dominate and destroy: "Rasmus kicked the horrible black weapon so that it flew into a corner. Then he picked it up with trembling hands, as if it were a poisonous snake. He could hardly bear to hold it ... he wanted to be sick" (Lindgren 131). Rasmus and Oscar use honorable, boy-sleuth style methods, whereas the cowardly criminals rely on their weapon: "Oscar was as strong as a bull, much stronger than Liander. But Liander had his terrible gun which he was aiming at Oscar. If it hadn't been for that..." (Lindgren 130). Commenting on the role of guns in children's mystery writing, Routledge suggests that the weapon serves as "a manifestation of a more general threat in children's detective fiction to eradicate or, at the very least, exclude childhood itself from the lives of adults and adult discourses" (71). Lindgren ensures the reader knows that, in the end, the rightful outcome is brought about more through the act of writing than violence, particularly through Oscar's second letter to the police (which the duo believed lost) that explains what truly happened. The adventure part of the novel appears to end abruptly when the sheriff mentions the fact that Rasmus is from the orphanage. Worried that he may be sent back to Vaesterhaga, Rasmus goes on the run again, with Oscar in pursuit. This series of events is the clue that the narrative still has another plotline to conclude, namely the hero's homecoming. As Knoth points out: "Lindgren convinces her readers that a child who goes looking for parents will certainly find them" (407).

Rasmus and the Tramp employs the classic motif of detective-and-sidekick against the "bumbling" cops. However, there is a twist in the tale, for Rasmus and Oscar are also under suspicion of having perpetrated the very crimes they are trying to solve. The search for truth is not simply about justice for the victims of crime; it is also justice for the sleuths whose social status, age, and marginality unfairly typecast and frame them: "Rasmus's eyes filled with tears. He knew that the sheriff would never believe a tramp" (Lindgren 129). As the criminals attempt to "frame" the detective and his sidekick, who are forced first into hiding, then into chasing them, Lindgren's suspenseful, well-paced language engages the reader's response, illustrating Routledge's idea that "in children's detective fiction, children and childhood are threatened not only by adult criminals, but also by the rational process of detection itself, which serves adult authority's need for order and conformity" (64). It could be argued that, as with all crime fiction, the interrogation of moral codes is compromised by the very portrayal of crime and violence, and by the structuring of narrative pleasure through detection and regulation of excess. However, Knoth argues that "Lindgren recognizes the central, yet conflicting longings of childhood — to have the security of a loving family but also a measure of adventure and excitement" (407). Lindgren's novel thus successfully negotiates the balance between the boy sleuth's successful solving of crime, thereby meeting his and our need for adventure and comedy violence, and the emotionally satisfying ending which rewards the boy detective with a family for his insistence on justice and loyalty to Oscar.

Conclusion — A Double Quest

Lindgren's portrayal of the boy detective Rasmus adds energy and charm to the character, and introduces new dimensions of generic experimentation into children's literature, an aspect of her work that critics have praised. Lindgren's generic blend suggests that "the work of [contemporary writers] testifies to the continuing impact of the detective paradigm on contemporary literature, and to the continuing openness to subversion and renewal" (Marcus 264). The detective teamwork by Rasmus, the courageous, fun-loving, and loyal one-off boy detective, and Oscar the loveable scruff of a tramp, who unexpectedly finds himself playing the part of the reticent, "sensible" adult, is only possible because both are streetwise and possess survival skills acquired through their experiences of marginalization. Both are vulnerable because they are inherently good, yet this keen sense of fairness eventually enables them to prevail. Through her portrayals, Lindgren interrogates literary genre, gender politics, and class issues as they are brought to bear on masculine identities. Lindgren's twin narrative strategies of adventure and affect add complexity and diversity to her boy sleuth and to children's mystery writing: "What is so pleasurable in Astrid Lindgren's stories has ... to do with her ability to anchor them securely in a genre, and at the same time to break its rules" (Edström 21). *Rasmus and the Tramp* is a crime fiction which provides thrills and suspense without giving nightmares, and gives an emotionally authentic portrayal of a boy sleuth whose double quest for justice and a home is as exhilarating as it is exciting.

NOTES

1. The first Swedish edition appeared in 1956. All references here are to the English translation from 1961. The book is also commonly translated as *Rasmus and the Vagabond*; both versions of the title abound in English.
2. Also discussed in Silvey 266.
3. Translation studies presents a discipline in itself with a number of differing perspectives and approaches; this essay can but merely acknowledge the existence of this area of concern.
4. Also cited in Edström 51.
5. Marcus cites Walter Benjamin, *Charles Baudelaire: A Lyric Poet in the Era of High Capitalism* (London: Verso, 1983). 48, as the origin of this idea.

WORKS CITED

"Bad Press Slows Adoption of Boys." BBC News online, 8 November 2008. http://209.85.229.132/search?q=cache:dn_5aTvsIyoJ:news.bbc.co.uk/2/hi/uk_news/7718572.stm+older+boys+difficult+to+place+adoption&cd=14&hl=en&ct=clnk&gl=uk Accessed 14 October 2009.

Delamater, Jerome, and Ruth Prigozy, eds. *Theory and Practice of Classic Detective Fiction*. Westport, CT: Greenwood Press, 1997.

Earnshaw, Stephen. *Just Postmodernism*. Amsterdam: Rodopi, 1997.

Edström, Vivi. *Astrid Lindgren: A Critical Study*. Stockholm: Rabén & Sjögren Books, 2000.

Geherin, David. *Scene of the Crime: The Importance of Place in Crime and Mystery Fiction.* Jefferson, NC: McFarland, 2008.
Greaney, Michael. *Conrad, Language and Narrative.* Cambridge: Cambridge University Press, 2001.
Kerouac, Jack. *On the Road.* 1957. London: Penguin Classics, 2007.
_____. "The Vanishing American Hobo." 1960. *Lonesome Traveler.* London: Penguin Modern Classics, 2007. 148–160.
Knoth, Maeve Visser. "Astrid Lindgren." *Children's Books and Their Creators.* Ed. Anita Silvey. Boston: Houghton Mifflin, 1995. 406–408.
Lindgren, Astrid. "I Remember..." *Signal* 57 (1988): 155–169.
_____. "Never Violence." http://www.atlc.org/Resources/never_violence.php. Accessed 14 December 2009.
_____. *Rasmus and the Tramp.* London: Methuen, 1961.
Marcus, Laura. "Detection and Literary Fiction." Ed. Martin Priestman. *The Cambridge Companion to Crime Fiction.* Cambridge: Cambridge University Press, 2003. 245–268.
Nikolajeva, Maria. "Children's Literature." Ed. Donald Haase. *The Greenwood Encyclopedia of Folktales and Fairy Tales.* Westport, CT: Greenwood Press, 2008. 185–194.
Novy, Marianne, ed. *Imagining Adoption: Essays on Literature and Culture.* Ann Arbor: University of Michigan Press, 2004.
Pyrhönen, Heta. *Mayhem and Murder: Narrative and Moral Problems in the Detective Story.* Toronto: University of Toronto Press, 1999.
Routledge, Christopher. "Children's Detective Fiction and the 'Perfect Crime' of Adulthood." *Mystery in Children's Literature: From the Rational to the Supernatural.* Eds. Adrienne E. Gavin and Christopher Routledge. Houndmills, Hampshire, UK: Palgrave, 2001. 64–81.
Rowland, Susan. *From Agatha Christie to Ruth Rendell.* Houndmills, Hampshire, UK: Palgrave, 2000.
Rubinson, Gregory. *The Fiction of Rushdie, Barnes, Winterson and Carter: Breaking Cultural and Literary Boundaries in the Work of Four Postmodernists.* Jefferson, NC: McFarland, 2005.
Saraga, Esther. "Dangerous Places: The Family as a Site of Crime." Eds. John Muncie and Eugene McLaughlin. *The Problem of Crime.* London: Sage, 2004. 191–238.
Silvey, Anita, ed. *Children's Books and Their Creators.* Boston: Houghton Mifflin, 1995.
Svoboda, Frederick Joseph. "Detective Sidekicks." *The Guide to United States Popular Culture.* Eds. Ray B. Browne and Pat Browne. Bowling Green, OH: Bowling Green University Popular Press, 1990. 230.
Wannamaker, Annette. *Boys in Children's Literature and Popular Culture: Masculinity, Abjection, and the Fictional Child.* London: Routledge, 2008.

8

The Power of Three: Alfred Hitchcock's Three Investigators Series

ALAN PICKRELL

In 1964, the publishing firm Random House introduced a new detective series for boys (Mattson 53). By that date, television had established itself firmly as an entertainment medium and, as a result, sales of juvenile books were in decline, since young people preferred the novelty of watching television to reading. To remain competitive in the market place, the Stratemeyer Syndicate had been engaged in a massive rewriting project to update its top performers, the Nancy Drew, Hardy Boys, and Bobbsey Twins series. At the same time, publisher Grosset & Dunlap was engaged in thinning out its offerings by discontinuing once popular series like the Judy Bolton, Cherry Ames, Ken Holt, and Vicki Barr books, while other juvenile publishers, such as Cupples and Leon, were disappearing from the scene altogether. Most publishers would have agreed that the time was not ideal to launch a new juvenile series, especially one aimed at boys since, traditionally, boys' books never sold as well as books for girls.

This new series, however, based itself on the popularity of a director of mystery and suspense films, who also hosted a television anthology program. Cashing in on his popularity in the United States, Alfred Hitchcock also loaned his name to a group of mystery and suspense anthologies for adults in addition to a monthly mystery magazine. Hardback anthologies for young people were also sold under his sponsorship. This new boys' series even borrowed his name: Alfred Hitchcock and the Three Investigators. From 1964 until 1987, forty-three titles in the series were published. An attempt to continue the series with the characters as older teens lasted from 1989 through 1990 and numbered eleven more volumes plus five novelty volumes in which the characters figured. Against all seeming odds, the books became highly successful for nearly twenty years and are still extremely popular in Germany, where new volumes are currently in production. In fact, Ingo Peters in "Reception as a Transcultural Process: Robert Arthur's *Three Investigators* and their German Success" argues that the phenomenal success of the books in Germany means that they were unsuccessful in the U.S. However, as most series book specialists would attest, a publishing run of nearly twenty-five years with a total count of forty-three volumes is anything but a failure. The books also have been translated to and published in many other languages and countries — further proof of their wide appeal.

Since so many of the tried and true series were failing and being discontinued, what was it that made this series a success? If Stratemeyer and his Syndicate form the ideal against which all series books are measured, certainly there are some influences that can be traced, not only from the Syndicate, but from a host of other successful books, authors, and series. Fiction factories like those of Eugene Scribe, Alexandre Dumas père, and Edward Stratemeyer made the process of analyzing successful plots and literary efforts a science. So how did the Three Investigators series become so successful that it ran to forty-three volumes in its original incarnation, when other new attempts at series, like the Christopher Cool, TEEN Agent series, died before they really started? Peters seems to have a notion of the workings of the series when he points out that the three boy sleuths always work in unison and have perfected working as a team (148). The real clue is perhaps found in the number of investigators that originally delineated the series, as well as Freud's theory of integrated personalities which based itself on three primary components of the psyche. In other words, the three sleuths work as one because they combine to make one.

Three has long been seen as a magical, mystical number in astrology, numerology, and other such arcane studies. Three is a religiously significant number: think of the Holy Trinity (Father, Son, and Holy Ghost) or the Holy Family (Mary, Joseph and Jesus.) Three is also a powerful number in literary circles: Arthur, Guinevere, and Lancelot; Athos, Porthos, and Aramis; Harry, Ron, and Hermione. Three is also an important number psychologically: there are three aspects of action (mental, verbal, and physical) common to human beings, and Freud, the father of psycho analysis, conjectured that there were three components of self: ego, superego, and id. In crafting his Three Investigators, creator Robert Arthur has contributed to this continuing legacy of threes. This is especially evident in the physical and psychological manifestations of each character, which in turn primarily represent one of the three human actions and one aspect of Freud's ideal functioning self.

Thus as a united whole, the Three Investigators represent just that—*one united whole*, a highly functioning individual who continues the literary, historical, and mythical tradition of three while adhering to the key psychological aspects of the number as well.

In both a logical and an arcane sense, the number three seems a perfect number for a cast of characters. It is wholly symmetrical, a center flanked on each side by supports. In the annals of series books, three was the number of the Rover Boys, the number of the Hardy Boys plus Chet, their comic relief buddy, and of course, the Three Musketeers who, in reality, turned out to be four close friends. In the Nancy Drew books, Nancy and her friends, George and Bess, comprised the charmed number of sleuths. In the mythology of numbers, three and four are "perfect" numbers. Three represents the Trinity while four represents the four corners of the earth, and the sum of the two equals the lucky number seven. From ancient times, the triangle, the visible symbol of the number three, was used to create the pyramids that were said to capture the power of the universe at their apexes and radiate it to the areas beneath those points. Later, the form was used in an upside down construction to become the paradigm for the Hegelian Dialectic, which was thought to be a panacea to cure the ills of society. From the Jungian perspective, the number three represents completeness, since it is a configuration of the past, present, and future. Significantly, there are also three aspects of action (mental, verbal, and physical) performed by human beings. Certainly acquaintances, as well as literary characters, might be described according to their actions. An intellectual personality might be described as primarily acting by mental exercise, while an athlete might be described as being a physical person, descriptions based on actions. Furthering the concept of three as completeness, Freud, the father of psychoanalysis, conjectured that there were three components of self: ego, superego, and id. Thus the well-balanced personality is composed of these three aspects of self in proportional inclusions.

Additionally, there is certainly an arcane aspect to the number three. According to tradition, the Magi numbered three. While Scripture itself never specifically states that the Wise Men, who were astronomers and magicians, were three in number, it does reference three symbolic gifts brought to the infant Messiah. This is not intended to compare The Three Investigators to the Magi; yet many of their adventures bear titles which suggest arcane happenings and supernatural doings, so like the Magi, The Three Investigators delve into mysteries of both the natural and the supernatural world. Moreover, three seems to be a magic number on its own. The third time's the charm, as has often been said.

Thus, within the context of an ideal number for literary character heroes, three seems to be a perfect balance. In such a triadic relationship, there is generally one character that is an acknowledged leader and is flanked by two subordinate characters. Each of those subordinates has a distinct and separate personality and set of abilities and talents. Given such a distribution and diversity, the separate and distinct characters can be assembled into a team which operates as a single organism. Although there are moments in any series which represent disruptions due to individual egos or misunderstandings, once those disturbances and distractions are cleared up, the unit is restored to purpose, so that usefulness and progress are resumed.

Drama of the Grecian Golden Age utilized three performers who portrayed all of the roles of a play with the aid of a chorus. The actors, designated as protagonist, deuteragonist, and triagonist, changed characters by altering masks and costumes, but together they created a unified impact and mythos. It could be argued that, in modern literature, characters might be considered fragments of what proves to be a whole when those characters work together in unison for a single purpose or common goal: i.e., three characters might each represent one facet of Freud's id, ego, and superego, so that the individual fragments total up to a whole and healthy human self. As well, each of these characters might primarily represent one force or form of action (verbal, mental, physical) individually, but when enacted in unison, would comprise a complete action.

What is more, the number three allows for synchronicity ("ready, set, go!"; "lights, camera, action"; "1,2,3, pull!"). The count of three frequently coordinates; three strikes and the batter is out. Events occur in triplicate, deaths occur in three, and three on a match is unlucky. "If at first you don't succeed, try, try again" and the third time will be successful. Human beings learned the need to synchronize early in human history, and sailing chants such as "Yo, Heave, Ho" reflect the need to work together to raise the sail. Ready on "Yo"; everyone pull on "Heave"; and rest on "Ho." Eventually the sail makes it to the top of the mast with the combined effort of all present.

Literature and theatre frequently make use of three characters who work together for a common cause. As previously mentioned, the characters of Arthur, Guinevere, and Lancelot and Harry, Ron, and Hermione are classic examples of this cooperation, as are Luke, Han, and Leia. However, triads that include members of the opposite sex have a vastly different energy and dynamic from those comprised of the same sex. Romantic attachments, misunderstandings, jealousies, and/or perceived betrayals are not integral to single-sex triads, and don't seem to disrupt the sense of unity. It is difficult to imagine Chet Morton complaining to Joe Hardy, "But you like Frank best!"

The same is true of either George or Bess in the Nancy Drew books. Somehow, single-sex groups just seem more idealized for younger readers while mixed groups seem to connect better with older readers. Plus, if group dynamics remain relatively harmonious amongst a group of people with similar interests, who also possess abilities that are complementary one to another, there are fewer distractions, and more attention can be paid to the project at hand.

The Three Investigators series utilized the components of several successful series, in the annals of juvenile and adult literature. Certainly, the Syndicate inspired the author, Robert Arthur. According to Seth Smolinske on "The Three Investigators" web site, Arthur wanted to produce a series he thought would be similar to, but better written than, the Hardy Boys and other items of juvenile fiction of the day. Following the Stratemeyer example, Arthur used the charmed number three for his characters, and followed the Syndicate policy of ending his chapters with a cliff hanger to keep his reading audience turning pages. Perhaps, however, an even more notable influence on the series was the work of Leo Edwards (Edward Edson Lee 1884–1944), who wrote five popular boys' series: Andy Blake, Jerry Todd, Poppy Ott, Trigger Berg, and Tuffy Bean (Cochran 8). Edwards' characters were based on youngsters that he knew in his small hometown, and readers enjoyed their exploits because they did all manner of things that boys like to do: they played pirate, floated rafts, fished, camped out, played detective, and solved minor mysteries. Like a number of other boys' series authors, Edwards never identified the ages of his characters, although judging from their interests and activities, Edwards's boys seem to be about the same age as Hitchcock's Investigators — hovering just beyond their early teen years. And, like many of their predecessors, they never aged, either. The device of never specifying the ages of the heroes allows a wider section of audience to identify with the boy protagonists. Not quite as young as the Bobbsey Twins, but not quite as old as the Hardy Boys, the Jerry Todd characters and The Three Investigators are not quite old enough for drivers' licenses and not quite old enough to be distracted by members of the opposite sex. They are, however, old enough to feel restricted by their comparative lack of mobility, or mobility dictated by how far they can ride their bikes, and to envision life careers and possibilities while succumbing to daydreams based on their own heroism and acclaim (Wawrzenski 6). In addition, there are other, more direct, connections between Arthur and Edwards. Two titles in the Investigators series are titles that Edwards used in two of his series: from the Jerry Todd series comes *The Mystery of the Whispering Mummy*, and from the Poppy Ott series comes *The Mystery of the Stuttering Parrot*. Of course, the ethos, plots, and subject matters of the Edwards and Arthur volumes are vastly different, and while the Todd books may comprise a minor mystery in some volumes, not every volume concerns a mystery. There is one other likely similarity between the two series. In the first Jerry Todd book, *Whispering Mummy*, Jerry joins an organization known as the Juvenile Jupiter Detectives. The name of Arthur's lead investigator is Jupiter Jones. In modern times, the name Jupiter, unless used in either astrological or mythological terms, is too unusual to be a coincidence, especially given the replication of titles. Therefore, it would seem that the originator of the Investigator series has crafted an homage to Edwards in this new series. Readers tend to forget that there was a *Tom Sawyer* series and not simply a single book, and that *Huckleberry Finn* was a spin-off from the Sawyer book, just as Poppy Ott was spun-off from the Jerry Todd books. Some critics, Betsy Byars and Wiley Lee Umphlet among them, have felt that Jerry and Poppy were created in the images of Tom Sawyer and Huck Finn. If, indeed, Jerry and Poppy were the literary heirs to and, at the time, the contemporary versions of the all-American boys Tom and Huck, then The Three Investigators continued in that entire tradition of boyhood adventures in caves and cemeteries within the 1960s through the 1980s, and Jupiter and his friends become incarnations of Tom and Huck in California for a new generation.

While Jupiter Jones may derive his name from a Jerry Todd book, nothing much else about Jerry resembles Jupiter, because "Jupe" follows the pattern of the intellectual detective. This does not imply that Jerry or the Hardy Boys are dunces, but Jupiter's intelligence surpasses clever and moves into the Encyclopedia Brown/Brains Benton territory. Rather than being merely intelligent, Jupiter occupies the realm of the intellectual, following the grand tradition set by Edgar Allan Poe's detective Auguste Dupin and leading to the most popular intellectual detective of all time: Sherlock Holmes. Like Holmes, Jupiter reads, observes, and comprehends. The popularity of Holmes is such that tribute pastiches are still written about him. There is a real fascination with him and his deductive reasoning, and it is easy to identify the Holmesian method with that of the Investigators: observation, analysis, and hypothesis. Systematically strike out everything that is false, and what is left, no matter how implausible, is true.

While a major difference between Holmes and Jupiter might appear to be in numbers (Jupiter has two assistants and Holmes had only Watson) this is actually not quite true. Holmes' attitude toward Lestrade changed over the years so that the Scotland Yard man made up a frequent part of a triumvirate, as did Holmes' brother, Mycroft. There were also those times when a third member of the party was made up of a local constable, or perhaps a client like the Baskerville heir. Jupiter, like Holmes, is very much a consulting detective, delegating as much work as he can to give himself time to ponder. He is also very much in charge, planning details of the investigation and drawing conclusions. Also like Holmes, Jupiter plays his cards close to his vest and frequently does not even let his own comrades know what he is thinking or doing. Holmes was also a master of disguise and make-up, and Jupiter's early years in theatre have made him an accomplished actor and voice imitator. These talents are immensely useful in solving cases.

One unfortunate characteristic places Jupiter among the ranks of another popular type of literary detective. Jupiter's stage name in his early show business years was "Baby Fatso," which he now despises as being demeaning and undignified. Unfortunately, he has retained a stocky build that tends, actively, toward the pudgy. Jupiter prefers to avoid physical labor and exercise when possible, but is capable of performing physically when called upon to do so. For example, when racing away from the threats of Terror Castle, in the first book of the series, Jupiter manages to keep right up to Pete, the acknowledged athlete of the trio. In point of fact, Jupiter's physique and intellect are at war with the accepted image of the heavy boy in juvenile literature. Fat boys are usually sidekicks and comic relief characters rather than "leading" characters. In fact, Edward Stratemeyer produced the perfect stereotypical fat boy when he created Chet Morton, boon companion to the Hardy Boys. From the beginning it was clear that, in addition to being *the* Hardy Boys, Frank and Joe were, quite simply, *hardy* boys. As idealizations of American youth, Frank and Joe are active, eager, bright, athletic, and handsome. They are all boy and capable of taking care of themselves in any given circumstance. Chet, on the other hand, presents a countenance variously described as "good-humored," "good natured," or "pleasant," but he is never presented as "handsome." In fact, his face is usually red from the exertion of carrying his weight about, and he tends to perspire heavily. Most heavy characters are usually a bit dull in wit and stereotypical in their likes and dislikes; they also display a decided preoccupation with food of any kind. Frequently these characters are the butts of jokes or ribbing by their more normally-sized companions. A notable exception to this description is the character of Mark Tidd in Clarence Budington Kelland's series by the same name. In fact, Mark knows how he, as a fat boy, is perceived by others, and rather encourages them in that opinion so he can more easily thwart their efforts to take advantage of him. Mark studies human nature and is singularly wise in the ways of other human beings and their perceptions. Mark (Marcus Aurelius Fortunatus Tidd, his full name given him by his father, a student of the fall of the Roman Empire) bears a classical Roman name, as do Jupiter and his uncle Titus Andronicus Jones, and Kelland avoids sharing Mark's age with the audience, to make his character more universally accepted by various age groups.

Fat detectives are not unknown within the realms of adult fiction, either. Agatha Christie's Hercule Poirot, he of "the little gray cells" and another intellectual consulting detective, is usually described and portrayed as a plump little dandy who loves his creature comforts, while Nero Wolfe is just simply enormous and tries to avoid ever leaving his home because of the effort and inconvenience involved. Wolfe is also addicted to his own creature comforts, which include, most significantly, a private chef. When Wolfe needs a first-hand report, he sends out his right hand man, Archie Goodwin, to bring back a description. Like Wolfe, Jupiter would far prefer to send out his own Archies instead of doing the legwork himself.

As an orphan, Jupiter shares another characteristic common to many leading characters in juvenile series, one that seemed dear to the heart of Edward Stratemeyer, who probably adapted it from the works of Horatio Alger. After all, Stratemeyer did write some Alger titles after Alger died. Many of the heroes of both books for boys and girls are semi-orphans, lacking one parent or the other. Jupiter, however, is a full-blown orphan. Both of his parents were killed in an auto accident, and he lives with his aunt and uncle who own and operate one of the larger junk/salvage yards in or around Rocky Beach, California, a suburb of Los Angeles. While many orphans, like Harry Potter, are at the mercy of their guardians, this has not been Jupiter's fate. Aunt Matilda and Uncle Titus are well-intentioned and make sure that Jupiter has enough to eat, clothing to wear, and a roof over his head, but other than that, they tend to overlook him in the hustle and bustle of every day life. Jupiter couldn't be more pleased by that fact, and takes every opportunity to "disappear." Next to the fence that surrounds the junkyard and concealed from view by piles and stacks of junk is an old mobile home. It can be reached and entered by any number of secret and circuitous routes. The trailer is guarded with various alarms of Jupiter's devising. This is the official headquarters and office of The Three Investigators and contains their files, a typewriter, and a makeshift laboratory. Few clients are invited into this sanctuary, since that would violate the group's secrecy and privacy elements. The trailer allows Jupiter to have a private spot where he can retreat and have some time to himself as well as a place to think about cases. This is also, in part, due to laziness. Jupiter is hiding from the possible work that his aunt and uncle might have in mind for him.

Like the adult detectives Poirot, Wolfe, and Holmes, Jupiter is not modest about his own intelligence and abilities. In Freudian terms, Jupiter represents the critical, questioning, moralizing aspect of the self which Freud designated the super-ego. This is further reinforced by the fact that the other two members of the trio are somewhat subservient to Jupiter who, to a certain extent, expects them to be his menials. Jupiter's association with a form of action is definitely the verbal component. He is the spokesman of the triad, and his ability with words and communication of information is superior. He delegates what is usually thought of as mental activity (research and information gathering) to one of his subordinates. The whole concept of investigating and solving mysteries began with Jupiter, and the group's headquarters belongs to him alone, so he is definitely in charge.

Investigator number two is Pete Crenshaw. Pete is the brawn of the organization. Athletically oriented, Pete is big for his age and muscular. He definitely prefers action to intellectual study or reasoning things out. Because of his size, Pete is always Jupiter's pick for any dangerous assignment which may necessitate physical prowess, co-ordination, or agility. Pete always achieves and completes his assignments, but he does so at a cost to himself, since he carries a secret. Pete's secret is his lack of self-confidence and his innate fear of being caught by the subject of his surveillance, or else failure in some other way. Interestingly enough, Pete is never able to admit his fears to others. His sometimes surly demeanor is not the result of his own disposition, but rather a way to hide the fact that he is afraid. He simply says that he doesn't want to do a thing rather than confessing he is afraid to do it. In this fashion, he is able to maintain his masculine identity through his athletic prowess rather than fearlessness. Thus it is to his credit that, in spite of his fears, he always comes through. Still, his instinct is for self-protection, and there is more self-generated emotional content in Pete's make-up than there is in either of the other investigators. Pete might be said to represent the id component in Freud's theory of self. Pete manages to hold himself in check and balance and never allows instinct or emotion to wholly rule him. Needless to say, in the world of action, Pete is the physical component to complement Jupiter's verbal skills. While Jupiter may talk to clients and interview suspects, it is Pete upon whom Jupiter depends to accomplish physical assignments such as climbing locked gates or crawling through culverts, all tasks that Jupiter would not like to do or thinks he would look foolish attempting.

In addition to Pete's personal usefulness to the team, he brings a world of valuable information to the group via his father's profession. Mr. Crenshaw is a special effects artist at a film studio. When he shares his knowledge with the boys, they are often, as a result, able to penetrate hoaxes being perpetrated on their clients and are frequently able to create some illusions of their own to trap various criminals. When a beach area is terrorized by a sea serpent, for example, the boys penetrate the mystery because of a similar special effect that Mr. Crenshaw had supervised for a film. The Investigators then turn the tables on the instigators and solve the case. Mr. Crenshaw also gives the boys some pointers about make-up and special props which aid their investigations.

The third investigator is Bob Andrews. Jupiter refers to him as "Records." Bob, who has a job at the local library, excels at research and record keeping. Jobs such as these are best for Bob, who is recovering from an accident which left him with one leg in a brace. This hindrance makes it difficult for Bob to keep up physically with the other two boys, especially Pete. Still, Bob is determined to be a contributing member of the group. He is small in stature, on the thin side, and studious by nature. In modern parlance, Bob would probably be known as a "geek." If it were possible to pair up Bob's adventurous spirit with Pete's physical prowess and strength, then a kind of unstoppable super investigator would emerge, but since that can't happen, Bob's talent for organization is his most valuable skill. Even though he has the heart of a tiger and the tenaciousness of a terrier, Bob's physical self just can't match up with his psyche. Consequently, Bob would seem to represent Freud's notion of the ego, and with his talents for research and analysis, his contribution to the action is that of the mental. Bob's handicap makes him physically and psychologically vulnerable. The addition of Bob provides the glue to make the group become a cohesive unit that is the equivalent of a whole and well-balanced personality or self. This fact alone accounts for a large portion of the success of the series: not only the fictional success of the boys solving crimes, but the financial success of the books themselves.

Robert Arthur, the creator of the books, died a short way into the series. Arthur wrote commercially and for the radio. He was an advisor to Hitchcock's television show and wrote a number of mystery stories for Hitchcock's magazine. It was he who thought of using the cachet of Hitchcock's name to sell the series. After Arthur's death, the series was continued by various different authors writing under their own names, since the series never had a "house" author name like those that the Syndicate provided. The reasons for the rather phenomenal success of the books have much to do with the name of the famous personality attached to them, although Hitchcock was never a "hero" in the sense that the Whitman authorized stories that utilized the names of famous movie and sports were. While the books never made a fortune in royalties for Arthur, most juvenile series authors, like Leo Edwards for example, had to work with several series at the same time to make ends meet. The books also continued a tradition begun by the best examples of juvenile boys' books by making use of interesting mysteries, humor arising from repartee and irony, non-perfect characters with whom readers could identify, and cliff-hanger chapter endings. Then, too, the titles of the volumes were evocative of the supernatural and rife with the promise of real thrills for the reader, especially when that promise was coupled with the name Hitchcock. Finally, given Freud's theory of self, the number of The Three Investigators becomes a representation of one whole person, and that complete one person is capable of a total and complete action. Jupiter is verbal; Pete is physical; and Bob is intellectual. Thus three combine to make one unified and complete focus. The various symbolisms and uses of the number three combine to make the series what it is: perfect in itself.

WORKS CITED

Arthur, Robert. *The Secret of Terror Castle*. New York: Random House, 1964.
Byars, Betsy. "Leo Edwards and the Secret and Mysterious Order of the Freckled Goldfish." *Leo Edwards Homepage*: Articles. n.d. 5 Mar. 2009. http://www.Smallbytes.net/~4lees/Leosite/index.html.
Cochran, Keith. "Leo Edwards Borrowers." *Yellowback Library* 111 (1993): 8–9.
Conan Doyle, Arthur. *The Original Illustrated Sherlock Holmes*. Secaucus, NJ: Castle, 1982.
Kelland, Clarence Budington. *Mark Tidd*. New York: Grosset & Dunlap, 1913.
Mattson, E. Christian, and Thomas B. Davis. *A Collector's Guide to Hardcover Boys' Series Books*. Newark, DE: MAD Book Company, 11–15.
Peters, Ingo. "Reception as a Transcultural Process: Robert Arthur's *Three Investigators* and their German Success." *Transcultural German Studies*. Eds. Steven D. Martinson and Renate Schultz. Bern: Peter Lang, n.d. 143–163.
Smolinske, Seth. "What and Who Are the Three Investigators? A Brief History." *The Three Investigators*. 3 Oct 2000. 15 Mar 2009. http://www.threeinvestigatorsbooks.com/TheThreeInvestigators.html.
Umphlett, Wiley Lee. "The Jerry Todd/Poppy Ott Books: Leo Edwards Celebration of American Boyhood." *Leo Edwards Homepage:* Articles. n.d. 5 Mar 2009. http://www.smallbytes,net/~4lees/Leosite/index.html.
Wawrzenski, Mark. "The Three Investigators: Then and Now." *Yellowback Library* 79 (1991): 5–8.

9

Clashing Genres: (No) Sex and (No) Violence in the Christopher Cool, TEEN Agent Series

MICHAEL G. CORNELIUS

The tail end of the 1960s saw the last, final creative gasp of the famed Stratemeyer Syndicate. During the decade, the last few of the Syndicate's original seventy-five series were created and released; though the company would survive until 1987 (when it was sold to Simon & Schuster) in the final twenty years of its existence the Syndicate only continued producing those series still in print (such as Nancy Drew and the Hardy Boys) or created new versions of formerly popular series, including two revisions of the Tom Swift books. Creatively, the Syndicate seemed to finally run out of fresh ideas.

The remaining few original series produced by the Stratemeyer Syndicate all had something in common; unlike series from previous decades, which were largely derivative of trends in juvenile or adult readership, the series spawned in the 1960s were largely works derivative of filmic (television and motion picture) popular culture. Western-themed series like Bret King and Linda Craig (which ran from 1960 to 1964 and from 1962 to 1964 respectively, though Linda Craig was briefly revived in 1981) were inspired by popular television shows like *Bonanza, Gunsmoke,* and *Wagon Train,* shows that ruled the Nielsen ratings in that decade. Similarly, the Christopher Cool, TEEN Agent series, which ran from 1967 to 1969 and produced a total of six volumes, was enormously derivative of the James Bond books and, even more directly, the very popular James Bond film series. The books themselves even winkingly refer to the Bond series on numerous occasions; when asked in the first book, *X Marks the Spy*, if he is a secret agent, Chris "sarcastically" replies, "Sure, 007 himself" (34). In a subsequent volume, when Chris is asked a question by his superior and gives no reply, his boss peevishly retorts, "Are you still there, Mr. Bond?" (*Department of Danger* 20). Given the popularity of the Bond books and films, it is no surprise that the Syndicate saw the spy series as source material for a new adventure for boy readers, and critically, the books were a success. John Axe wrote of the series, "The books were just as fresh and exciting for youngsters as the James Bond books were for adults" (38). Despite this critical praise, however, the Christopher Cool, TEEN Agent series ran only three years and six volumes before the series was ended in 1969. From the Syndicate perspective, this marked a distinct failure, a premature demise for a series based on one of the most popular genres — the spy thriller — of its time. Axe believes that the lack of sales for the Cool books can be blamed on the general decline in readership of juvenile books that occurred in the 1960s, as television and other forms of mass media supplanted and surpassed text as the main form of children's entertainment. Axe writes: "Television had taken over as the primary entertainment medium for young Americans by the late 1960s and they no longer bought [series] books in large numbers" (38).

Yet another reason for the demise of the Christopher Cool series may be in the clashing nature of the books' dual, dueling genres. The Christopher Cool books were both a spy series and a boy sleuth series; while on the surface these two genres might seem to overlap (spy series are, after all, overwhelmingly male in representation, and both are designed to attract a significantly male readership), the reality is that the two genres are distinct enough in several key areas to create a clash in genric intention that ultimately negated the fulfillment of one genre in favor of the other. As a result, rather than creating a type of genric synchronicity, the two clashing mediums actually disrupted one another, so that one genre impeded the creative fulfillment and expectations of the other. As Glenna Andrade notes, "Genre is both a literary focus and a social construction" (164). She continues: "Even though many stories incorporate elements of other genres, such as when a romance includes detective elements or when historical fiction integrates adventure hero qualities, each hero remains central within the formula of his or her own genre" (164). Andrade cautions that genres can become combative, especially if the standard elements of one genre preclude the fulfillment of the standard elements of the other. This, according to Andrade, results in a "suppression and disruption" of genre and character that creates a disharmony in the united work (165).

This type of genric disharmony is plainly evident in the Christopher

Cool series. In the books, the world of the spy thriller clashes with the social mores of the boy sleuth; the result is a type of "cold war," and, as such, tension is created between the genres that ultimately allows for the fulfillment of neither. This is especially true in the way the books handle genric conventions regarding sociality, sex, and violence. The spy thriller tends to embrace these last two aspects; indeed, one could hardly imagine a James Bond book or film without multiple sexual and sexualized women and lots of gunplay. Boy sleuth books, however, embrace a wholesome approach towards both the opposite sex and violence; in these books, malt shop dates replace nighttime liaisons, and fists fly instead of bullets. Plus, the spy thriller relies on its solitary hero, a lone figure fighting to preserve social order; in boy sleuth books, social groups win out, and thus the dynamics of the hero's relationship to both his world and his genre differ drastically. In the Christopher Cool series, it is the conventions of the boy sleuth genre that win out; as such, readers who imagine they are picking up a junior James Bond may be sorely disappointed at what they find. It is this literary disharmony that hastened the demise of the series, since the expectations of the readers could not be effectively met. For Christopher Cool, clashing genres result in the one "cold war" that he could not ultimately navigate or escape.

One of the key conventions of the boy sleuth book that emerges within the Christopher Cool series is its emphasis on sociality. Sociality is an important construct to both boys' and girls' series books. In both, the social success of the sleuth(s) reflects the normativity of a youth who indulges in generally abnormal behavior. Searching for clues, questioning suspects, and being overly concerned with social justice are not the hallmarks of typical teen-aged young America. The fact that the sleuth has friends — and, indeed, is often the leader amongst his or her friends, the proverbial most popular kid in school — reassures the reader not only of his or her relative normativity but, in fact, argues that their sleuthing actions render them ultranormative, creating a model for both other characters in the tale (who usually follow the sleuth's example) and readers (who, as Betsy Caprio and others have shown, often write wistfully of their own desires to act like the main detective). In girl sleuth series, friends often reflect aspects of their gender that are more generally and stereotypically drawn than the main sleuthing character reveals. Bess Marvin and George Fayne, for example, the best friends of Nancy Drew, reflect both extreme girlishness and extreme tomboyishness. Bess is cowardly; George, hyperactive. George is abrupt; Bess is sweet. Nancy is the normative center; for a character who does incredibly abnormal things, Nancy appears positively usual when sandwiched between her two best friends. As Ilana Nash concludes: "This triumvirate of characters flatters

Nancy by comparison and suggests that the ideal girl is she with no vulnerabilities, no appetites, no overt feelings, and perfect self-discipline" (39).

Ultimately, in many girl sleuth books, such as in the Dana Girls, Vicki Barr, Shirley Flight, and Cherry Ames, the large coterie of friends is sloughed off; as the girl sleuth grows into womanhood, she leaves her chums behind, working largely alone or replacing friends with a more familial grouping. Boy sleuths, however, rarely make the same transition; while they often begin their series with a large group of chums, that group is generally maintained through the end of the series. For boys, groups do more than express the normativity of the main character(s); for boys, groups enact codes of masculinity, fashioning gender-performative characteristics that mark the male throughout life. According to Jay C. Wade and Chris Brittain-Powell, males are "dependent on a male reference group for [their] gender role self-concept" (323). The authors continue: "The gender role self-concept is one's self-concept with regard to gender roles and includes one's gender-related attributes, attitudes, and behaviors" (323). As such, "males identify with other males to the extent that they feel psychological relatedness to a particular group of males or to all males" (324). For boy sleuths like Chris Cool, their gender role self-concept generally falls into the "Reference Group Dependent status," which "is characterized by feelings of psychological relatedness to some males and not others, a conformist ego identity, dependence on a male reference group for one's gender role self-concept, and thereby rigid adherence to gender roles, stereotyped attitudes, and limited or restricted gender role experiences and behaviors" (325). The groups thus become a way for the individual to claim a larger construct of manhood in an environment that reflects both how he identifies himself and how the world perceives him in a way that will ultimately define or re-define his role as male. These groups tend to alter or proscript behavior, homogenize values and beliefs, and aid in the self-fashioning of a masculine identity. Thus it is no surprise that the groups of boy sleuths found in series books tend to act and think alike; the group itself is designed to create a unilateral mode of being. For a member of the group,

> he would define his maleness or masculinity based on other like males or his peer group, which would tend to be homogeneous in character. For example, such feelings and beliefs may be present in a man who is a member of a college fraternity, who will only socialize and be friends with other men in his fraternity, and incorporates the fraternity's image of masculinity as his own; or a man who has sexist and prejudicial attitudes because this is what he has learned from other males in his environment with whom he identifies, and to have such attitudes is consistent with being a part of "the group" [Wade and Brittain-Powell 325].

Boy sleuths create groups around them that reflect their own values of social justice and share the same yearning for adventure and mystery. However, it is not that sleuths find like-minded young men as themselves to join their group; rather, behavior becomes proscripted upon membership. Peer groups have long been seen as modes of modifying individual behavior; boys' series books are no exceptions. Thus much of Chris' actions in the series emanate from the group he belongs to, not just the values that reflect TEEN but the behaviors of his partner the other agents he works with closely. For all boy sleuths, socialization is thus a way to not only normalize unusual (though socially beneficial) behavior but also to create a larger structure around said behavior to further validate its existence.

This homogeneity, though, creates a series of superstructured individuals who are, quite literally, just like the next guy. For the most part, one boy sleuth is like another, though a few series do create external differentiation amongst the sleuths. The Three Investigators series is perhaps most famous for this, as the three young male sleuths, the intellectual, overweight leader Jupiter Jones, the rangy, athletic Pete Crenshaw, and the bookish and (at least in the beginning of the series) temporarily disabled Bob Andrews are, visually, nothing alike. The boys, however, share the same intrinsic values, gender roles, and societal beliefs; their differences, while seemingly vast, are truly only skin-deep. This is by design. The group works to contain and curtail adolescent male behavior; by remaining part of the group, the text can ensure that no one member goes too far astray. A lone individual fighting for social justice — as James Bond so capably demonstrates — is a far more discursive and dangerous figure than a group of males working towards the same cause.

In conscripting Chris' behavior, his social group reflects the grander design of the Stratemeyer Syndicate itself, which eschewed violence in favor of tension derived from the potentiality of violence, a promise that generally went unfulfilled in Syndicate books. "Wholesome" is hardly the type of word one would ascribe to the Bond series, and yet it was deemed important for the Chris Cool series to adhere to the at-times rigid strictures set forth by the Syndicate formula (Herz 13). The books themselves are centered around Christopher Cool, TEEN Agent. TEEN is an acronym for the Top-secret Educational Espionage Network, a branch of the Central Intelligence Agency (CIA). As its mission, TEEN recruits the best and brightest students from America's top colleges and universities to fight against the forces of evil — and in late 1960s Cold War-America, that usually meant Communist spies or, even more fantastically, operatives of TOAD, a malevolent organization bent on nothing less than world domination. Chris himself is a lean, blond-haired, blue-eyed sophomore at Kingston University (an Ivy League *nom de plume* substituting for Princeton University). Chris is a master linguist (quite literally fluent in dozens of languages) and one of the most brilliant students at Kingston (though his professors are led to believe he prefers discotheques to study hall, since his spy activities take him away from campus so frequently). After being recruited for TEEN, Chris receives intensive training in "electronics, photography, cryptography, flying, scuba diving, karate and aikido" (*X Marks the Spy* 4). Thus trained, Chris is ready to tackle villains worldwide, including such dastardly men as The Chiller and Dr. Death, all while doing his best to preserve the Cold War balance of power and the American way of life he so effortlessly represents. The Christopher Cool, TEEN Agent series ran for six volumes, all published under the Stratemeyer pseudonym of Jack Lancer. According to John Axe, the first three volumes were actually penned by James "Jim" Duncan Lawrence, a prolific Syndicate ghostwriter who also wrote volumes in the Hardy Boys, Tom Swift, and Nancy Drew series and who would later pen the newspaper comic strip adventures of master spy James Bond himself. Jerry Mundis wrote the next two volumes, and Richard Deming the last. The six titles in the series are: *X Marks the Spy* (1967); *Mission: Moonfire* (1967); *Department of Danger* (1967); *Ace of Shadows* (1967); *Heads You Lose* (1968); and *Trial by Fury* (1969).

For the most part, the Christopher Cool series adheres to the conventions of the Stratemeyer boy sleuth book. Like most of Stratemeyer's boys' series, the book actually revolves around a male peer group or, as in the Rick Brant and Ken Holt series, a duo. Chris' partner, Agent Geronimo Johnson, is almost as omni-present as Chris in the series, and is often depicted as the more competent of the two spies. The books reflect patriarchal pro-American attitudes, and both spies work diligently to uphold the status quo and the American way of life. The books are educational, proffering instruction on the varying places Chris and Geronimo travel, and generally wholesome. While the series does include more direct violence than the Hardy Boys does (though it bears pointing out that Chris and Geronimo, as college sophomores, are older than the Hardy Boys by a couple of years), violence is still depicted in a manner befitting a boy sleuth series. Chris and Geronimo do not carry guns, instead using an anesthetic weapon called a "sleepy sliver" to incapacitate their foes; when confronted by thugs wielding pistols and knives, the TEEN spies use their training in martial arts to disarm their foes before knocking them out with a well-placed aikido chop. Like other boy sleuths, Chris and Geronimo detain their foes, rather than kill them; villainous rogues and fellow spies are generally captured, not killed. When killing does take place, it does so away from the reader's gaze, and is always the handiwork of the villains; Chris and Geronimo never kill in the series, no matter what danger they find themselves or the world in. Perhaps most interestingly, both boys come from a disadvantaged socio-economic background: Chris' father has been missing for two years at the series' start, rendering Chris a virtual orphan with no parental source of family income; Geronimo, a Native American raised on a reservation, would likely also have an impoverished background. Yet for both boys, largely because of their spy duties, finances are not an obstacle, and they have equal access to fast, expensive cars, can travel anywhere in the world on a whim or a hunch, and enjoy the use of a host of wardrobe items and technological gadgets that complement their work. TEEN must even sponsor their Ivy League tuition, since neither ever expresses any concern about paying for next semester's classes.

Interestingly, the Chris Cool books also adhere to many of the conventions of the spy thriller as well. In fact, on the surface, the spy genre has much in common with boy sleuth series. Both are highly masculine genres; both are concerned with restoring order and upholding the patriarchal status quo; both operate from a strongly pro–Western ideology and focus on duty to country, capitalism, and democracy. In their analysis of Jerry Palmer's seminal work *Thriller: Genesis and Structure of a Popular Culture,* John G. Cawelti and Bruce A. Rosenberg suggest that "the thriller is determined by the interplay of two major elements: an individualistic competitive hero and a conspiracy that threatens the orderly fabric of society" (3). James Chapman further codifies the genre when he notes that spy thriller narratives must contain three facets: political content; an ideology of national identity; and fantastic, nearly outrageous plots that utilize bizarre and grotesque villains as counterpoint to the lone spy figure who acts as cynosure of the story (25–32). James Bond, of course, was not the first spy thriller series. According to Clive Bloom, "the formal origins of the spy genre lay hazily within an amalgamation of the imperial adventure tale and the detective novel. Both forms emerged in their proper state in the last quarter of the nineteenth century and were themselves responses to social pressure" surrounding emerging colonial and post-colonial tensions and domestic socio-economic and class pressure and the rising public fascination with sensational crime (1). Bloom further places the spy thriller series as directly "tied to *international* political and social tensions" (1, italics original). Thus, Bloom argues, the deconstruction of imperialistic empires coupled with the rising awareness of global authority created a tension that, in literature, was alleviated by the figure of the secret agent, the lone wolf working for the "right" side whose purpose was to halt those elements in the emerging world that wished to threaten the rapidly crumbling old order. Thus such tales, like boy sleuth books, work to restore and uphold "the established social order" (Cawelti and Rosenberg 3).

The James Bond book and film series belong to a subgenre of spy thrillers that Bloom labels "adventure-romance" (1). Indeed, many critics believe that Bond creator Ian Fleming fashioned a wholly new genre when he invented Bond: James Chapman writes that "the Bond series is a genre (or at the very least a sub-genre) in its own right," while Cawelti and Rosenberg note that Fleming "creat[ed] a new formula [in Bond] that would be widely imitated in novels, on film, and in television" (22, 150). The first Bond novel, *Casino Royale*, was released in 1953, with eleven subsequent novels and two short-story collections to follow (plus numerous pastiches written by subsequent authors with permission from Fleming's estate). Sales of the early books were respectable, though hardly best-seller status. When the series was issued in paperback its popularity took off, and with the advent of *Dr. No*, the first Bond film, in 1962, the series finally achieved the rarified status it still maintains today. By 1967, the year the first Christopher Cool book was released, Bond novels were selling over a million copies a year in Great Britain alone (Chapman 23).

Unsurprisingly, because of his immense popularity and unique status amongst the spy thrillers of his time (most new spy works since then are often seen as being derivative of, or reactionary to, Bond), Bond has been the subject of much critical scrutiny. Chapman argues that Bond is "an essentially conservative hero, a defender of the realm, committed to preserving the institutions and society of his country.... Bond himself is frequently constructed through imagery which enforces notions of patriotism and duty" (29–30). Cawelti and Rosenberg write that Bond represents "goodness without ambiguity ... [facing] a series of supremely sinister, evil, and grotesque villains" (128). Charles Taliaferro and Michel Le Gall note that "Bond is moved by a concern for justice and protecting the innocent" (97). Hence, in many respects, Bond makes for a logical if adult extension of the boy sleuth; both have the same motivation, the same desire for justice, and work to uphold the same patriarchal status quo. Thus it is no surprise that the Stratemeyer Syndicate created a boy sleuth version of Bond.

The series have many more tangible elements in common than social values on justice and Western society. In fact, the similarities between the two series reflect the indebtedness of the Christopher Cool series to its adult progenitor. For example, Bond's boss, the man who gives him his marching orders, is M; Chris Cool's boss is Q, which not only continues the mono-letter representation of the shadowy head figure but also alludes to the Bond gadget-master, also named Q. Christopher Cool's Q is so like Bond's M that he even employs a "usual fake British accent" (*X Marks the Spy* 2). No reason is ever given for this affectation, though the nod to Bond is easily identifiable. Also easily identifiable is the relationship both series has to spy gadgets, technology, and modes of transportation. In Chris Cool, the gadget-master is named Pomeroy, though the fussy, quirky genius is an obvious pastiche of Bond's Q (whose real name, Major Boothroyd, is not unlike "Pomeroy" in its basic sound components). In both series technology and transportation play a vital role. According to Fred Erisman, technology in boys' series literature is designed to proffer "the picture of American youth as mechanically competent" (14). Erisman notes that technology and a technical education was a way to become "universally acknowledged and respected" (15). Russel B. Nye, writing about the Tom Swift, Boy Inventor series, suggests that what made that series so popular is that "Tom Swift grasped the technology of the machine age and brought it under control" (83). Erisman echoes this when he suggests that in these books, "technology is something that *can* be, and *must* be, mastered" (24). Likewise, Bond is also a master of the technological: "Bond is at home with, and identified by, his association with technological accoutrements. His relationship with modern gadgetry is that of the competent technocrat. He exhibits in fact an amused sense of supremacy over these symbols of the present and future" (Bloom 88). In both series, mastery of such technology implies mastery of the larger world and the self: "Bond's 'gadgets' are recognized as one of the functional characteristics of heroism" (Zani 173). By demonstrating their ability to utilize even the most complex machinery around them, both Bond and Chris Cool illustrate their ability to master the complex world they seek to maintain and control.

Transportation is also a key element to both series. For boy sleuths as well as girls, transportation implies "freedom" (Nash 36). Nancy Drew's roadster, for example, "not only allows her mobility, it frees her from the chafing ritual of begging her father from permission to use his car" (Nash 36). For boy and girl sleuths alike, such freedom bridges the world to adulthood while also providing autonomy from it. Sleuths like the Hardy boys and Christopher Cool often have a host of transportation options before them: fast cars, motorcycles, well-equipped spy vans, powerful speedboats, and even light aircraft. Their ability to martial such technology, master its use, and gain access to it whenever desired reflects their mastery and dominance of the larger world around them, and their importance in that world's extended social hierarchy.

Likewise, Bond is famous for his association with cool, sleek cars and other such similar modes of transport. For Bond, however, his car goes beyond simple representation of freedom. As an adult, Bond has already gained the freedom boy and girl sleuths manifest through their vehicles; for Bond, a car is no more significant than any other technology, something to be mastered, dominated, and controlled. Yet Bond's choice of car is significant. His famous Aston Martin, popularized in the film versions of the series, reflects a materialistic, aggrandizing side of the character that seems antithetical to the covert secrecy required of a master spy. Bond's car shouts "Look at me!" whenever it zooms past, not "Forget I was ever here." It inspires envy, not nonchalance. Bond himself is unapologetically materialistic, not only in what he drives, but in his sartorial and gastronomic habits as well. In *Casino Royale*, Bond explains, "You must forgive me ... I take ridiculous pleasure in what I eat and drink. It comes partly from being a bachelor, but mostly from a habit of taking a lot of trouble over details" (61). As Suzie Gibson points out, "There is a fluency expressed here between Bond's attitude toward consumable items and his work" (52). Though Fleming argues that Bond's attention to detail is what makes him so exceptional as a master spy, the inverse also seems to be true as well, namely that Bond's work has caused him to not only appreciate the finer things, but to expect them. Presumably, Bond counteracts the need for secrecy that surrounds his work and his life with an ostentatiousness that belies his occupation. Thus such overtly masculine symbols as fast, fancy cars represent Bond himself. In the Chris Cool series, the cars are likewise fast and furious. Though Nancy Drew drives a roadster and the Hardy boys have a sensible van, Chris and Geronimo have a fleet of sports cars at their beck and call. In the series, descriptions of vehicles are presented in rapturous, glowing, almost pornographic detail: "[Chris] headed for a bulletlike Jaguar on the parking lot near the dormitory. The 4/2 liter engine purred like a well-fed pussycat, then broke into a full-throated jungle roar as the gleaming black Jag show down the driveway into Madison Circle.... A leather-jacketed motorcyclist stared enviously at the sleek car" (*X Marks the Spy* 1–2, 4). This envy offsets the covertness that surrounds Chris' real self; the Jaguar allows other men to openly admire him even though, on the surface, he must continue to act as any other all-American college youth.

Another area in which the two series correlate is in their depiction of antagonists, especially by focusing on villains as members of minoritorialized groups, as distinctly different from the normative, white, Anglo-Saxon hero of the tale. Michael Woolf suggests that Fleming's villains are "racially ambiguous" and reflect "the other" (93). Cawelti and Rosenberg continue this thread when they write, "The villain's basic falsity is symbolized by his dubious racial heritage. Where the hero is pure Anglo-Saxon, the villain is invariably from an 'inferior' race or some curious racial mixture.... The blatant racial symbolism ... establish[es] the fundamental opposition of hero and villain" (128). Umberto Eco and Oreste del Buone, in *The Bond Affair*, argue that the Bond novels are based on a series of oppositional, archetypal relationships: between Bond and M, between Bond and the woman, and most especially, between Bond and the villain, who represents the overriding inherent tension "between the Free World and the Soviet Union, England and the non–Anglo-Saxon countries represent[ing] the primitive epic relationship between the Chosen race and the Lower race, between Black and White, Good and Bad" (59–60). The emphasis on "other" can be seen in the descriptions of the villains themselves in the Bond series, as in this description of Dr. No: "The bizarre, gliding figure looked like a giant venomous worm wrapped in grey tin-foil, and Bond would not have been surprised to see the rest of it trailing slimily along the carpet behind" (*Dr. No* 127). Similar descriptions abound in the Chris Cool series. In the final book of the series, *Trial by Fury*, the chief antagonist, codenamed the Komodo Dragon, is described to Chris thusly: "[P]hysically he is horrible. He is gross, bloated, disgusting. Despite his brilliance, he eats like a pig — or rather like his reptile namesake, bolting his food down in enormous quantities" (162).

Later, when Chris first spies the villain for himself, his reaction is just as telling: "He had the face of a savage Buddha" (166). In both descriptions the emphasis is on those physical characteristics that represent the Dragon as a figure in direct opposition to the TEEN Agent himself. The Dragon's girth suggests his willingness to disregard societal boundaries. As Jana Evans Braziel and Kathleen LeBesco note, "The corpulent [has often been seen] as an encoded surface that signifies the subtext of the psyche. Frequently the fat body is read as the corporeal presencing of other, presumably more intrinsic, incorporeal qualities or characteristics — the signifying of latency and lack" (3). Large bodies are often used to represent greater, blacker marks of the soul, excesses of morality that reflect the physical excesses the antagonist is obviously willing to indulge in. "Fat equals ... transgression"; a large body is often seen as being marked by sin (Braziel and LeBesco 3). Chris' initial thought on meeting the Komodo Dragon is likewise indicative of the villain's otherness; not only does Chris emphasize his size (by comparing him to the traditionally corpulent form of the Buddha) but also his ethnographic heritage. The reference marks the Dragon's face as non–Western, though, as the reader learns, the antagonist's ethnic background is Chinese, and not Vedic Indian as was the Buddha's. The implication here is that, to Chris, all non–

Westerners look alike, and most are not to be trusted. This attitude is reflected numerous times in the series. When visiting Djakarta in the same book, Chris notes that the city is "struggling to cast off ancient ways and make [itself] into a modern metropolis" (30). This salient sentence firmly encapsulates the imperialist attitude of the series, that the "ancient," non-Western "ways" of this Eastern capital must be sloughed off and Djakarta must be transformed into a carbon copy of a Western capital before it can be modernized and thus, from the book's perspective, made suitable in Western eyes.

Interestingly, the Christopher Cool series also places a huge emphasis on the non-Anglo-Saxon background of many of Chris' supporters and helpers in the series as well. The most obvious of these is Chris' partner Geronimo, whose Native American heritage is mentioned time and again in the series. Geronimo is Apache, and Chris, the master linguist, is fluent in the language himself, so the two boys often converse in Apache when they don't wish their conversation to be overheard. Likewise, Geronimo's nickname for Chris, "*choonday*," is described as an Apache word for "friend." On the surface, then, it appears as though Geronimo's role as "other" is celebrated in the series, and his differentiation, and that of other characters in the books, may counterbalance the traditionally xenophobic attitudes of spy thrillers like Bond.

However, Geronimo's "otherness" is *overly* emphasized in the series. While his nickname for Chris is the Apache word for friend, Chris' nickname for Geronimo is "redskin," a horrible epithet that he not only uses frequently throughout the series, but one that the omniscient narration of the books habitually uses to describe Geronimo as well. The books also refer to Geronimo as "the Apache" and "the Indian" as often as by his own name; he is also called a "copper-skinned youth" (*X Marks the Spy* 1) on numerous occasions, and the books continually "compliment" Geronimo by emphasizing his otherness. In the first book, Geronimo's attraction to becoming a spy is described thusly: "Geronimo [came] from the greatest race of guerilla fighters in history, with the blood of Apache war chiefs in his veins" (*X Marks the Spy* 3). Chris joined TEEN to find his missing physicist father, but to the more "savage" Geronimo, the attraction is not a chance to save his family or the world, but "the deadly business of cold-war espionage" itself (*X Marks the Spy* 3). The books continually revel in Native American stereotypes: "All the same, his [Geronimo's] instinct had never let them down. Indians had some way of scenting an enemy, like a coyote sniffing poisoned bait" (*Mission: Moonfire* 128). The continued emphasis on Geronimo's distinctly non-Anglo-Saxon heritage is designed to create an opposition not to his enemies, who actually share a similar differentiated ethnic background, but to his partner, thus ensuring that, while the boys remain relatively equal in their spy abilities and in importance to the plots of the books, Chris is the character elevated to heroic status, since he represents not only the intended readership of the book but the traditional white, male, Anglo-Saxon hero of twentieth-century spy thrillers and boy sleuth books.

Other characters whose ethnicity, race, or gender differs from Chris' likewise find these differences emphasized throughout the texts. When fellow TEEN agent Beauregard Tatum makes his first appearance in the series, he is referred to — not once, but twice — as "the Negro" before his name is actually used (*Department of Danger* 23). Though labeled one of TEEN's "most remarkable agents," Tatum "did his best to disguise a brilliant mind with an air of flamboyant foolery" (*Department of Danger* 23). This allows the books a chance to emphasize his otherness through language, dress, and action (Tatum refers to fellow agents as "cats" and greets people with "What cooks?," the books' construct of 1960s African American vernacular) (*Department of Danger* 23). Women receive a similar treatment: Spice Carter and Yummi Toyama, two female TEEN agents, are generally left out of the series' emphasis on action. In the fifth book of the series, *Heads You Lose*, Spice and Yummi complain that Chris and Geronimo receive an exciting assignment while they are left to interview over a hundred employees of a governmental agency. When Spice laments, "Is this a job for a spy?," Geronimo replies, "I think it's very nice ... feminine, dull, and appropriate" (14). When Spice angrily aims a karate blow at Geronimo, he parries her blow easily "with a laugh" (14). The scene illustrates the disdain both the series and the agency has for female agents, who exist to be captured, rescued, and marginalized like any typical damsel in distress. As such, the two women's female-ness is emphasized over and over, again creating an opposition to main hero Chris. In fact, the series is highly cognizant of these differentiations: at one point, Yummi says to Geronimo, "Us minority types have to stick together," suggesting not only the emphasis on demarcation between ethnic, racial, and gender groups in the series but the role to which members of the non-male, non-white, non–Anglo-Saxon demographic are generally subscribed (*Ace of Shadows* 108).

Thus the Christopher Cool series does adhere to James Chapman's main precepts for the spy thriller genre. The plots generally revolve around political upheaval and the East vs. West or Soviet vs. NATO dichotomy that is also found in Bond; the books emphasize an ideology of national identity that is essential not only to the mission but to Chris' own subjectivity as well; and the plots are of the outrageous, "take-over-the-world" variety led by grotesque villains and evil organizations bent on the destruction of democracy, freedom, and the British/American way of life (S.M.E.R.S.H. and

S.P.E.C.T.R.E. in Bond, TOAD in Chris Cool). However, one of Chapman's criterion for the genre is *not* met by the Chris Cool series. Chapman emphasizes that the spy is a solitary individual, a lone figure that exists outside of the boundaries of society (though he surrounds himself with the finer trappings of it) in order to more ably preserve said society. Key to understanding this aspect of Bond is his recognition of his own role as "anti-hero" (Chapman 22). As an anti-hero, Bond is able to adopt the methodology of the series' antagonists — most notably through his license to kill — while still working for truth, justice, and the proverbial American/British way. As Cawelti and Rosenberg note, "While killing is the most important crime or sin legitimated by the [Bond novels,] it is significant that Bond is called on to perform a number of traditionally disreputable acts as he pursues his profession: at various points he must become a gambler — even a cheater at cards — a seducer, a thief, a swindler" (135). Though Bond sometimes struggles with his moral ambiguities in the novels, in the film series, no murder is complete without a pithy quip, a nonchalant dusting of the clothes, and a wry smile. The seduction of an enemy agent or an innocent by-stander is a victory, not just for Bond, but for the society he represents. The fact that all Bond films end in those three elements — the death or destruction of most of the antagonists (often an entire army is wiped out), a wry joke at the villain's expense, and the final seduction of the infamous Bond "girl" — validates Bond's moral transgressions because of the consequences that would ensue if he acted otherwise. For Bond, the ends quite literally justify the means, and in many ways, because Bond works alone, sanctioned by his government but generally outside of its confines or prying eyes, what he does goes unmarveled and unremarked upon by anyone but the all-too-willing-to-play-along members of the audience. Thus Bond is able to bend the will and morals of the status quo in order to preserve it.

Unlike boy sleuths, who rely on socialization to help form their subjective identities, Bond has no similar need for male company. This would place Bond into Wade and Brittain-Powell's "No Reference Group," which "is characterized by a lack of psychological relatedness to other males, an unintegrated or undifferentiated ego identity, an undefined or fragmented gender role self-concept, and confusion, anxiety, alienation, and insecurity associated with gender role experiences" (324). Wade and Brittain-Powell suggest that men who belong to the "No Reference Group" feel isolated from larger male communities, not wanting to belong to any but often being forced to pledge membership to one group or another to enact the role of male. Bond, however, is a male who generally lives outside of society's grasp; when he seeks company, it is generally women who comfort him. Bond demonstrates both a lack of desire and ability to interact with other males. Most of his male-male interactions in his world result in violence; the few that don't, such as those with M or Q, are still fraught with tension and unease, as Bond simply (and often, poorly) plays the role of dutiful secret agent in order to be sent out on his next assignment.

Bond's attitude towards male socialization in particular and towards men in general is reflective of his hypermasculinity, a profile of masculine behavior that typically involves high levels of aggression and violence, as well as "destructiveness, low tolerance for delay of gratification, crime, drinking, and similar dispositions" (Broude 103). Garry Chick and John W. Loy suggest that such behavior results in overtly and overly stereotyped masculine behavior, the kind demonstrated in Bond's constant bedding of different women, in his attitudes towards fast cars, alcohol, gambling, and hedonism in general. A hypermasculine male does not work well within a larger societal group because his behavior is antithetical to the operational dynamics of the group itself; unless the group is bent on destruction, hypermasculinity threatens the stability of the unit. For Bond, of course, and for all spy thriller heroes, hypermasculinity is an asset; it creates a condition within the spy to behave recklessly, abandon caution, and enjoy aggression. As a set of personality traits, hypermasculinity is ideal for the successful spy.

Thus Bond's individuality is a key to his success; however, Christopher Cool does not spy alone. He always travels with a partner, and often teams up with other spies, from both TEEN and the CIA, in order to successfully complete his missions. Like all boy sleuths, Chris works within and from the group mentality; his behavior is thus constrained, his values more in line with societal values as a whole. It is this key difference between the two series where the clashing ethos of the two differing genres is most readily evident; the boy sleuth culture demands male socialization, while the spy series requires that the agent work alone. Caught between two worlds, Chris chooses the former genre, and the result is a demarcation of his sleuth and spy identities. Ultimately, Chris cannot be both, at least not successfully, and still meet the narrative expectations both genres entail.

Perhaps the most obvious manifestation in both works of how sociality impacts the action is in regards to violence. The Bond novels, and even more so the films, fairly revel in violence; as previously noted, Bond's "commission as a spy frees him from responsibility and gives him license to do things he could not ordinarily do without serious consequences. James Bond ... has the 'license to kill'" (Cawelti and Rosenberg 13). Bond is also a continual victim of substantial violence. Charles Taliaferro and Michel Le Gall describe the depiction of violence in the Bond novels and films as rising to levels of "sadism," noting that "the issue of sadism is perhaps best addressed through the depiction of torture. Bond is subjected to systematic, sustained torture in many of the books ... [and] a few movies" (98). For Taliaferro and Le Gall, violence works at "merging the torturer and victim," not only confusing the morality of the violence in the series (Bond is free to return that which is visited upon him) but also allowing the audience to take some amount of pleasure from the deaths of the villains: "We are intended (in the film and book) to enjoy Dr. No's sliding down a pipe into a vat of heavy water" (Taliaferro and Le Gall 97). By their very nature, the spy thriller genre is violent, but the violence is not designed to disgust or repulse the reader. Rather, it allows us to revel in the destruction of our fears, those elements that we believe exist that seek to ruin our way of life, and to take some grim satisfaction in our own superiority, that "our man" has won the day and that the comic villain has come to his appointed and expected end. By reveling in such violence, we are complicit in its action; any violent recourse or reaction, of course, stuns us with disgust. When one of Bond's allies is assassinated or eliminated, or when Geronimo is poisoned (as he is in *Heads You Lose*), we recoil in horror and disgust; when Bond eliminates an entire army of villainous henchmen, or when the notorious madman the Chiller is killed in the first Christopher Cool book, we exult in victory. The "us-vs-them" dichotomy of the genre creates this contradicting set of reactions that allows us to both revel in violence and recoil from it. The end result is that it is only what is done to *us* that matters; what we do to "them" only belies that "they" certainly deserved it.

Boy sleuth books, however, can never be truly overtly violent. In his instructions to Leslie McFarlane, the ghostwriter on the first Hardy Boys books, Edward Stratemeyer wrote that text should contain "not quite such strong language and not much pistol play ... it will pay to liven it up here and there with a bit of fun or horseplay on their part" (Greenwald 49). Even though Stratemeyer penned those instructions in the mid–1920s, the same rules of the Stratemeyer Formula still applied forty years later. The series goes out of its way to lessen any potential violence, especially on the part of Chris and his fellow TEEN agents:

> "Our mission is to stop Cascabel," Geronimo said. "Any way we can?"
> "Wrong. We want him alive — captured — delivered to our government ... [h]e has a lot to pay for, an awful lot."
> "Understood," Chris said [*Heads You Lose* 11].

Whereas Bond has a license to kill, Chris only has a license to detain — a decidedly tougher task when traipsing through the Amazonian jungles of Ecuador.

Detention is a key reading of the Chris Cool series. When captured, as he is in nearly every book, Chris is usually detained and threatened with violence, but rarely does he suffer any actual physical manifestation of it. Geronimo is one time shot, but the chilling moment turns out to be a false alarm — he has been implanted with a tracker, not struck by a bullet. When the boys do face physical peril, it is usually dealt with briefly (knife-wielding assassins are easily judo-chopped into unconsciousness) or comes as the result of non-direct confrontation (Geronimo is once poisoned, but is quickly cured at a local hospital.) In fact, during the entire series, Chris' actions never result in a death, something the books are keen to stress. In *X Marks the Spy*, for example, Chris is forced to blow up a laboratory to prevent a villain known as the Chiller from shooting down the President of the United States' airplane. In the aftermath, the TEEN agents share an unusual concern:

> "Is anybody — well — you know — dead?" Spice asked falteringly, not wanting to look around herself.
> "I believe they all will recover from their injuries," the French secret agent replied [175].

In fact, the book explicitly states that the Chiller was injured but could recover from his injuries; however, he refused medical treatment and died, taking his nefarious plans for world conquest to his grave. Conveniently, Chris's actions in causing the villain's death are forgotten, as the ultimate act that led to the man's demise was by his own hand, and not Chris'.

The lack of allowable violence manifests itself in other ways in the series, too. As previously noted, the boys do not carry guns, but rather rely on anesthetic weapons to incapacitate foes. The TEEN agents also have a host of defensive weapons, designed to facilitate escape, rather than the more offensive weapons common to the Bond novels and films. Spice's concern over dead enemy agents bent on destroying America would hardly be echoed by Bond; however, they are a manifestation of the primary genre of the Christopher Cool, TEEN Agent series. The moral code to which all boy sleuths must adhere is much more rigid and austere than anything Bond must endure. In a world where "horseplay" replaces gunplay, such standard spy activities as smoking and drinking are strictly forbidden. Where Bond enjoys a martini ("shaken, not stirred"), Chris and Geronimo, though of the legal age to consume alcohol for the time period and traveling in a foreign country, enjoy *apfelsaft*, an apple-cider drink, rather than anything alcoholic. Even the TEEN leader, Q, drinks milk instead of scotch, perfectly capturing the wholesomeness of the boy sleuth genre's moral code. These subtle shifts reflect a type of "code-switching," an attempt to maintain key aspects of the derivative genre (the spy thriller) while simultaneously satisfying the conditions of the originating genre (boy sleuth books). The result, however, is far from harmonious; indeed, it is absurd to imagine the head of a spy agency drinking milk. At its worst, the Christopher Cool series falls into such parodical moments unintentionally but damagingly, for it is moments like this that demonstrate the inability of the two genres to merge cohesively into one fulfilled topos.

Most indicative of the clashing nature of genre between the James Bond and Christopher Cool series is the way in which each handles the issue of sexuality. For Bond, sexual conquest is both a means to an end and a part of his job; whether bonus or expected payment, the fall of both the virtuous and villainous Bond girl is an expected aspect of any Bond saga. In Chris Cool, however, women are generally viewed as a source of constant anxiety; like a nervous, fumbling teenager, Chris may often speak of women in sexualized tones, but the threat of actual physical contact renders him squeamish and inert. Ultimately, for Bond, women represent an object of desire, something to be conquered, used, and generally discarded; for Chris, women represent an object of anxiety, something to be avoided as much as possible.

Yet the treatment of women in both series does have some similarities. In both, women often are introduced to the story as an object—something to be looked at, subject to the male gaze. According to Sarah Bromberg, this perspective "allows men to unconsciously oppress and coerce women in order to satisfy their fantasies," while ultimately demonstrating male dominance in both the sexual and social order (296). The objectification of women in the spy thriller is not just incidentally dehumanizing; as women often act the part of assistant or aid to the antagonist, this process of dehumanization is key to the spy's ability to commit whatever action necessary to successfully seduce, overcome, or destroy the woman. Thus women are often introduced in both series as the object of the male gaze—Ursula Andress' famous entrance in the film version of *Dr. No* (a scene repeated by Halle Berry in *Die Another Day*) is the perfect illustration of this. The woman emerges from the liquid element, silent, her moist flesh and form on display for all appreciative male eyes. Similar scenes abound in the novels as well, as the literary version of the above scene indicates:

> It was a naked girl, with her back to him. She was not quite naked. She wore a broad leather belt round her waist with a hunting knife in a leather sheath at her right hip. The belt made her nakedness extraordinarily erotic. She stood not more than five yards away on the tideline looking down at something in her hand. She stood in the classical pose of the nude, all the weight on the right leg and the left knee bent and turning slightly inwards, the head to one side as she examined the things in her hand [*Dr. No* 67].

The eroticized nature of the scene, the silence of the woman, and the presence of leather and a weapon, suggesting danger, titillation, and sadomasochism, all highlight the way in which women are viewed in the Bond series. As Bloom succinctly puts it, "Bond's women are never chaste" (86).

Similar scenes abound in the Chris Cool series, though never are they as erotically tinged as in Bond. In fact, there is "never any overt sexual conduct in any of the Christopher Cool books" (Axe 38). Rather, these scenes in the Chris Cool books read almost as a pastiche of those in Bond, as if Chris knows he is supposed to objectify the women he encounters, but is not sure of the properly salacious way to do it. One woman, for example, is referred to as a "blonde morsel" when Chris first spies her (*X Marks the Spy* 21). Numerous scenes objectifying women are handled in similarly juvenile fashion. Referring to a stewardess he met on a plane trip to Indonesia, Geronimo mutters, "Running Fawn is my dish" (*Trial by Fury* 37). Yet a mere page later, Geronimo points towards the most beautiful of a group of dancing girls and says to Chris, "Dig that one," demonstrating his lack of true intent — sexually or otherwise — towards either (38). During an earlier mission, Chris and Geronimo await a group of dancing "Circassian Slave Girls," about whom Chris murmurs, "May help to pass the time" (*Mission: Moonfire* 4). Thus while the boys continually joke about the women who are the objects of both their and the narrative's gaze, when confronted with actual evidence of female sexuality, both the boys and the narrative become chaste, unsure, and nervous. Hence women represent not the object of the male gaze in the Chris Cool series but rather a simulacrum of the gaze itself. Their desire to look at the female form ratifies the normativity of both Chris and Geronimo, reminding us that they are hot-blooded all–American college students and spies. However, when confronted by actual female sexuality, the boys tend to become embarrassed and fumble insecurely, activity wholly unbecoming a trained spy and certainly not found in their progenitor James Bond. In both *Mission: Moonfire* and *Heads You Lose*, Chris and Geronimo are confronted by Spice Carter and, in the second, both Spice and Yummi, wearing only bathing gear (specifically bikinis in the latter), but both the boys' eyes and the narrative gaze shies away from describing the female body and instead focuses on descriptions of their eyes, face, and hair only, as if to look below the neck would be unseemly and untoward. Similar scenes are abundant in the series. In *Trial by Fury*, Geronimo stammers nervously when a woman kisses him on the cheek (100). In *Department of Danger*, an undercover Chris finds himself threatened while dancing with a beautiful TOAD agent named Pamela, who tells him that the pin on her dress is a poison-dart gun aimed right at Chris. Taken aback, the TEEN agent finally responds,

"Sorry, you'll have to aim higher.... I'm wearing bulletproof underwear. Sort of a nylon-and-steel-mesh body stocking" (102). The sexual nature of Chris' joke defuses the situation, and seems almost worthy of a quip straight from Bond; the indication that Chris is now the object of the woman's gaze (both as a potential victim and sexual partner) is amusing and smacks of self-confidence. Yet the line also seems tinged with a palpable sense of dread, as the TEEN agent worries that a beautiful woman might, indeed, desire him both violently and sexually, combining the two things his series works so diligently to eschew. The reaction, far from being the smooth chatter of a seductive Bond, is the nervous reply of a virginal schoolboy, afraid of and titillated by the predatory, experienced woman who has made him the object of her desire.

For Bond, such an encounter is commonplace; many of the infamous "Bond girls" enter the narrative connected to the chief antagonist. In films like *Dr. No*, *Goldfinger*, and *Thunderball*, the heroines — in this case Honey Rider, Jill Masterson, Pussy Galore, and Domino — are "saved from evil by Bond" (Taliaferro and Le Gall 102). Sex with Bond thus becomes morally redemptive for each woman, who then plays a small but vital role in aiding Bond in overcoming his foe and her former associate. Taliaferro and Le Gall explain:

> Before the intervention of Bond ... these women are depicted as being of questionable virtue despite their denial of having sex with the evil protagonist. Nevertheless, the novels and the films exhibit a clear literary topos for the role of women which follows a course of development from whore to mother: from enslavement to seduction, sex, and ultimately the redemption of these 'lost women' along with the absolution of their sin and guilt from association with the criminal mastermind [103].

Through his sexual intervention, Bond creates a situation where the woman (if she survives the adventure) is now morally secure enough to re-enter society. Since Bond himself cannot exist within the society he serves and protects, it allows him perfect cover to leave the woman behind, morally cleansed and unerringly discarded. Cawelti and Rosenberg note, "Those who are not literally destroyed are symbolically eliminated, for the romance invariably breaks up before the next adventure" (143).

In this scenario, women in the world of Bond continually remain objects; whether morally redeemed or not, they are always a prize to be conquered, the subject of the victor's spoils in the hero's contests with the series' antagonists. Bond himself seemingly views these women as nothing more than the rewards for his labor; when the labor is done, so is his need of them. He moves on, to the next mission and to the next woman. Bond's attitudes towards women are key to the fashioning and reading of his subjectivity, especially his overtly masculine subjectivity. In Bond, the "character's unusual sexual attractiveness [is] a sign of his heroic prowess ... sexual chastity and restraint are no longer meaningful symbols of manliness and heroism" (Cawelti and Rosenberg 142). Bond's sexual prowess is thus viewed as an extension of both his aggressive masculinity and essential male-ness; Bond's relationships with women emphasize both his normativity and his super-normativity, in that it reinforces traditional masculine desire and demonstrates Bond's ability to function in yet another arena beyond the average male.

The boy sleuth's general lack of sexual knowledge and interest in attaining it is supposed to emphasize the "boyness" of the sleuth, the innocence that reflects the moral code attached to the boy sleuth genre. For girl sleuths, sexuality is a harbinger of womanhood which, for much of the twentieth century, meant taking on the traditional roles of wife and mother and leaving behind the role of detective and independent feminine/feminist agent. Boy sleuths, on the other hand, faced no similar proscriptions; while not a regular part of series literature or juvenile literature in general, sexuality was always an expected aspect of a growing male's learning curve. By the college years, especially in the late 1960s, one would expect a male to acknowledge his own sexual desire, even if he chose not to act on it. But the Christopher Cool books, because they still belong to the boy sleuth genre, eschewed any acknowledgement of the boys' own sexuality, even if this willful sexual ignorance ran counter to the generic conventions of the spy series. Thus for Chris, women become an object of anxiety, and not desire; for him, subjecting women to his own gaze is an action he performs not out of any yearning but only because it seems expected of him to do so. This results in numerous scenes in the series that are both discomposing and awkward when it comes to Chris expressing and repressing his own sexuality. The most illustrative scene that reflects Chris' view of women as an object of anxiety occurs in the first book of the series, *X Marks the Spy*. In an episode that mirrors a scene right out of Bond, Chris overhears a young woman on the telephone using what he believes is a key code word related to his current mission. Deciding that a romantic overture would make for the best ruse to interrogate the suspect, Chris approaches the college-aged young woman by asking, "Excuse me, but aren't you a Cliffy?" (70). The narrative assures us that the young woman is unattractive: "The girl giggled nervously, displaying buck teeth. She had stringy, mouse-colored hair and was wearing fancy sunglasses. With her sunglasses off, she looked even worse. Chris wished she had left them on" (70). For Chris, the rest of the luncheon date was excruciating;

when he finally uncovers that girl had not used the code word after all, he laments, "Now he might be stuck with this female the rest of the day" (71). Though Chris manages to extricate himself after the meal, he later bumps into the young woman again and is forced to endure another meal with her.

For Bond, such an encounter, even with an unattractive female (though the only unattractive females in Bond are those operative henchwomen, such as Rosa Klebb in *From Russia with Love*, whose gender is almost irrelevant, since Bond himself never views them sexually) would represent a further chance to extricate information through any means necessary, usually seduction; this seduction would also validate Bond's heroic prowess as alpha male and reward him for his services to country and crown. In Chris Cool, the TEEN spy willing to give his life for his country and do whatever is necessary to achieve his mission (though he is generally disallowed from killing, he demonstrates his willingness on occasion to do so) balks when confronted with a member of the opposite gender who views him romantically. For the rest of the series, Chris generally avoids similar encounters with women; when wooing another potential source of information in *Mission: Moonfire*, Chris's dates always include Geronimo, ensuring that the situation never becomes too awkward sexually speaking. Though Spice Carter and Yummi Toyama would seem like plausible romantic matches for Chris and Geronimo, the four only interact while working, and even then, never go on anything that is even a facsimile of a date. When Chris finds himself alone with Pamela, her threatening sexuality disarms him; quickly, he brings her back to his group to ensure the protection of his larger, male-dominated social unit.

Ultimately, the lack of success for the Christopher Cool, TEEN Agent series may have as much to do with failed genric expectations as demographic shifts in late 1960s readership. For while both the James Bond and Christopher Cool series adhere to Chapman's three basic elements for a spy thriller series, as many critics have rightly noted, Bond is a subgenre unto himself; to mimic Bond must mean utilizing, responding to, or acknowledging the violence and sexuality inherent to Bond and post–Bondian imitators. As Chapman notes, "Bond novels offered a fantasy which provided scope for the gratification of repressed desires, whether they be focused on fast cars, food, drink, women, or all of those" (37). The expectations of male readers — even teen male readers — were thus met not only by the international action and ideology of national identity inherent to the genre, but also through the materialistic, chauvinistic, and aggressive tendencies displayed by the lone spy anti-hero. The Christopher Cool series, however, found itself grappling with the conventions and expectations of clashing genres and a dual readership; in the end, the boy sleuth genre won out, removing those elements that distinguished Bond and made him the cultural zeitgeist he is today. Without an acknowledgement of sex and violence — even in some anemic, safe-for-the audience form — the Chris Cool books failed at being a spy series and thus, ultimately, failed at being a boy sleuth series as well.

WORKS CITED

Andrade, Glenna. "Hermione Granger as Girl Sleuth." *Nancy Drew and Her Sister Sleuths: Essays on the Fiction of Girl Detectives.* Eds. Michael G. Cornelius and Melanie E. Gregg. Jefferson, NC: McFarland, 2008, pp. 164–178.
Axe, John. "Christopher Cool TEEN Agent: The Series and Its Cover Art." *Susabella Passengers and Friends.* Jul 2005: 36–43.
Bloom, Clive. "Introduction — The Spy Thriller: A Genre Under Cover?" *Spy Thrillers: From Buchan to le Carré.* Ed. Clive Bloom. New York: St. Martin's Press, 1990, pp. 1–11.
Braziel, Jana Evans, and Kathleen LeBesco. *Bodies Out of Bounds: Fatness and Transgression.* Berkeley: University of California Press, 2001.
Bromberg, Sarah. "Feminist Issues in Prostitution." *Prostitution: On Whores, Hustlers, and Johns.* Ed. James E. Alias, Vern L. Bullough, Veronica Elias, and Gwen Brewer. Buffalo: Prometheus, 1998.
Broude, G. "Protest Masculinity: A Further Look at the Causes and the Concept." *Ethos* 18 (1990): 103–122.
Caprio, Betsy. *Girl Sleuth on the Couch: The Mystery of Nancy Drew.* Trabuco Canyon, CA: Source Books, 1992.
Cawelti, John G., and Bruce A. Rosenberg. *The Spy Story.* Chicago: University of Chicago Press, 1987.
Chapman, James. *License to Thrill: A Cultural History of the James Bond Films.* New York: Columbia University Press, 2000.
Chick, Garry, and John W. Loy. "Making Men of Them: Male Socialization for Warfare and Combative Sports." *World Cultures* 12.1 (2001): 2–17.
Eco, Umberto, and Oreste del Buone. *The Bond Affair.* London: Macdonald, 1966.
Erisman, Fred. *Boys' Books, Boys Dreams, and the Mystique of Flight.* Fort Worth: Texas Christian University Press, 2006.
Fleming, Ian. *Casino Royale.* New York: Signet, 1960.
_____. *Dr. No.* New York: Signet, 1958.
Herz, Peggy. *Nancy Drew and the Hardy Boys.* New York: Scholastic Books, 1977.
Lancer, Jack. *Ace of Shadows.* New York: Grosset & Dunlap, 1968.
_____. *Department of Danger.* New York: Grosset & Dunlap, 1967.
_____. *Heads You Lose.* New York: Grosset & Dunlap, 1968.
_____. *Mission: Moonfire.* New York: Grosset & Dunlap, 1967.
_____. *Trial by Fury.* New York: Grosset & Dunlap, 1969.
_____. *X Marks the Spy.* New York: Grosset & Dunlap, 1967.
Nash, Ilana. *American Sweethearts: Teenage Girls in Twentieth-Century Popular Culture.* Bloomington: Indiana University Press, 2006.
Nye, Russell B. *The Unembarrassed Muse: The Popular Arts in America.* New York: Dial Press, 1970.
Palmer, Jerry. *Thrillers: Genesis and Structure of a Popular Genre.* New York: St. Martin's Press, 1979.
Taliaferro, Charles, and Michel Le Gall. "Bond as Chivalric, Comic Hero." *James Bond and Philosophy: Questions Are Forever.* Eds. Jacob M. Held and James B. South. Chicago: Open Court, 2006, pp. 95–108.

Wade, Jay C., and Chris Brittain-Powell. "Male Reference Group Identity Dependence: Support for Construct Validity." *Sex Roles* 43.5/6 (2000): 323–340.
Woolf, Michael. "Ian Fleming's Enigmas and Variations." *Spy Thrillers: From Buchan to le Carré*. Ed. Clive Bloom. New York: St. Martin's Press, 1990, pp. 86–99.
Zani, Steven. "James Bond and Q: Heidegger's Technology, or 'You're Not a Sportsman, Mr. Bond.'" *James Bond and Philosophy: Questions Are Forever*. Eds. Jacob M. Held and James B. South. Chicago: Open Court, 2006, pp. 173–186.

10
"The Perfect Hero for His Age": Christopher Boone and the Role of Logic in the Boy Detective Narrative

Nicola Allen

It has often been noted that Mark Haddon's novel *The Curious Incident of the Dog in the Night-Time* (2003) gives voice to a previously marginalized perspective in that the narrator and protagonist (Christopher Boone) is a teenage boy living with a high-functioning type of autism known as Asperger's syndrome. The text utilizes typographical innovations such as the insertion of diagrams and the deliberate avoidance of a purely chronological chapter ordering (Christopher prefers prime numbers because "prime numbers are like life. They are very logical but you could never work out the rules" [15]). The novel also references complex mathematical material in order to accurately render Christopher's world for the reader. This results in the text being visually reminiscent of much postmodern textual practice; however, the side-effects of some of the symptoms of Christopher's condition mean that, in many ways, Christopher also forms an example of a traditional hero. Christopher's Asperger's Syndrome manifests itself in an inability to repudiate logic, and this means that he is extraordinarily brave when logic dictates that this is necessary in order to solve a mystery (he overcomes his immense fear of strangers and his phobia of negotiating a route on public transport, for example, in order to get to the truth). His condition also means that Christopher is unable to tell lies. He explains this to the reader:

> A lie is when you say something happened which didn't happen. But there is only ever one thing which happened at a particular time and a particular place. And there are an infinite number of things which didn't

> happen at that time and that place. And if I think about something which didn't happen I start thinking about all the other things which didn't happen [24].

Despite outlining the reason for his inability to tell lies, these undoubtedly "heroic" characteristics work against the text's seemingly postmodern oeuvre, and to some extent, revalidate the traditional male protagonist archetype.

Christopher's heroism eventually pays dividends and he succeeds, not only in solving the mystery of who killed the dog, but also in securing a lasting reconciliation with his estranged mother, proving himself to be capable of much more complex emotional engagement than his parents previously believed. Thus, while it is true that the novel successfully utilizes the marginalized voice of its narrator in order to comment upon the partiality of the traditional detective figure, in giving its protagonist a "happy ending," the book also reinstates a traditional narrative structure. Indeed, Christopher's journeying to his mother's flat forms a contemporary re-telling of a structure outlined by Joseph Campbell in *The Hero with a Thousand Faces*, in which Campbell suggests that "the adventure of the hero normally follows the pattern of [...]: a separation from the world, a penetration to some source of power, and a life enhancing return" (35). Christopher's initial lack of agency in his own narrative and unquestioning belief in his father's lie that his mother is dead, followed by the discovery that he is in possession of superior abilities in math and science and the confidence that he gains from his journey to the address that he finds on a letter from his mother (thus uncovering the "truth" about what happened), certainly fit into the pattern described by Campbell. This chapter suggests that there is then something of a bifurcation of effect in that the text becomes at once seemingly liberating, liberal, and radical, while simultaneously containing elements that remind the reader of the much older, traditional, quest narrative structure.

Haddon's novel, therefore, follows an ancient pattern set by the oldest tales imagined and made archetypal by the success of works such as J. R. R. Tolkien's *Lord of the Rings* trilogy (1954–55), the *Disc World* books (1983–) by Terry Prachett, and J. K. Rowling's Harry Potter series (1997–2007). The key difference lies in the book's protagonist. Christopher is a fifteen-year-old boy living with autism and Savant Syndrome who tries to find out who has killed his neighbor's dog. Christopher has exceptional logical and mathematical reasoning but limited social skills. Early on in the novel, Christopher confides:

> I find people confusing. The first main reason is that they do a lot of talking without using words. The second main reason is that people often talk using metaphors.— He was the apple of her eye [Haddon 8].

This provides the reader with the first of many articulations of what it might be like to experience life as Christopher does. These glimpses into Christopher's world provide some of the more powerful, emotionally charged moments in the narrative. His condition aside, however, Christopher largely fits the profile of a boy detective; in terms of age and background, he is fifteen years old, from a middle class home, and lives with his father. Christopher's middle-class upbringing, and the fact that his father plays a central role in his life, means that he has much in common with numerous earlier boy detectives, from the Hardy boys and Tom Swift to Rick Brant and Encyclopedia Brown. However, unlike many young detectives, Christopher's investigating gets him into trouble, and ultimately the very act of "detective work" has to be undertaken secretly as his father forbids him from seeking out the answers to his mystery.

The book also engages with, rather than simply following the conventions of, traditional detective fiction, and, as such, the text represents a metafictional engagement with the genre. Christopher finds solace in the detective novels of Arthur Conan Doyle and references Sherlock Holmes several times, most movingly when he realizes that his father has lied to him about his mother's death. Christopher explains how Holmes works as a buffer against emotional trauma in such situations: "I thought that I had to be like Sherlock Holmes and I had to detach my mind at will to a remarkable degree so that I did not notice how much it was hurting inside my head" (164). The book's title is also taken from Doyle's short story "Silver Blaze" (1894). For Christopher, the detective figure represents an opportunity for a positive re-reading of his inability to intuit other people's emotions as well as provides him with the opportunity to move beyond the confines of the limited world of home and school. It is because he has a mystery to solve that Christopher forces himself to speak to people outside of his immediate comfort zone: "I don't like talking to strangers. But I'm doing detective work" (Haddon 20). Throughout, he uses Holmes to represent the ultimate positive incarnation of the triumph of reason over emotion; this allows Christopher to reconfigure his social limitations as strengths. When a teacher suggests that Christopher likes math because "it was safe ... it meant solving problems, and these problems were difficult and interesting but there was always a straightforward answer at the end," Christopher suggests that the teacher doesn't really understand numbers (Haddon 81). He uses "The Monty Hall Problem" to explain why in a game show with a prize behind one of three doors, one should always change one's choice of doors once the choice has been narrowed down to two, despite the fact that this seems counterintuitive. He concludes:

> And this shows that intuition can sometimes get things wrong. And intuition is what people use in life to make decisions. But logic can help you work out the right answer. It also shows that Mr. Jeavons was wrong and numbers are sometimes very complicated and not very straightforward at all. And that is why I like The Monty Hall Problem [Haddon 82].

Christopher's desire to prove to the reader the importance of analysis and logic forms one of the ways that the novel leads the reader into Christopher's psyche; yet the detective genre itself forms one of the more significant means by which Haddon gives the reader a sense of how Christopher engages with the world. Christopher explains why the genre is so important to him (and why he has chosen to write a murder mystery himself), thus highlighting the form's unique status as the most "logical" genre within fiction:

> This is a murder mystery novel.
> Siobhan said that I should write something I would want to read myself. Mostly I read books about science and math. I do not like proper novels. In proper novels people say things like, "I am veined with iron, with silver and with streaks of common mud. I cannot contract into the firm fist with which those clench who do not depend on stimulus." What does this mean? I do not know. Nor does Father. Nor does Siobhan or Mr. Jeavons. I have asked them [Haddon 4–5].

Here, Christopher expresses through implication the appeal that the detective genre holds for him. He demonstrates how everyone else that he knows is unable to decipher the quote from the "proper novel;" thus Christopher reveals empirical evidence that his position on "proper" novels is not as solipsistic as it may first appear.

It is evident from his actions, and from what he tells us, that what is of paramount importance to him is reason. There is no intuition, no guesswork, and no hunches in his detection, or, indeed, his life as a whole — only rational calculation. Even Christopher's jokes promote the importance of mathematics and logic:

> And this is the joke. There are three men on a train. One of them is an economist and one of them is a logician and one of them is a mathematician. And they have just crossed the border into Scotland (I don't know why they are going to Scotland) and they see a brown cow standing in a field from the window of the train (and the cow is standing parallel to the train). And the economist says, "Look, the cows in Scotland are brown." And the logician says, "No. There are cows in Scotland of which one at least is brown." And the mathematician says, "No. There is at least one cow in Scotland, of which one side appears to be brown." And it is funny because economists are not real scientists, and because logicians think more clearly, but mathematicians are best [Haddon 69].

In foregrounding Christopher's positive reconfiguration of his own perspective, the novel fulfils one of the central tenets of detective fiction, as Glenna Andrade argues: "Detective fiction has always placed its focus directly on the central investigating figure: the texts are plot driven, but the plots are often formulaic enough to allow the sleuth figure to shine through as the cynosure of the text" (165). Andrade argues that the genre is therefore useful as a device for creating female-centered narratives in which "the tables are turned" and the usually male-centric world of figures such as Sherlock Holmes is replaced by a female perspective, as is the case with female sleuths from Miss Marple to Trixie Belden and beyond. *The Curious Incident of the Dog in the Night-Time* also responds to this element of detective fiction and extends its ability to create a narrative space for previously marginalized or untold perspectives. Christopher, in fact, actively and knowingly responds to the genre's ability to foreground and authorize the central detective figure as a means of creating an identity outside of the limitations of his condition, and yet in doing so the text also resituates the male figure at the center of the genre and instigates a different kind of battle for equality.

Christopher is a figure who, in many ways, shares some of the processes of marginalization that the girl detective faces, and yet the trajectory of his story follows that of the traditional hero (rather than heroine). Thus, although his condition means that his father takes an active, protective role in Christopher's everyday life, and as such, Christopher has to negotiate his way through the very difficult task of convincing those around him to grant him the freedom that other boy detectives might take for granted, Christopher's is essentially a quest narrative that places him within, rather than at odds with, that tradition. Such a text holds immense potential for a reconfiguration of previously marginalized voices. Ruth Gilbert notes that one of the reasons that the novel has enjoyed such popular and critical success is that Christopher's Asperger's Syndrome always positions him at a distance from that which appears "obvious":

> This creates both comic moments (how to understand a raised eyebrow) and emotionally charged scenes (when Christopher rejects his father). Like the alien observer in Craig Raine's poem "A Martian Sends a Postcard Home," Christopher's emotional dislocation means that he can describe the world around him with remarkable and sometimes startling perception [Gilbert 245].

Chana Kronfeld discusses this process of giving voice to marginalized perspectives in her text *On the Margins of Modernism*, when she emphasizes the socially redemptive possibilities of such a strategy and suggests that "writing from a marginal position can — perhaps must — destabilize the norm of the literary and linguistic system by marking the unmarked, charging the neutral, colorizing the colorless, particularizing the universal" (72). This approach to the marginal regards the process of creating and making popular novels that detail the experience of marginality as a political act that can help to counter the prejudices of the mainstream, and by radicalizing the novel form (one which is essentially concerned with ideas), Kronfeld suggests that such novels may ultimately have the effect of allowing people to revise their social and political views, albeit secondarily or tangentially. In one sense the book fulfills this function as it centers a previously marginalized experience, and yet, in other ways, the novel is surprisingly "traditional" in its form. Andrew Stickland hints at this duality within the text, implying that it can be regarded as containing the potential for socially redemptive possibilities while also, in some areas, maintaining stereotypes: "Unfortunately, given the protagonist's affliction, the book may well end up simply reinforcing the stereotype of the mathematically gifted social inadequate" (Stickland).

Stickland raises a pertinent point, and yet his notion that Haddon risks reinforcing "the stereotype of the mathematically gifted social inadequate" can be countered by the fact that Christopher uses his love of science and math as a way of positively rendering himself as central detective figure in his own narrative. His scientific brain is one manifestation of Christopher's Asperger's Syndrome; while the condition does override his emotional response to his mother being hospitalized ("Mother is in the hospital: 'Can we visit her?' I asked, because I like hospitals. I like the uniforms and the machines"), it also lends Christopher his savant abilities (Haddon 20). Christopher's aptitude in the fields of science and math afford his emerging adult masculinity the space to develop (almost) free from the social constraints that would inevitably modify and curtail his reliance on logic, and force him to instead embody a less wholly "masculine" identity. Since Christopher cannot access intuition and empathy and can only process information in a Holmesian logical manner, he is afforded a space in which to explore the uses and limitations of such an approach.

Indeed, Christopher's love of math and science and his distrust of fiction could easily be regarded in gender specific terms, as Sylvia Walby notes: "Education is considered to continue this process [of differentiating gender identities], both in terms of the formal curriculum, since boys and girls usually study different subjects, and in the hidden curriculum, in what they pick up informally.... Boys are more likely to take science and craft subjects" (92). Therefore, when Christopher aligns himself with Holmes as a positive rendition of the opposite of intuition, he also aligns himself with a very "masculine" hero figure.

At many other points in the novel, the symptoms of Christopher's condition also happen to ascribe him a traditionally "masculine" heroic identity, since the qualities that he lacks (empathy, intuition, etc.) are often thought of (however parochially) as traditionally "feminine" qualities. Thus while he differs from boy detectives in terms of his limited freedom, Christopher actively exhibits many of the attributes that a "traditional" hero should have: he is truthful, honest, and brave, and above all he stops at nothing to solve the mystery that he has uncovered. As noted above, these traits mean that Christopher occupies a space that is extremely close to the traditional hero, both the traditional detective hero figure (such as Holmes) and, more broadly, the hero of any conventional quest narrative. It is his condition that means that Christopher can only be truthful, yet he reminds us of the human impulse to regard this as a heroic trait; he says, "I do not tell lies. Mother used to say that this was because I was a good person. But it is not because I am a good person. It is because I can't tell lies" (Haddon 10). Christopher's mother here enacts an inevitable facet of the reader's response to a protagonist who cannot lie, in that she constructs this as a part of her son's heroic appeal, and reminds the reader that to have a protagonist who is so honest, truthful and brave that he forms a very conventionally heroic central character is a rarity in contemporary fiction. Therefore, despite the fact that it is Christopher's condition which causes many of these qualities, his mother reminds the reader just how easy it is to romanticize such a figure.

The reader, however, is made aware that Christopher's reaction to emotions forms an extension of his identification with Holmes. For Holmes, logic and reason triumph over empathy and intuition every time, and reminding the reader of this specific heroic manifestation of these attributes allows Christopher to build a world in which he, too, can triumph. The book actively acknowledges the complexities of Christopher's attempted validation of the Holmes figure, and ultimately the text demonstrates that life without the ability to intuit other people's emotions is fraught with difficulty. In fact, Christopher's "real" journey is one of self-discovery in which he begins to negotiate his way through the difficult world of adult emotions, rather than attempting to avoid them. By the end of the text, Christopher has utilized his hard-won freedom to gain some independence and respect, yet his still largely unchallenged assumption that his parents' marriage failed because of the difficulties of looking after him has not been wholly resolved in his own mind. As such, Christopher hopes that the family unit can be reinstated now that he is more independent: "I used to think that Mother and Father might get divorced. That was because they had lots of arguments and sometimes they hated each other. This was because of the stress of looking after someone who has Behavioral Problems like I have" (Haddon 22).

However, the reader remains aware that there may be other reasons for the breakup, and it is hinted that the problem may lie with Christopher's father's controlling behavior rather than with Christopher:

> When I went to school on Monday, Siobhan asked me why I had a bruise on the side of my face. I said that Father was angry and he had grabbed me so I had hit him and then we had a fight. Siobhan asked whether Father had hit me and I said I didn't know because I got very cross and it made my memory go strange. And then she asked if Father had hit me because he was angry. And I said he didn't hit me, he grabbed me, but he was angry. And Siobhan asked if he grabbed me hard, and I said that he had grabbed me hard. And Siobhan asked if I was frightened about going home, and I said I wasn't [Haddon 43].

The situation that Haddon presents the reader with implicitly reveals the limits of detecting; through his powers of deduction Christopher is able to locate his mother, but he is unable to decipher the complex reasons for his parents' divorce. He cannot understand the emotions he is faced with, nor fully comprehend the reasons for his mother's present poverty, but these are deliberately complex issues which also baffle the adults in Christopher's world. His failure to understand or account for these factors, then, connects rather than distances Christopher, from the other characters, yes, and ultimately, from the reader as well.

Christopher's predicament and his final (partial) triumph over adversity serves as a reminder of just how unnecessary Christopher's marginalized status is. Indeed, Haddon constantly draws parallels between Christopher's experiences and a more general, almost "everyman" experience. As Christopher reminds us,

> everyone has learning difficulties because learning to speak French or understanding relativity is difficult and also everyone has special needs, like Father, who has to carry a little packet of artificial sweetening tablets around with him to put in his coffee to stop him from getting fat ... and none of these people are Special Needs, even if they have special needs [Haddon 64].

It is not so much that the text universalizes Christopher's experience; rather, it highlights how common the perception of marginalization is. This aligns Haddon's position with that of Alan Sinfield, who associates the evocation of the marginal perspective with a growing skepticism concerning the idea that European and North American humanism can lead to a universal culture. He notes:

> At first sight, the "man" of European and north American humanism, in whose name "good" culture was allegedly produced and has usually been read, seems to include everyone; that is why this seemed the culture for welfare capitalism and left culturalism to proclaim. But in practice "man" always has a centre and a boundary. The function of the concept after all is to distinguish man from not man, and this means that someone is marginal and someone gets left out [300].

This reading of the inevitable construct of a cultural center and a margin within fiction reminds us of the efficaciousness of rendering something as central within the novel. Sinfield's very insistence that "someone is marginal" can be read as a counter to the humanist ideal of a universalizing culture that finds a voice is what Malcolm Bradbury terms the "traditional" form of the novel. Moreover, Sinfield identifies in this process of making someone marginal a reduction or effacement of subjectivity, thus implicating such a centralizing "liberal" culture in a dehumanizing process, a denial of rights and agency. Fiction can and has found itself implicated in that process, and it becomes possible that a text can break down some barriers whilst leaving intact, or even partially reinstating, others. Bradbury argues that the prime theme of the novel of manners that forms the benchmark of the "traditional" form of the novel is "the ethical conduct of man in a society relatively stable and secure" (32). The general ethos of such a text would largely substantiate the notion that the social and moral worlds are both rationally definable and contiguous: "It explores dissonances between ethical absolutes or social virtues and the particular individual experience of these and since it ends with a restoration, that replacement of the social norms, the giving back of sons to fathers and lovers to lovers" (Bradbury 32). Thus within Bradbury's concept of a traditional form, although a text may contain moments which challenge the invisible systems that govern dominant ideologies, there is always an element of a return to a recognizable (and therefore ideologically similar) world at the happy resolution of the text.

Haddon's text adheres to the model that Bradbury outlines above, in that it works as an interesting affirmation of a partially (but not wholly) reconstructed patriarchy; the text poses some challenges at the level of ideology but ultimately retains something of the "traditional" novel that Bradbury identifies. Christopher represents a different type of "head of the family" (he is socially awkward because of his autism and is ultimately neither benevolent nor selfish, as his inability to intuit the responses of those around him lead him only to think in terms of logic rather than strategy), yet he successfully comes to represent the renewal of the family unit with himself as the central figure. Christopher concludes his narrative by reminding the reader of his victory with the triumphant lines, "I went to London on my own, and I solved the mystery of who killed Wellington. And I found my mother and I was brave and I wrote a book and that means I can do anything" (268). This ending is suggestive of a more inclusive version of the hero quest narrative.

In re-visiting older narrative forms and evoking the Holmes archetype, Haddon critiques these traditions within detective fiction, but the text also reminds the reader of their usefulness and continued role as a point of identification for Christopher and, therefore, the novel partially revalidates them. Christopher draws upon the strength that identifying with Holmes brings, and despite his autism and the initial refusal of his teachers and parents to see him as a potential rival for control of the family unit, Christopher eventually becomes the commanding force. His final triumph over the other male characters in the novel, and particularly his ability to usurp both his father and Mr. Shears (his mother's new partner) as dominant figures in his mother's life, means that Haddon expands the parameters of patriarchy to depict a more inclusive model but also, interestingly, to some extent reaffirm it, as Christopher's journey very closely follows that of a "traditional" hero.

In the novel, Christopher acts out what Anthony Easthope describes in *What a Man's Gotta Do* as the essential difference between dominant cultural notions of masculinity and the lived masculinities that construct engenders. Easthope suggests that "clearly men do not passively live out the masculine myth imposed by the stories and images of the dominant culture. But neither can they live completely outside the myth, since it pervades the culture" (167). Christopher's journey into solving the crime of the dog "murder" leads him to encounter and negotiate his own way through the different masculinities on offer. Christopher ultimately rejects the models he observes around him (his father, Sherlock Holmes, Mr. Shears, the Reverend Peters), eventually finding his own path, though interestingly doing so through the medium of taking control of the emotional life of his family in a way that supports a positive rendering of a reconfigured patriarchal order that sees him usurp his father and take control of the family unit. In some ways, he is demonstrating Kate Millett's argument in *Sexual Politics*: "Perhaps patriarchy's greatest psychological weapon is simply its universality and longevity ... patriarchy has a [still more] tenacious or powerful hold through its successful habit of passing itself off as nature" (58). For most of the novel, the adults around Christopher attempt to forge a space for him to exist outside of the dominant ideological structures; he attends a "special school" that is supposed to shelter him from the pain and confusion of the outside world, since he is deemed unable to cope with the complexities of it. Yet, of course, there is no escape from dominant ideologies. Ultimately, Christopher still is compelled to act out a modified version of the hero quest and to take his rightful place as male head of the household. Once his father proves himself to be dishonest, and therefore unfit to lead, Christopher has no choice but to step in and take control, not only of his own future, but of his family's as well.

The adults around Christopher allow him limited opportunities to exercise his emerging desire for self-determination, and this means that Christopher both feels the injustice of his father's control and himself rejects this type of authority. Christopher challenges traditional patriarchy, particularly when it seems illogical, eschewing the traditional model of the family unit and deciding to pay someone to look after him: "When I've got a degree in math, or physics, I will be able to get a job and earn lots of money and I will be able to pay someone who can look after me and cook my meals" (58). In asserting that he will instigate a financial reward for his day-to-day care, Christopher distances himself from the patriarchal family model that Walby describes: "The family is considered to benefit capital by providing a cheap way of providing the day-to-day care of workers.... It is cheap because women as housewives do this for no wage ... thus capital benefits from the unequal sexual division of labor within the home" (4). Christopher is made aware of the need to pay someone to look after him when his father has to take over the duties that a mother would more usually perform. This unusual situation and Christopher's awareness that looking after "someone with behavioral problems" might require particular care and attention allows Christopher an insight into the workload that a mother figure would usually undertake within the household, and he articulates the desire for a more fair exchange in return for this labor (22). Christopher's sense of fairness here marks him as a particularly appealing character, and goes some way to allying the reader with Christopher, and, to some extent, against his father. As such, the reader is sympathetic to Christopher's familiar adolescent desire for greater autonomy.

Regardless of his desire for greater freedom, Christopher is not afforded the status of adolescent and is denied the freedom to explore his emerging sense of independence despite taking his A level math exam three years early, doing so (in part) to assert his aptitude: "I am going to prove that I'm not stupid. Next month I'm going to take my A level in math and I'm going to get an A grade" (22). Christopher's perception that he needs to demonstrate his capabilities in order to win back the mother who has deserted the family unit perhaps echoes the dynamic found in girl detective series such as the Trixie Belden series, of which Michael G. Cornelius notes, "The purpose of mystery solving ... is to ensure that familial units function and thrive in the happiest ways possible" (9). Christopher's quest begins to fulfill this function once the real mystery concerning his father's deceit and his mother's whereabouts becomes clear. Unlike his hero, Holmes, who acts for the good of society and keeps law and order, Christopher's quest is much more personal and intimate. Christopher thus enacts a quest to become almost an "alpha male," figure, protecting his emotionally vulnerable mother and ensuring that justice (in the form of truth) prevails.

As Ruth Gilbert notes, the archetypal detective novel constructs a competition between the criminal and the detective "as they both struggle to possess meaning in the narrative. The criminal 'writes' the crime and the detective must 'read' the signs left behind (clues) correctly in order to solve the mystery and restore order" (242). There is another dimension to this story, however, since it is Christopher's father who is revealed to be the "criminal." This means that one of Christopher's most fundamental needs is no longer being met; he no longer feels safe at home in the company of his father (his primary caregiver). Christopher's quest for a narrative is ultimately successful, and although Haddon highlights the limitations of Christopher's reliance on an identification with the figure of Holmes, the detective narrative itself not only forms a point of identification for Christopher, it also allows him a space within which he can construct an identity for himself outside of the limiting label of someone with "special needs." Ultimately it is his engagement with, and search for a place within, the detective genre that allows Christopher the space to "grow" into adolescence, taking more risks and gaining valuable independence as he does. The novel ends on a positive note: Christopher has achieved an "A" grade on his A level math exam and is looking forward to repeating this success in the science subjects next year. This happy ending creates something of a bifurcation of effect, then, in that the text contains elements that suggest that the form has been radicalized while also containing elements that remind the reader of the much older (and in this text, much less challenged) quest narrative structure. In essence, Haddon's novel works to reform (rather than replace) the traditional genre, and it does so from within, demonstrating to the reader how desirable an appropriation of the figure of the hero and a place within those traditions is for his protagonist.

WORKS CITED

Andrade, Glenna. "Hermione Granger as Girl Sleuth." Eds. Michael G. Cornelius and Melanie E. Gregg. *Nancy Drew and Her Sister Sleuths: Essays on the Fiction of Girl Detectives.* Jefferson, NC: McFarland, 2008. 164–179.

Bradbury, Malcolm. *Possibilities: Essays On the State of the Novel.* Oxford: Oxford University Press, 1973.
Campbell, Joseph. *The Hero with a Thousand Faces.* London: Harper Collins, 1993.
Cornelius, Michael G. "Introduction: The Mystery of the 'Moll Dick.'" Eds. Michael G. Cornelius and Melanie E. Gregg. *Nancy Drew and Her Sister Sleuths: Essays on the Fiction of Girl Detectives.* Jefferson, NC: McFarland, 2008. 1–11.
Easthope, Anthony. *What a Man's Gotta Do: The Masculine Myth in Popular Culture.* London: Routledge, 1990.
Gilbert, Ruth. "Watching the Detectives: Mark Haddon's *The Curious Incident of the Dog in the Night-Time* and Kevin Brooks 'Martyn Pig.'" *Children's Literature in Education* 36.3 (Sept. 2005): 241–253.
Haddon, Mark. *The Curious Incident of the Dog in the Night-Time.* London: Vintage, 2003.
Kronfeld, Chana. *On the Margins of Modernism.* Berkeley: The University of California Press, 1996.
Millett, Kate. *Sexual Politics.* New York: Doubleday, 1969.
Sinfield, Alan. *Literature, Politics and Culture in Postwar Britain.* London: Continuum, 1997.
Stickland, Andrew. Review of *The Curious Incident...* 10 November 2003. 25 September 2009 <http://plus.maths.org/issue27/reviews/book4/index.html>.
Walby, Sylvia. *Theorizing Patriarchy.* Hoboken, NJ: Wiley Blackwell, 1990.

11
Has the World Outgrown the Classic Boy Detective?

JOHN FINLAY KERR

Boy detectives have laid down their magnifying glasses, so to speak, in the "putting away of childish things," and are not as popular as they once were. Sleuth youths like Tom Swift, the Hardy boys, the Three Investigators, and Encyclopedia Brown now seem woefully outdated: they are pie-eyed and wholesome and utterly WASP, and their mystery-solving is laced with stereotyping, class-bias and patriarchal values.[1] On the whole, the genre is intended for an earlier era and a less critical generation of young readers. Their do-good attitude seems saccharine today, supplanted in children's literature by increasingly acerbic and morally ambiguous children's books like the Lemony Snicket series. The halcyon days of the archetypal boy-detective, the unabashed summers of his youthful enthusiasm, appear to have passed.

However, not all boy detectives have entirely left the scene. Instead of interrogating the older icons, this essay is an investigation of modern literature and fresh perspectives into the boy sleuth, to show how the boy detective is currently regarded and self-reflexively reinvented. In this, he will be investigated from three directions. Firstly, the figure is discussed as tragically estranged in a modern world, through the character of an autistic boy savant, Christopher Boone, in Mark Haddon's *The Curious Incident of the Dog in the Night-Time*. Secondly, what happens to the classic boy detective when he grows up is interrogated, through the character of Billy Argo in Joe Meno's *The Boy Detective Fails*. Thirdly, how does the classic figure fare when updated, as in the instance of the recent resurgence of the Hardy Boys series. Finally, these tripartite lines of investigation (boy detectives in today's world, boy detectives in adulthood, and modernized boy detectives) allow for a triangulation of the archetype's current position, helping to pinpoint these boy wonders in the present.

Boy Detectives in Today's World

The Curious Incident of the Dog in the Night-time modifies the boy detective archetype radically by depicting a sleuth who is also a sufferer of autism (or more accurately, Asperger's syndrome, as his language is intact; hence the first person narrative). This introspection allows the main character to cast his detached skills of observation over the type of protagonist he consciously embodies: that is, he scrutinizes the boy detective like only a boy detective can — from within (in fact, "autism" comes from the Greek word for self, "autos"). Being a savant gives a real-world rationale for this particular boy detective's exceptional brainpower, his eidetic memory and his knack for lateral thinking. Yet his obsessive, intense skills of deduction are also turned inwards on himself, and is used by Haddon to dissect assumptions of the genre.

Writing a boy detective tale from the perspective of an autistic youth shakes up a narrative that would be highly conventional if it followed a classical order (a crime is discovered, solved, and order restored). However, here the caper takes on elements that are more in common with works by writers such as Dave Eggers and Jonathon Safran Foer, who write innovative, postmodern fictions beyond the cultural turn. *The Curious Incident* employs a nonlinear structure and an unconventional delivery of information, especially in the first few chapters. It emulates Boone's own mental processes of observation and deduction. For example, even the chapter headings are given in prime (rather than consecutive) numbers, restructuring the novel around idiosyncratic ways of thinking. Although initially confusing, once this is explained by the narrator, it becomes perfectly obvious, as answers to puzzles should be. This post-modern mystery case extends this convention onto the codes of composition.

Other highly self-reflexive and unconventional aspects of the book include the textual inclusion of sidelines and inserts, diagrams and figures, appendices and wry footnotes.[2] These are tessellated within the narrative, paradoxically at once both implemental and tangential — that is to say, they are integral precisely *because* they are departures, becoming telling evidence of curiosity and mental subjectivity. Boone's erratic regurgitation of knowledge makes him the real Encyclopedia Brown. The same post-modern deployment of a variorum of additional information — a nonlinear collection of "special features" that are almost hypertextual — is used in *Extremely Loud and Incredibly Close* by Jonathon Safran Foer to delineate the thinking of another odd, unusual boy detective, who is just as monumentally displaced in the post–9/11 world.[3]

The new focus, then, is clearly being put on the boy detective's own ontology: on the inner-workings of his mind, on what drives him, his *raisons d'être*. In Boone's curious case, this fascination is with fictional detectives, leading to an increasingly introverted examination of the genre. Mystery novels are his *idée fixe*, and Boone emulates their protagonists with an autistic obsessiveness. This schema is apparent in his actions, his narration (which is contextualized as a school writing project) and most importantly his responses to the people inside what is known as the "mesosystem" (see Bronfenbrenner): a child's immediate community of home, school, peers and neighbors, who are recast by the wannabe boy detective in the stereotypical roles of suspects, informants, witnesses and associates. Boone overtly models his life around the reassuring constraints of mystery fiction. This results in an astute deconstruction of the genre from within. He is encouraged at school to "write something I would want to read myself," but Boone notes how he also "wanted to write about something real" (5, 6). Like many people with autism, Boone is ill at ease with lies and fabrications (he considers mystery novels to be puzzles — as abstract and hypothetical — and not necessarily as fictions). In many ways, the genre in which Boone is writing actually dictates his own self-development and his investigation into who killed the titular dog.[4]

Although filled with thrilling encounters and baffling mysteries, boy detective stories always remain one step removed from real jeopardy; they feature tame and nominal dangers, the literary equivalent of trained tigers.[5] Their protagonists are helpful and enthusiastic, their moral beliefs never shaken. They never address the social realities of crime or its repercussions. Blows are only ever glancing. Cases generally involve catching thieves, smugglers and spy rings, or if the boys are lucky, finding treasure. Order is immanently restorable, the crimes reversible, the victims duly compensated. The brutality of the poodle skewered on a gardening fork in *The Curious Incident* seems out of place in the world of the boy sleuth, but it is the fulcrum of this new school of searing self-investigation, and triggers the transition into a modern world with higher stakes. Haddon revives the boy detective by making reality all too real for him, such that his busy mind is at a disorientating loss and struggling to comprehend.

Thus, for this genre, *The Curious Incident* is unprecedentedly primal. Being "on the case" leads Boone to uncover his mother's infidelity, his father's violent side (he is the dog-murderer, the culprit, but for sympathetic reasons), and Boone's own guilt at being at the center of all this. The boy detective himself is in this case the cause, and the motive, for violence. For Boone, the wholesome endeavor of playing at "private investigator" turns into something extremely real and incredibly personal. It subverts the traditional narrative justice of boy detective cases (the Hardy boys, for example, would never find that Laura Hardy had an affair, or that their father Fenton was a criminal). Boone's discoveries, like the slaughter, are irrevocable in destroying innocence.

The Curious Incident makes the figure of the boy detective more relevant for modern readers by making him self-conscious and more believable. Boone is a pedantically reliable narrator. As he says, unlike other people, "the pictures in my head are all pictures of things that really happened" (98). Boone is fundamentally predisposed to find lying practically impossible (24). He recalls dialogue and events verbatim, sometimes without fully understanding them. Self-referentially, Boone even lays bare the genre's basic formula: "In a murder mystery novel, someone has to work out who the murderer is and then catch them. It is a puzzle. If it is a good puzzle you can sometimes work out the answer before the end." (5).

To try to make sense of the dog's death, Boone uses all the conventions in the Junior Detective's Kit: drawing up lists of suspects, interviewing them, and searching for clues. More importantly, however, on account of his autism, the real world itself resembles one large mystery for Boone. He already has to scrupulously decipher meaning from everyday life, to make sense of his surroundings and other people's speech and expressions, through "detective work." He carries in his pocket a diagram of smiles and frowns explicitly to decode others' feelings. Although Boone is a highly functioning child, as a sufferer of autism, he needs to work consciously at grasping the "theory of mind" (which comes automatically to most people, and means the ability to recognize the autonomous mental states of others as separate from our own).

Obviously, this is essential to sleuthing: being able to infer other people's states of mind, comprehending their motives, and whether they are guilty or innocent. Boone deals with his problems in understanding others as a puzzle, because "if something is a puzzle there is always a way of solving it" (145). Haddon makes this similar to the classic ontological dilemma of the detective: the difference between what the sleuth knows versus what other participants (witnesses, suspects, victims, and culprit) in the mystery might know, and recognizing that someone involved knows something the detective does not, and thus enquiries must be made. Hence Boone approaches getting to know new people as a sort of private-eye interview, grilling them earnestly for information.

Boone is a natural detective, with his clinical detachment, his compulsion to investigate, his clear-cut sense of right and wrong, and his dogged pursuit of the truth. He has extreme skills of observation and an exceptional memory, and the ability to notice the most seemingly inconsequential of details (which usually contain the most important clues). He quotes his idol, Sir Arthur Conan Doyle's Sherlock Holmes, in saying "the world is full of obvious things which nobody by any chance ever observes" (92).⁶ Boone admires Sherlock's talent of "detaching his mind at will" and his ability to logically put together "strange and apparently disconnected episodes" (92). This mentality resonates with the symptoms of Boone's own childhood developmental disorder. He is meticulously methodical in everyday life — such as when working out a schema for how to catch a train — and refers to this as doing "detecting" (212). He relies on detached, deductive chains of reasoning to make sense of ordinary things, events and interrelationships: "Father looks after me when I get in trouble ... *and* he looks after me by cooking meals for me, *and* he always tells me the truth, *which means* that he loves me" (109, italics mine).

In *The Curious Incident*, the boy detective novel evolves to a level of self-awareness not associated with the traditionally "earnest" genre. Haddon offers an appropriately estranged new perspective on familiar themes. Boone even comments indirectly upon the evolutionary imperative to change, and those three conditions that must be met in order to survive: replication, mutability, and heritability (203). The same might be said of those literary genres that last over time. If so, then *The Curious Incident* clearly replicates and adapts its own genetic/genric lineage in carrying on the heritage of boy detectives.

However, transcoded within this postmodern permutation is the suggestion that to be a boy detective nowadays, to be that complex combination of naïve and highly observant, must be a social and developmental liability. Boone is a disadvantaged pariah, flummoxed by a confusing and unwelcoming world. Haddon makes the position of the junior detective synonymous with autistic aloneness. It is equated with a qualitative impairment or developmental disorder, as if boy detectives have failed to successfully mature or "keep up" with their literary peers and other concurrent derivatives of detective fiction. In doing so, Haddon suggests that, in the current climate, something about the essence of the icon is now thoroughly self-defeating.

The Boy Detective Grows Up

Joe Meno's adult novel *The Boy Detective Fails* further suggests that the precocious private-eye is fundamentally and fatally flawed. The icon matures into a fallible adult, failing to live up to his early crime-solving potential. As an institutionalized man, he investigates the existential mystery surrounding the suicide of his childhood partner in detecting: his own kid sister. His failure is rooted in his complete and utter genius, which is perceived as being a disadvantage in life. Indeed, it is Billy Argo's previously unrivalled success, his overconfidence, that leads to his inevitable downfall. In this, Meno suggests how the boy detective cannot mature, because he is defined by a liminal age — a specific moment of youthful activity — as well as by an earlier cultural era.

In the majority of new children's books, when boys go detecting, it is incidental, and done simply to advance the plot. They are not explicitly boy detective books. While vestiges still remain in say, the Harry Potter series, said character is first and foremost a boy-wizard, and the mysteries that he solves are subordinate to the magic.[7] The fictional figure of the boy detective, and what he embodies — that spirited, self-righteous and patriarchal putting right of lawlessness — has been outmoded. More recent interpretations in the genre (such as *The Dead Boy Detectives* in the *Sandman* comic book series) tend to be more textually savvy and to emphasize "failure studies," the jaded erasure of the presumptuous junior detective. These newer entries in the boy detective genre exhibit innovative cynicism and play textual games. They cannot be as easily ingenuous, so they are instead ingenious. The boy detective is the puzzle now, his existence the mystery.

As part of this ironic decoding of the detective icon, Meno's book includes a cipher ring on the back flap, with parodically cheerful instructions to "✂CUT OUT AND DECODE!✂". It then directs readers to sequences of scrambled letters at the bottom of select pages. Using this cardboard-spinner, the reader may feel like a bit of a prat. It is akin to being a grotesquely overgrown kid, trying to read one's first chapter-book with the help of a dictionary — except in reverse, as the code-breaker is designed to help readers get back into a juvenile frame of mind, of play.[8] It mimics belonging to a boy detective fan-club with a special member's ring and kit. It is embarrassingly fun at first, but grows tiresome. Significantly, this accords with the boy detective becoming predictable and stale. Yet (or maybe even because of this) the encrypted text contains one of the novel's most heartbreaking disclosures, which non-interactive readings would miss.

The ring also permits Meno to put readers through their paces as vicarious boy detectives. Using the tool establishes an immediate identification with the character, making adult Billy more accessible than the squeaky clean wunderkinds. He is invested with contemporary doubts and insecurities (specifically, *The Boy Detective Fails* reacts to post–9/11 anxieties). Marshall McLuhan theorized that inanimate objects can become extensions of peoples' minds, their thought-processes and identities: here, it is the quiddity of the boy detective's toolbox that absorbs conscious attention, the immediate sense of self. Readers temporarily become boy detectives (and old ones at that, estimating the average age as being similar to that of the author and protagonist). This fosters a self-aware empathy with the moribund figure, in how futile and ridiculous it now feels to be "doing boy detective work" at thirty years old.

This is one of many interactive, postmodern touches in *The Boy Detective Fails*. Like *The Curious Incident*, Meno's absurdist work commences with a postmodern use of non-ordinal chapter numbers. It also begins well beyond the end of the boy detective's career (past the point of his effectiveness) with Chapter Thirty-One, entitled "The Mysterious Identity of the Boy Detective," which recaps and satirizes cliché childhood cases. This overview even features a "missing" subchapter that simply says we are "getting ahead of ourselves" and leaves the rest of the page mysteriously blank (16). Later, another absent chapter, in a truly self-referential feat, just apologizes gleefully for its being irreplaceable and stolen, as if the book itself— and by extension the icon — is eroding in the reader's hands.

Meno also rejects Standard English in favor of an innovative use of written language. His writing appears raw and uncorrected — creative and generative — rather than grammatically correct, in order to intercept with deeper and more randomized emotional truths. The text is thoroughly non-normative, which is at odds with the would-be stabilizing force of the detective, who throughout this caper — his existential crisis — is as out of his depth as Alice was in Wonderland. Logic works against him, and equally confounds the reader.

Yet the most radical departure comes in the passage of time and age; this boy detective fails because he has grown up, and is now a "boy, defective." He is fundamentally at odds with his identity. The earlier exploits of Billy and his youthful sidekicks are epitomized in that "all foul riddles, all wild hoaxes, all staged problems were solved quickly, with joy, fondness, and surrender" (15). This bromide perfectly predicts the fatal flaw: that boy detectives triumph over surrendering adults, whom they either foil (criminals) or put to shame (the authorities). So whatever is to become of these prodigies when they become adults, and no longer need fake moustaches and spirit gum from their kits? What happens to them when they outlive their usefulness and their cultural appeal?

Their defining achievements in childhood are thus self-defeating; the character is doomed from the start. They have been pitched prematurely against the adult world, which — in a symbolic inversion of the child's nursery — they have power over to admonish and correct. Boys can tell off adults, and show how comprehensively they know the rules. Meno follows this through to its conclusion: that this condemnation must turn inward when they become one of the adult population themselves (and either a criminal or a failure). Their whole world goes wrong: their status quo is upended, overturning their innate, childish prerogative to administer discipline and reproach. As an aged-boy detective, Billy cannot deal with the uncontrollable adult world. Transversely, Boone is automatically stuck as a boy detective precisely *because* he is lost in this modern world (and must, to his detriment, still rely on detecting to get by).

Yet it is more than just a matter of age, of youth versus experience (although this does apply to the genre and its aging readerships). If it were mere chronology, boy detective tales would be revitalized by the next wave, by a new generation of kids. As it is, the most notable new boy detective characters are in adult fiction and adult-orientated pop (i.e., ironic) culture, like the Adult Swim animated series *The Venture Bros*. No, the waning popularity of the boy detective, his metaphorical loss of purpose, is just as much due to world-changing events and to cultural climates of insecurity.

Accordingly, in *The Boy Detective Fails*, buildings disappear without warning. The cityscape is unsafe, unprotected. As Meno describes: "We live in a town that is disappearing, and worse, like the buildings, our hope is gone and we are no longer surprised by anything" (35). The anxiety and neuroticism of new boy detectives is symptomatic of a general malaise, in response to the grim realities of modern life and of paranoia. In both *The Curious Incident* and *The Boy Detective Fails*, the world is depicted as being an unwelcoming and frightening place, which their trumpeted childhoods (and by extension, the genre's innocent origins)[9] leave them ill-equipped to face. As a victim in *The Boy Detective Fails* ponders, "she already knew ... she was at the whim of the general disorder and unimaginative meanness of the world around her" (46).

The simple restoring of order ("so easy," one might say, that "a child can do it"), that sense of closure that boy detectives can offer up on a platter when they solve a crime, now appears trite and out-of-keeping.[10] Narrative justice is no longer settled by just working out who the culprit is; crimes remain irreversible. As with the dead dog in Haddon's novel, Meno's book involves shock violence against animals: unusually graphic and unconventionally cruel (by comparison, the traditional crimes in the genre are pragmatic and goal-oriented, such as theft, ransom or smuggling). In both animal cases, the boy detective is forced to confront violence for its own sake: meaningless and indecipherable. The most plausible answer as to why these things happened is that it is an unkind world; thus, the boy detective becomes nihilistic instead of self-righteous.

Both stories start with animal cruelty as a sort of sacrificial opening to putting the boy detective himself on the autopsy slab. Importantly, the deaths are the loss of loved pets, as if signalling the end of childhood innocence. The titular "curious incident" is a transition of sorts into adulthood; after solving this case, Boone abandons the boy detective vocation to become a mathematician at a university. Billy is not so lucky. After hospitalization in his teens, he doggedly investigates his sister's death. His first new case, however, is the beheading of a schoolgirl's pet rabbit. The girl is a pariah and suspicion falls on her hateful classmates. It is the "tall poppy syndrome," it seems, which makes the boy detective (a pariah himself) treat other people with suspicion.[11]

However, it is not only a world of hateful people, a Hamlet-like "sea of troubles" that signals the demise — or at least the disabling — of the boy detective. Instead, it is something implicit to crime solving that backfires against him: specifically, the unavoidable committing of errors. As Billy teaches his rabbit-less client, sleuthing works on the logical assumption that people make mistakes, which then obviously become clues. He says:

> The only thing all men have in common ... is their inherent capacity to make mistakes. We will always fall short. We will always fail at our grand schemes; we can trust that there will always be a clue or a fingerprint or some sign. That is what we must now find [82].

This regression towards slip-ups is presented as a certainty, the movement towards chaos, towards the uncontrollable (which is what *crime* is): the descent into disorder. Paradoxically, it is *also* the basis for restoring order in the genre (because things ultimately go awry for the criminals; they slip-up), but it is founded upon a fallacy. Billy, as an upholder of the law, clings to this one security in an uncertain world (that eventually people make mistakes) without realizing the irony that if they keep going long enough, boy detectives, too, will come to make mistakes, just like the very villains they face.

Thus, their self-righteousness has a limited shelf-life, a liminal age — that is, it lasts until they know better. In *The Curious Incident*, Boone touches upon this briefly in one of his tangents about chaos theory and games of chance. It may seem insignificant, a random interjection about systemic decay, but it is actually a shrewd and relevant observation, as given enough trials and time, it is unlikely the boy detective will remain unblemished, or perpetually infallible.

The double-bind of the boy detective, then, is that his fresh-faced innocence cannot last forever. Eventually he has to grow up and face disillusionment in himself. The same demoralizing might be said of the genre, which turns to cynicism and self-mockery as it gains increasing textual knowingness. In *The Boy Detective Fails*, Billy struggles ineffectively to continue his childhood successes after the death of his sister Caroline. It is as if one of the classic Bobbsey Twins were to be murdered (certainly this is what Meno plays upon). Given that siblings in such pairs are each a reflection of the other, the death is a psychic annihilation that effectively disintegrates the boy detective's self. Again, like *The Curious Incident*, the murderer is (in part) himself, although unwittingly — which almost makes it worse, a detective so flawed as to not detect his own involvement. Even more tragic, this crime is a suicide, impossible to mend. Not that this stops Billy from trying: "The moment he found out, the boy detective began to reconstruct the crime scene in miniature, determined to prove that his sister Caroline was the murder victim of some masterfully plotted and nefarious revenge scheme" (25).

Curiosity here does not solve his identity crisis; it only exacerbates it. Even in his thirties, Billy is referred to as "the boy detective" more often than by his name. A constant contradiction in terms, he cancels himself out. The role of the boy detective, the position that defined him and in which Billy's personal worth was formerly invested, turns against his psyche like a mental illness. Indeed, Billy suffers major depressive and obsessive compulsive disorders. Meno not only links this to being an overly intelligent child ("This is what a boy detective does: he is always counting, estimating, recording. He cannot stop") but also as the ultimate, unsolvable crime that a boy detective will face, as it is "perpetrated within the shady, secret underworld of Billy's mind" (47, 43).

Billy's story is not dissimilar to the fate and current state of the boy detective icon in modern culture as "moribund." Billy is unsparing in his angst, but this reflects on the contemporary condition of the genre: the solipsistic, introspective cases of this new century tend towards self-aware angst. The new perspectives on the boy detective are acidly tongue-in-cheek: "postmodern postmortems," investigating and dissecting the character as a type, and as culturally moribund. They seem to be investigations into the cultural cause of death for classic boy detectives, the self-destruction of the icon.

While *The Curious Incident* and *The Boy Detective Fails* are cases in which this is especially salient and overt, they are not isolated instances. The close analysis presented here of these two texts comes about because are they are interesting in themselves and in relation to the entire genre simultaneously. Also, they represent the two main "temporal rifts" encountered in updating the boy detective: that is, one primarily addresses a shift to the modern world (*The Curious Incident*) and the other the issues facing a grownup boy detective (*The Boy Detective Fails*). However, there are many notable others.

Consider, for example, the film *Brick* (2005), in which the boy detective is hardened into the film noir private-eye, transposing and merging both into the drug culture of a contemporary California high-school. Even Batman's sidekick Robin the Boy Wonder — that superhero of boy detectives — has since 1984 evolved into the more mature (and slightly jaded) crime fighter Nightwing, who is uncomfortable with his past as Batman's protégé (and subsequent Robins have either died, been replaced, or become villains like the murderous antihero Redhood, or even a genetic reincarnation of Batman's main nemesis, the Joker, in the DVD *Batman of the Future: Return of the Joker* [2000]). It seems that some form of estrangement is increasingly necessary in handling the iconic status of the boy detective now; otherwise they are hard to take seriously. *The Boy Detective Fails* may (somewhat sadistically) put the archetype through electroshock therapy, but at the same time, it tries to resuscitate him.

The archetype is also often played with and parodied in popular culture. The adult cartoon series *The Venture Bros.* features not only the titular sweater-vested spoofs of the Hardy Boys, but also a grown-up boy detective (Billy Quiz Boy) who is really just a diminutive man with an enlarged head. While attempting to prolong his reputation indefinitely, Quiz Boy is a walking punch-line. The character is perhaps a cautionary example for the titular youngsters Dean and Hank Venture, who are already ridiculous with their irritating "gosh darn it" swearing and do-good attitude (often cheering their annoying catchphrase: "Go team Venture!").[12] The comedy stems from putting the duo in situations where their outmoded inquisitiveness and innocent principles are painful to watch. To modern tastes, the boy detective appears as a ready-made, pre-packaged joke.

The Secret Files of the Diogenes Club, a collection of short stories by the author and academic Kim Newman, also features a physically distorted and emotionally stunted "man-as-boy" detective (an exact opposite of the boy-acting-as-adult, as if becoming the imago inverts the archetype).[13] Except unlike the genial Billy Quiz Boy of *The Venture Bros.*, Newman's invention Clever Dick is a super-villain. First described as a lisping child sleuth holding "a magnifying glass the size of a lollipop" (155), Dick is exposed as a brat *and* an accomplice to murder. Significantly, Dick is on the verge of puberty (his villainous scars as an adult are the result of adolescent acne). Disgraced, he resurfaces in another short story as a power-crazed, cryogenic-obsessed scientist with an inferiority complex. Dick's mania for cryogenic suspension is an apposite metaphor for the frustrations and fallibility facing a boy detective who has to eventually grow up. Here, the twisted boy detective is redescribed as now of "pensionable age, but ... frozen inside ... still eleven, and poisonous" (244).

Evidently, the consensus is that the boy detective cannot be kept in immaculate stasis.[14] He changes, or the world around him does. Neither is conducive to the continued spotless appearance of the boy detective. Appearances of jaded, aged, parodied or hilariously outdated boy detectives in the key texts and a collection including *Brick*, *Batman* and *The Venture Bros.* demonstrate the various ways in which the disjuncture of changing times can go horribly wrong for the archetype.

The Rebooted Boy Detective

There is, however, a third option to relocating boy detectives into the modern world and confronting them with "culture shock," or featuring the boy detective as an adult who is now a "passé prodigy." This third possibility can actually hold fast to the old-fashioned conceits of the genre, with no (or minimal) arch self-consciousness in the text. Instead, the figure of the boy detective and the format of the fiction as well are renovated and updated, bringing both into the twenty-first century. These are the texts that branch out into newer media forms where their simple restoration of order can still appear original, such as the recent revivals of the Hardy Boys series in techno-savvy books, comics, and computer games. Examples include the reality TV-show themed mystery Hardy Boys (*Brothers Undercover*) *Deprivation House* (2008), the trendy Japanese-style comic books, and the multimedia narratives of Hardy Boys computer and touch-screen console games, all of which incorporate new fads and technologies.

Deprivation House, one of over twenty books in the relaunched Hardy Boys series, is particularly mentionable for involving the *Big Brother* television phenomenon, which was nonexistent during earlier runs. The mystery is basically "Boy Detectives versus Reality Television," a clash that revitalizes the classic Hardy Boys adventures while pointing out the disparity between entertainment cultures then and now. Much of their detective work in this case is to discern artifice from reality (such as in the prologue, set in a conventional "haunted" amusement park) and involves their abilities to read and interpret entertainment content. *Deprivation House* makes several references to an increased new media literacy, and to the teaching of critical viewing in schools. As Frank (the more uptight, older and traditional of the brothers) says to Joe:

> "Have you ever considered the possibility that you watch too much TV?"...
>
> "Have you ever considered the possibility that you don't watch enough?" Joe shot back. "You don't even know who Ripley Lansing is — and she's the center of our case" [12].

Thus, the Hardy Boys encounter the cult of celebrity and the real-time mystery of which television contestant will win. As in Ben Elton's *Dead Famous*, the show is a closed-room mystery with a twist. In the Hardy Boy's adventure, the house is peopled with bloggers and thinly-disguised celebrities (akin to Paris Hilton) mingling with the undercover detectives, who are there to foil a death threat. The elimination challenge is centered on the idea of spoiled youths living in a Beverly Hills mansion, where they lose a modern luxury every day. This provides a contemporary cultural context for the basic egotism and arrogance of the boy detectives (while simultaneously complicating their secret mission, as everything is recorded live on multiple television cameras).

Like other narratives in this revived series, *Deprivation House* employs multiple perspectives, basically channel changing between Joe and Frank, the split storytelling making for a punchier narrative. Each brother is identified at the start of the chapter by a silhouette, which is taken from the photographic cover in an attempt to make the pair more than just "sibling ciphers," and give them more personality within the limits of the writing. However, much as the new authors try to stay true to the original characters, the series still buys into the modern take of boy detectives as maladaptive. For example, Joe describes Frank as "compulsively organized. I'm talking compulsive as a psychiatric disorder" (7).

In addition to the popular culture references in the reality television premise, these revived boy detectives of years ago name drop everything from *Life of Pi* to YouTube in trying to attract young, modern readers and convince them of their continued relevance. The books still feature their father Fenton Hardy, their semi-absent mother and disapproving Aunt Trudy (formerly Aunt Gertrude), yet also fold in references to the present day and popular culture. The brothers now exist in a world of iPods and EpiPens. Joe refers to his detective's intuition as his "Spidey sense," effectively extemporizing on the superpowers of the comic book hero Spiderman (76). This persists into the new comic books, too, which are perhaps more simpatico and in tune with what is popular today.

The Hardy Boys comics (beginning in 2005) are presented as the *new* adventures of a *vintage* crime-solving duo. Joe and Frank are now equipped with the latest gadgets. This stance is almost double-jointed; appealing at once to the legacy of Edward Stratemeyer's characters while also rebooting them, playing to both the past and the cutting-edge. The blurb promises the Hardy Boys "as you've never seen 'em;" a paradox given the comic book's appeal is based on their instant recognizability, their iconic status, as well as on their apparently contradictory modernization, in effect pitching both ways simultaneously. In a depiction of the medium truly equalling the message, the comics are even being delivered to readers by mobile phone technology (Powers 2008).

Yet this unprecedented way of seeing the boys is not just in the techno-savvy updating. Visually, these comics are presented in an American version of manga (a Japanese style of cartoon drawing that has become increasingly popular in Western culture since the late twentieth century). This modern cross-pollination includes a visual grammar that is decidedly a conglomeration of American and Japanese styles: reading as American comics do (panels left-to-right) but using the Japanese iconography for actions and emotions. Thus, the alteration to the boy detective is not only in content but in the very form (and the choices made within that form), offering a more modern and globalized feeling to the book, while also avoiding some of the attendant problems of cultural claustrophobia levelled against the original series by looking farther afield, and internationally, for inspiration. Comics commentator Scott McCloud suggests that the more stylized or "cartoony" human faces are in comics, the more readily that readers might relate to them and identify with those characters (36). This effect could mean this manga approach makes the Hardys more accessible (counter to the characteristic aloofness of the boy detective seen in so much fiction nowadays).[15]

The new Hardy boys can use digital photos, PDAs, eBay and search engines (the comic panels that indicate scene changes even mimic Google Earth maps). Clearly, the brothers have adapted to technologies that would otherwise make the boy sleuths redundant. They have been turned into whiz-kids, part of the next generation, instead of adhering mulishly to the past. When Joe asks Frank how he knew how to hotwire a motorbike, his brother responds that "the internet is a wondrous place," showing their newfound skills are self-contingent — using technology teaches them how to use other technologies (7). They are being acclimatized. Why use a magnifying glass when one can scan and enlarge electronically?

The comics and new book series each make references to computer games, and it is fitting that the Hardy Boys have recently (2008) made their debut in playable media, which is the entertainment of choice for much of the youth market. Through games, the boy detectives' fictional world is being brought back to life as interactive simulations. As Frank says to Joe in the manga:

> Amazing, isn't it ... how a videogame can engage the mind — stimulate your imagination ... it's like it can bring you to a whole other world, a different reality right here in your own living room. What other medium can do that? [15].

Happily reading a book in the next panel, Joe shoots the reader a knowing look, and yet detective work is in fact in perfect sympathy with the ideals of exploring and investigating inherent to games and their narrative's dynamics. Indeed, playing on this affinity, in the *Brothers Undercover* novels, the junior sleuths receive their mission briefings on ersatz game cartridges. The medium of computer games opens up fresh possibilities for boy detectives, and gives them (and their followers) new worlds to explore in a mode that is unusually simpatico with their old-fashioned snooping.

The match seems felicitous — wiring a new connection between boy detectives and a youth market obsessed with digital media. Unfortunately, the Hardy Boys have so far failed in digital outings, with the first game being released (Hardy Boys: *The Hidden Theft* [2008]) receiving mostly negative buzz. Yet while *The Hidden Theft* is clumsy and poorly realized (and frustrated gamers with its slow, clunky and cumbersome PC interface), in theory, a boy detective mystery suits game play as *investigation*. Perhaps more than any other medium, computer games could conceivably change the method of transmission while leaving the archetype relatively intact. The whodunit element is effectively retooled; and indeed, *Hidden Theft* is being rejigged for the distinctive Wii console, with its more intuitive and bodily movement-based means of interaction. The product details for an upcoming second game (for Nintendo DS) entitled *Treasure on the Tracks* (2009) promises players will be actively involved with searching for clues and exploring environments, interacting with characters through dialogue options, as well as solving interactive puzzles as they control the Hardy boys to crack the case.

Again, this is another push for fostering — in any manner possible — an increased identification with boy detectives, before the gap gets too wide.[16] Through games, fans finally get to "play the part." In a metatextual sense, when the Hardy boys use computer interfaces and cell phones in-game, the players are vicariously using the technology within the game themselves. It is the players who search for the clues, who "interrogate" the suspects, who "solve and discover," in the guise of the boy detective. The flipside is that the boy detectives are along for the ride like empty avatars. Indeed, one of the major failings of first game is that the boy detectives appear lifeless. They are, on Freud's continuum of the uncanny, too corpse-like. Perhaps the failure to revive the boy detective through seemingly ideal interactive means could turn out to be the final nail in their coffins, confirming their demise.

Culturally, what do all these revenants and resurrections of the traditional boy detectives mean — from the troubled Boone and the depressive, disenfranchised Argo to the reanimation of the Hardy Boys franchise? Arguably, they demonstrate there are no boy detectives *in excelsis* left, no glorified representation of them that is as carefree and wonderful as the boys were once presupposed to be. The modern equivalents are apologetic and world-weary boy sleuths, stuck in indifferent and dislocating settings. Even the pluckiest have an aura of fatalism about them, of frustrations, self-conscious to the end of their own obsolescence. Yet why are there so many of these last ditch efforts to revive boy detectives then, to shift them into more current surroundings, if the only avenues available are through cynicism, or desperate attempts to reenergize them with technology? Do they fill a need, perhaps a different one than they originally met, a modern need for nostalgia? Alternatively, is it their culturally-induced "camp" value, something that makes them appeal to more adult perspectives? Or is it not any single reason, but a complex interaction between these factors? Maybe it is a mystery that stumps the boy detective in everyone; perhaps it would defy even the best of their kind to deduce the appeal. Yet clues, scattered around the cultural field like grisly remains, all add up. Has the world grown too old for boy detectives? Undoubtedly—yet secretly, we still want them back.

Notes

1. One of the defining tropes of the genre is its determinedly platonic justice (everyone is put in their place, and there is a satisfying reaffirming of hierarchy). They are usually ideologically reactionary. Of course, less than innocent subtexts have been scribed in the Stratemeyer series (see Michael Bronski's article "Nancy Boy") but these aspects were quite subliminal, if not unintentional; complaints leveled against "series books" at the time usually concentrated on their formulaic writing and perceived lack of quality (see Greenwald).

2. Features that are also seen in the innovative works of Eggers and Safran Foer.

3. Safran Foer's young protagonist acts as a stand-in detective, trying to restore sense to a damaged world.

4. The interplay here cannot be overstated: Boone is applying the rules of boy detective fiction, making him a meta-boy detective who ends up investigating the boy detective icon from the inside, because of his own introversion and his obsession with the archetype (and in doing this, he is being a detective.)

5. Of course, reviewers at the time would disagree! Franklin K. Mathiews, librarian to the Boy Scouts, advised in 1914 that the detrimental influence of boys' series books was "simply incalculable. I wish I could label each one of these books: 'Explosives! Guaranteed to Blow Your Boy's Brains Out'" (Mathiews, cited in Rehak 97).

6. This emulation of an adult is not out of character; boy detectives have modeled themselves on adult ones before (for example, the Hardy boys follow their father, and later their mysterious mentor, the special agent Arthur E. Gray). What is different here is that Christopher Boone reveres—and is self-referential about—an older predecessor in literature, who is his antecedent in more reflexive ways.

7. Magic, of course, is antithetical to mystery-solving, as it runs on the notion of wonder; a magician never reveals his tricks, while a detective cannot wait to spill the beans to everyone, preferably in a crowded room.

8. The reader has to keep "looking" the words up, and they are unfamiliar and dyslexic in appearance, perhaps reminding grownup readers of when reading was difficult, and each word had to be apprised of its meaning.

9. In such dashing, rip-roaring fare as R.L. Stevenson's *Treasure Island* (1883) and *Kidnapped* (1886), and J. M Falkner's smuggler's tale *Moonfleet* (1898), all of which spotlight inquisitive boy heroes, vibrant prototypes of the junior detective. The figure of the boy detective only becomes increasingly simplified and sanitized in American fiction of the early and middle twentieth century. In fact, *Moonfleet* (which departs from the Gothic novel in its focus on juvenile readers) presents perhaps one of deepest and complete characterizations of a boy sleuth, well before the regression to a "type."

10. Conceivably, this is influenced by — and a commentary upon — operating in a post 9/11 landscape.

11. It has been pointed out that this referent may be culturally specific; in New Zealand, it is a common term used to refer to the phenomenon — particularly in schools — of the resentment and cutting down of high achievers by their peers.

12. The Venture Bros. also have their own literary role model: *Giant Detective Boy*, an appropriately titled exaggeration of the stereotype, who features as a fictional character (and role model) within the show.

13. Readers may recognize the club from Conan Doyle's Sherlock Holmes stories.

14. When he *is* kept in stasis (like Kim Newman's Clever Dick) it backfires; stagnancy is still change.

15. *The Dead Boy Detectives* comics are also being given this treatment in a series of manga digests by Jill Thompson, which illustrates the modern appeal of this approach.

16. It is interesting that the Nancy Drew computer games from the same company (JoWooD and The Adventure Company), which are in the first-person, are far more successful (perhaps due to a closer, more seamless interactive identification, as she remains invisible during game play, allowing for a greater subjective transference).

WORKS CITED

Brick. Dir. Rian Johnson. Perf. Joseph Gordon-Levitt. Focus Features, 2006.
Bronfenbrenner, Urie. *The Ecology of Human Development*. Cambridge, MA: Harvard University Press, 1979.
Bronski, Michael. "Nancy Boy." *The Boston Phoenix*. 13 June 2002. Accessed 15 May 2009. <http://www.bostonphoenix.com/boston/news_features/other_stories/documents/02309513.htm>.
Dixon, Franklin W. *Hardy Boys Undercover Brothers: Deprivation House*. New York, NY: Aladdin Paperbacks, 2008.
Gaiman, Neil (creator), Ed Brubaker (writer) and Bryan Talbot (penciller). *Sandman Presents: Dead Boy Detectives*. New York: DC Comics/Vertigo, 2001.
Gaiman, Neil (creator), Jill Thompson (writer and penciller). *The Dead Boy Detectives*. New York: DC Comics/Vertigo, 2005.
Greenwald, Marilyn. "The Newspaper Reporter as Fiction Writer: The Tale of 'Franklin W. Dixon.'" *Proceedings of the 86th Annual Meeting of the Association for Education in Journalism and Mass Communication*. Kansas City: History Division, 2003.
Haddon, Mark. *The Curious Incident of the Dog in the Night-Time*. London: Random House Children's Books, 2003.
Lobdell, Scott (writer), and Lea Hernandez (penciller). *The Ocean of Osyria (Hardy Boys Graphic Novels: Undercover Brothers #1)*. New York: Papercutz, 2005.
McCloud, Scott. *Understanding Comics: The Invisible Art*. Northampton, MA: Kitchen Sink Press, 1993.
Meno, Joe. *The Boy Detective Fails*. Chicago: Punk Planet Books, 2006.
Newman, Kim. *The Secret Files of the Diogenes Club*. Austin: MonkeyBrain Books, 2007.
Powers, Kevin. "Nancy Drew and Hardy Boys on your Cell Phone." *Comics Bulletin* 24 (June

2008). Accessed 15 May 2009 <http://www.comicsbulletin.com/news/121436180863541.htm>.

Rehak, Melanie. *Girl Sleuth: Nancy Drew and the Women Who Created Her*. Orlando: Harcourt, 2005.

Safran Foer, Jonathon. *Extremely Loud and Incredibly Close*. London: Penguin Books, 2005.

The Venture Bros. Jackson Public (creator). Adult Swim/Cartoon Network. 2003.

About the Contributors

Nicola Allen has taught courses on contemporary British fiction, modernism and post–World War II fiction and film at Birmingham City University for several years as well as modules on feminism and creative writing at Northampton University. Nicola gained her Ph.D. in 2007 with her dissertation on post–1975 British fiction, and has since published *Marginality in the Contemporary British Novel* (Continuum, 2008). She has also written on "The Lapsarian World and Social Class" for *Critical Perspectives on Philip Pullman's* His Dark Materials (forthcoming, McFarland), and co-written with David Simmons "'Biting the Hand That Feeds You': *Survivor* (2000) and *Haunted* (2005) as Critiques of 'The Culture Industry'" for *Reading Chuck Palahniuk: Monsters, Mayhem and Metafiction* (Routledge, 2009). Nicola is currently co-editing a collection for Rodopi on twentieth century canonical British and American texts.

Charlotte Beyer is senior lecturer in English studies at the University of Gloucestershire, England. She has published several articles on Margaret Atwood's fiction and poetry, and her recent and forthcoming publications reflect both her long-standing interest in crime fiction and her interest in "crossover" writings using different genres and forms, such as life writing, autobiographical texts, and literary journalism. They include a book chapter and a forthcoming article on Willa Cather's journalism and a forthcoming article on Doris Pilkington's *Rabbit-Proof Fence* in a teaching context. She is currently writing on crime fiction.

Elizabeth D. Blum is an associate professor of history at Troy University in Troy, Alabama. She received her B.A. from the University of Texas, and her M.A. and Ph.D. in history from the University of Houston. Her first book, *Love Canal Revisited: Race, Class, and Gender in Environmental Activism*, was published by the University Press of Kansas in 2008. She is currently researching changes in environmental values presented to children in popular culture sources through the twentieth century.

Michael G. Cornelius is chair of the Department of English and Mass Communications at Wilson College in Chambersburg, Pennsylvania. He is the author/editor of nine books, including, with Melanie E. Gregg, *Nancy Drew and Company: Essays on the Fiction of Girl Sleuths* (McFarland, 2008), for which he wrote an article on technology and masculinity in Nancy Drew as well as the critical introduction. He has published extensively on girl sleuths and other subjects.

Fred Erisman is Lorraine Sherley Professor of Literature Emeritus at Texas Christian University in Fort Worth. A specialist in American popular literature with a particular interest in the social history of aviation, he held the Charles A. Lindbergh Chair of Aerospace History at the National Air and Space Museum, Smithsonian Institution in 2002–2003. He is the author of *Boys' Books, Boys' Dreams, and the Mystique of Flight* (TCU Press, 2006) and *From Birdwomen to Skygirls: American Girls' Aviation Stories* (TCU Press, 2009), as well as numerous articles on series books, science fiction, and detective and suspense fiction.

C.M. Gill earned a B.A. in psychology from the University of Texas at Austin and a master's degree in English from Texas State University in San Marcos, Texas. She currently teaches at Texas State University and Austin Community College and has published in *Texas Books in Review* and *Style: A Quarterly Journal of Aesthetics, Criticism, Poetics, and Stylistics*.

John Finlay Kerr is currently a Ph.D. student at the Australian National University and a graduate of Victoria University of Wellington, New Zealand. He writes and teaches on a variety of topics in literature studies, film and popular culture. In addition to his fiction, John has written for *Screen Education, Film-Philosophy, Screening the Past* and *Transformative Works and Cultures*. His main areas of research are fictions from the Victorian era onwards, spanning print, film and playable media.

H. Alan Pickrell is an Emory & Henry College professor emeritus of speech/theatre. His B.A. degree is from Belmont College, and he holds an M.A.T. from Vanderbilt University. He has done additional study at the RSC via Wroxton College, a British extension of Farleigh-Dickinson University, the University of North Carolina at Chapel Hill, and the University of Georgia. A past chair of the Dime Novel, Pulp, Series Book division of the Popular Culture Conference, he has written numbers of articles for *Yellowback Library, Newsboy*, and *Dime Novel Round-up*. He has contributed to several books about series literature, including *Nancy Drew and Her Sister Sleuths* (McFarland, 2008). Two of his major literary interests are the works of L. Frank Baum and the Allan Quatermain novels of H. Rider Haggard.

Christopher Schaberg is an assistant professor of English at Loyola University New Orleans, where he teaches courses on contemporary literature and critical theory. His article "Bird Citing: On the Aesthetics and Techno-Poetics of Flight" was recently published in the multidisciplinary journal *Nebula*, and he is currently working on a book about the culture of U.S. airports. Schaberg writes about literature and new media on his public blog "What Is Literature?"

Larry T. Shillock is an associate professor of English and an assistant academic dean at Wilson College in Chambersburg, Pennsylvania. His research interests include critical theory, the history of affect, the modern novel, and classical Hollywood cinema. He is a frequent writer for *The Bloomsbury Review*.

Brian Taves (Ph.D., University of Southern California) has been a film and television archivist with the Library of Congress for twenty years and won the Library's second Kluge Staff Fellowship, 2002–2003. He is the author of more than 100 articles and

25 chapters in anthologies, has edited three books and authored five more, most recently *Talbot Mundy, Philosopher of Adventure* (2005) and *P.G. Wodehouse and Hollywood* (2006), both from McFarland. He is a well-known authority on Jules Verne, particularly with his influential *The Jules Verne Encyclopedia* (Scarecrow, 1996). He is also writing a book on the film and television adaptations of Verne from around the world and a biography of silent-era movie pioneer Thomas Ince.

Index

ABC television network 63, 70, 72
Ace of Shadows (Christopher Cool) 148
Adams, Harriet Stratemeyer 72, 74
Adelia Applegate 26, 34
Adventures of Huckleberry Finn 137
Air Trails 118
Alex Upgrove 41
Alfred Hitchcock and the Three Investigators (series) *see* The Three Investigators (series)
Alger, Horatio 7, 139
Allen "Biff" Hooper 40, 58, 70, 80
al-Qaeda 52
American International Pictures 74
Ames, Florenz 64
And Then There Were None 83
Anderson, Richard 69
Andrade, Glenna 144, 171
Andress, Ursula 160
Andrews, Edward 70
Androgyno 4
Andy Blake 136
Appleton, Victor (pseudonym) 90, 100
Archie Goodwin 139
Aronson, Amy 44
Arthur, Robert 133, 136, 137, 141
Arthur E. Gray 195
The Assassins 52
Aston Martin 152
The Atkinson News 109, 112–115
Atterbury, Malcolm 70
Atwater, Edith 73
Aunt Jane's Nieces (series) 43
Axe, John 7, 144, 148
Axelrad, Nancy 70, 72

Baer, John 67
Barmet Bay 66
Barthes, Roland 33
Barton Swift 90, 91, 94, 96, 97
Batman 109, 113, 190. 191
Batman (1966–68 television series) 68

Batman of the Future: Return of the Joker 190
Bayport 21, 26, 31, 49, 57, 59, 66, 68, 69, 73–75, 78, 81
BBS Productions 83
Beauregard Tatum 155
Benjamin Franklin Pierce 2
Berry, Halle 160
Bess Marvin 40–42, 77, 134, 136, 145
Biff Hooper *see* Allen "Biff" Hooper
Big Brother 191
"Bill Barnses's" 118
Bill Bergson 121, 122
Bill Bergson, Master Detective 121
Billman, Carol 49
Billy Argo 180, 185–189, 194
Billy Quiz Boy 190
The Birth of a Nation 98
"Blackhawks" 118
The Blond Ones 72
Bloom, Clive 149, 161
Bob Andrews 16, 141, 142, 147
The Bobbsey Twins 8, 132, 136, 189
Boeing Air Transport 116, 117
Boeing B-9 Bomber 117
Boeing Model 40B-4 116
Boeing Model 80A 116
Boeing Model 221 Monomail 117
Boeing Model 247 116
Bomba the Jungle boy 8
Bonanza 75, 80, 143
Boston, Joe 72
The Boy Detective Fails 17, 180, 184–190
Boy Scouts 89, 96
Bradbury, Malcolm 175
Brainerd, Chris 83
Brains Benton 137
Braziel, Jana Evans 153
Bret King 4, 143
Brick 189–191
Brittain-Powell, Chris 146, 156
Bromberg, Sarah 160

Bronski, Michael 195
Bronx Zoo 98
Brooks, Peter 27
Brotman, Joyce 73
Buffy Summers 2, 3
Buffy the Vampire Slayer (film) 2, 3
Buffy the Vampire Slayer (television series) 2, 3
Byars, Betsy 137

C. Auguste Dupin 6, 7, 137
Cain, James M. 22
Callie Shaw 24, 28, 31, 40, 73, 80
Campbell, Carole Ann 65
Campbell, Joseph 168
Campfire Girls 89
"Campus Terror" (Hardy Boys television) 72
Caprio, Betsy 145
Captain Marvel 109
Carson Drew 74
Casino Royale (James Bond book) 150, 152
Cassidy, David 73
Cassidy, Shaun 73–76, 79
Castrone 4
The Caves of Fear (Rick Brant) 10
Cawelti, John G. 149, 150, 152, 156, 162
Central Intelligence Agency (CIA) 147, 157
Chandler, Raymond 22
Chapman, James 149, 150, 155, 156, 164
Cherry Ames 13, 43, 44, 132, 146
Chet Morton 21, 24, 26, 28, 32, 40, 42, 58, 65, 70, 71, 78, 80, 81, 134, 135, 138
Chick, Garry 157
Christie, Agatha 7, 83, 139
Christopher Boone 167–178, 180–184, 187, 194, 195
Christopher Cool (character) 4, 10, 13, 16, 144, 146–149, 151–155, 157–164
Christopher Cool, TEEN Agent (series) 133, 143–145, 147–165
Chubby 71, 80; *see also* Chet Morton
Chudacoff, Howard 104
Circle 4 Patrol (Tim Murphy) 108, 109, 111, 117
Clever Dick 190, 196
Clue?? 83
The Clue in the Diary (Nancy Drew) 38, 41
The Clue in the Embers (Hardy Boys) 63
Clues Brothers (series) 36
Clyde, Andy 67
Cole, David 78
Columbo (character) 83
Columbo (series) 72
Conan Doyle, Arthur 7, 169
Connelly, Mark 10, 39, 40, 43

Considine, John W., Jr. 63
Considine, Tim 63, 66, 68, 79, 80
Constable Riley 24, 81
Conway, Russ 65
Coogan, Peter 110
Cooper, James Fenimore 2
Cornelius, Michael G. 12, 41, 177
Cotten, Joseph 75
The Country Wife 4
Crane, Stephen 110
Crawford, Robert L. 20
Cronon, William 104
CSI 7
Cupples and Leon 132
The Curious Incident of the Dog in the Night-Time 17, 167–178, 180–184, 186–189
"The Curse" (Hardy Boys television) 78

"Da Doo Run Run" 76
Dainty Fidget 4
Dana Girls 8, 126, 146
Daring Wings (Tim Murphy) 108–110, 112, 114, 115
Dauphine 3, 4
Dave Fearless 4
Davy Crockett (television series) 63
The Dead Boy Detectives 185, 196
Dead Famous 192
Dead on Target (Hardy Boys) 76
Dean, Graham M. 108, 116–118
Deane, Paul 48
de Lauretis, Theresa 26, 27
del Buone, Oreste 153
DeLillo, Don 59
Deming, Richard 148
Department of Danger (Christopher Cool) 148, 161
Deprivation House (Hardy Boys) 191, 192
Derrida, Jacques 56
Detective Smuff 25, 26, 31, 33, 81
Die Another Day (James Bond film) 160
"The Disappearing Floor" (Hardy Boys television) 72
Disc World 168
Disney, Walt 62
Dixon, Franklin W. (pseudonym) 20, 51, 63, 72
Dr. No 153
Dr. No (James Bond film) 150, 160, 162
Dr. Zachary Smith 70
Domino 162
Don "Scotty" Scott 13
Don Sturdy 4
Douglas DC-1 117
Duff, Howard 75
Dumas, Alexandre père 133

Easthope, Anthony 176
Eaton, George C. 118
Eco, Umberto 153
Edström, Vivi 121, 125
Edwards, Leo 136, 137, 141
Eggers, Dave 181, 195
The Ego and the Id 22
Eilbacher, Lisa 73
Eisner, Will 118
Elton, Ben 192
Emerson, Ralph Waldo 93
Encyclopedia Brown 14, 137, 169, 180, 181
Epicœne, or the Silent Woman 3, 4
Eradicate "Rad" Sampson 99–101
Erisman, Fred 11, 47, 151
Erwin, Jhene 77
Esmond, Carl 75
Evanovich, Janet 6
Extremely Loud and Incredibly Close 181
Ezra Collig 25, 31–34, 81

The Fairview Boys (series) 13
Falkner, J. M. 196
Fenton Hardy 9, 20–26, 28–34, 42–43, 56–57, 60, 65, 66, 69, 71, 73, 74, 77, 79, 80, 82, 183, 192
Filmation 70–72, 78–82
Fleming, Ian 150, 152
The Flickering Torch Mystery (Hardy Boys) 71, 82
"The Flickering Torch Mystery" (Hardy Boys television) 72
Flight to Nowhere (Hardy Boys) 72
Foer, Jonathan Safran 181, 195
Fong, Brian 68
Footprints Under the Window (Hardy Boys) 43
Foucault, Michel 11, 12
France 2 77
Frank Hardy *see* Hardy Boys (characters)
Freud, Sigmund 22, 26, 30, 60, 133–135, 140–142, 194
From Russia with Love 164
Fuller, Gillian 58

Garis, Howard 90
Gates, Richard 69, 70
Gelbart, Larry 2
Gellar, Sarah Michelle 2
George Fayne 40–42, 78, 134, 136, 145
Georgetown University 60
Geronimo Johnson 13, 148, 149, 152, 154, 155, 158, 159, 161, 164
Gertrude Hardy 39, 65, 66, 69, 71, 73, 77, 79, 80, 192
Giant Detective Boys 196
Gibson, Suzie 152

Gilbert, Edmund 73
Gilbert, Ruth 171, 178
Gilded Age 15, 87, 88, 90–93, 95, 98, 102–105
Gilgamesh 5
Gillis, Jackson 64, 67
The Girl Aviators (series) 43
Girl Scouts 89
Goldfinger (James Bond film) 162
Grant, Madison 98, 102
Granville, Bonita 72
Gray, Colin 78
The Great Airport Mystery (Hardy Boys) 51, 56–60
The Green Hornet 68
Greene, Lorne 75
Griffith, Melanie 74–75
Grosset & Dunlap 36, 70, 71, 76, 81–83, 132
Guinevere 133, 135
Gunsmoke 143

Haas, Charles 65
Haddon, Mark 17, 167, 168, 170, 172, 174–176, 178, 180–182, 184
Haller, Daniel 74
Hamlet 5
Hammett, Dashiell 22
Han Solo 135
Happy Feet 86
the Hardy Boys (characters) 4, 8, 9, 10, 13–15, 17, 19–21, 23–26, 28–34, 36–40, 42–47, 51–61, 64–81, 90, 135, 151, 152, 169. 180, 180, 191–195
The Hardy Boys (Filmation television series) 62, 70
The Hardy Boys (Nelvana television series) 62, 77–80, 83
The Hardy Boys (series) 19, 20, 25, 28, 29, 33, 35–40, 42–49, 51, 55, 58, 60–61, 62, 66, 68–72, 74, 76, 78–81, 132, 134, 136–138, 143, 148, 158, 180, 191–194
"The Hardy Boys and Nancy Drew Meet Dracula" (Hardy Boys television) 75
Hardy Boys Casefiles (series) 36, 51, 53, 76, 77
Hardy Boys Digests (series) 36
The Hardy Boys Mysteries (television series) 75; *see also The Hardy Boys/Nancy Drew Mysteries*
The Hardy Boys/Nancy Drew Mysteries (television series) 36, 62, 69, 71–74, 76–83
Hardy Boys: Undercover Brothers 36, 191, 194
Harmon, John 67
Harry Potter 5, 19, 133, 135, 139, 168, 185

Hartsfield Airport 52
The Haunted House (Hardy Boys) 74
The Haunted Showboat (Nancy Drew) 41
Hawkeye 2
Heads You Lose (Christopher Cool) 148, 155, 161
Hecht, Albie 86, 87, 103
Heidegger, Martin 56
Henry Robinson 28, 31, 33
Hercule Poirot 6, 139
Hermione Granger 133, 135
The Hero with a Thousand Faces 168
Herz, Peggy 83
The Hidden Theft (Hardy Boys) 194
Highet, Fiona 77
Hilton, Paris 192
Hitchcock, Alfred 132, 141, 142
Holy Grail 5
Honey Rider 162
The Hooded Hawk Mystery (Hardy Boys) 63
Hoot 86
Hostages of Hate (Hardy Boys) 51, 53–57, 60
"The House on Possessed Hill" (Hardy Boys television) 74
The House on the Cliff (Hardy Boys) 42–43
Houston Daily Post 89
Huck Finn 137
Hurd Applegate 26, 28, 31, 33, 34, 64

Industrial Revolution 88
Inspector Lestrade 81, 137
The Interpretation of Dreams 60
Iola Morton 40, 65–67, 80
The Iowa City Press-Citizen 108
Ironside 83

James Bond (character) 83, 144, 147, 150–153, 156–158, 160–165
James Bond (series) 143–145, 147, 149–152, 156–158, 160–165
Jane Eyre 5
Jauss, Hans Robert 19
Jerry Gilroy 40
Jerry Todd 136, 137
Jill Masterson 162
Jim Foy 68
Joe Hardy *see* Hardy Boys (characters)
John "Red" Jackley 23, 30–33
John Watson, MD 137
Johnston, Janet Louise 75
the Joker 190
Jonson, Ben 3, 4
Jorgenson, Jamie 83
Judy Bolton 13, 43, 44, 132
Jupiter Jones 16, 137–140, 142, 147

Kalle Blomkvist *see* Bill Bergson
Kato 68
Kay Tracey 44
Keene Carolyn (pseudonym) 72
Kelland, Clarence Budington 138, 139
Kelley, Philip 83
Ken Holt 11, 13, 132, 148
Kerouac, Jack 123
Keystone Kops 120
Kidnapped 196
Kimmel, Michael 44
The King & I 68
King Arthur 5, 133, 135
Kingston University 148
Kirk, Tommy 63, 65, 66. 68, 79
Klein, Michael 78
Knoth, Maeve Visser 121, 125, 129
Kosleck, Martin 75
Kronfeld, Chana 171, 172

Lancelot 133, 135
Lancer, Jack (pseudonym) 148
Larson, Glen 72, 74
"The Last Kiss of Summer" (Hardy Boys television) 76
"The Last Laugh" (Hardy Boys television) 78
The Last of the Mohicans 2
Laura Hardy 21, 23, 31, 32, 39, 65, 69, 77, 80, 183
Lawrence, James Duncan 148
LeBesco, Kathleen 153
Lee, Bruce 68
Le Gall, Michel 150, 157, 158, 162
Lemony Snicket 180
Life of Pi 192
"Light Action in the Caribbean" 58
Linda Craig 143
Lindgren, Astrid 16, 120–130
Little Lord Fauntleroy 2
Lopez, Barry 58
Lord of the Rings 168
Lost in Space 70
Loubert, Patrick 78
Loy, John W. 157
Luke Skywalker 135
Lutz, Mark 78

M 150, 151, 153, 157
MacDonald, Donald 64
the Magi 134
Major Boothroyd *see* Q (James Bond)
Marcus, Laura 124
Mark Tidd 138
Marlboro Man 44
Martin, Pamela Sue 73
Mary Nestor 90

M*A*S*H 2
Mason, Bobbie Ann 39, 44
Matheson, Tim 69, 70
Mathiews, Franklin K. 195
Matilda Jones 139
McCloud 72
McCloud, Scott 193
McCoy, Horace 22
McFarlane, Leslie 20, 158
McGrath, Juliet 1
McMillan and Wife 72
McTeague 110
Meno, Joe 17, 180, 184–187, 189
Metro-Goldwyn-Mayer (MGM) 98
The Mickey Mouse Club 62, 63, 65–69, 72, 78, 79, 81, 82
Mike Hammer 83
Milland, Ray 75
Miller, J. Hillis 27
Millet, Kate 176
Miss Marple 6, 171
Mission: Moonfire (Christopher Cool) 10, 148, 161, 164
Mr. Damon 95, 96, 100, 101
Mr. Pinchwife 4
Moonfleet 196
Morley, David 9
Morose 3, 4
Morrison Ranch 65
The Motor Boys (series) 13, 43
The Motor Girls (series) 43
Mrs. Baggert 94
Muir, John 89, 95, 96, 104
Mundis, Jerry 148
Murder by Death 83
Murphy, Richard 69
My Three Sons 80
The Mystery at Lilac Inn (Nancy Drew) 38
The Mystery of Ghost Farm (Hardy Boys television) 66, 67, 81
"The Mystery of Jade Kwan Yin" (Hardy Boys television) 69
The Mystery of the Applegate Treasure (Hardy Boys television) 62, 63, 66, 67, 69, 82, 83
The Mystery of the Chinese Junk (Hardy Boys) 68–69
The Mystery of the Chinese Junk (Hardy Boys television) 62, 68, 69, 71, 79, 80, 82
"The Mystery of the Flying Courier" (Hardy Boys television) 76
"The Mystery of the Hollywood Phantom" (Hardy Boys television) 73
The Mystery of the Stuttering Parrot (Poppy Ott) 136

The Mystery of the Stuttering Parrot (The Three Investigators) 136
The Mystery of the Whispering Mummy (Jerry Todd) 136
The Mystery of the Whispering Mummy (The Three Investigators) 136

Nancy Drew (character) 8, 13, 15, 19, 36–38, 41–44, 49, 76, 77, 83, 126, 145, 146, 151, 152, 196
Nancy Drew (series) 36, 40, 41, 43–45, 48, 49, 62, 71, 73, 90, 132, 134, 136, 143, 148
Nancy Drew (television series) 77, 78
Nancy Drew and Her Sister Sleuths 12
Nancy Drew and the Hardy Boys Be-a-Detective Mystery Stories 77
Nancy Drew and the Hardy Boys Super Mystery Series 36, 77
Nancy Drew and the Hardy Boys Super Sleuths! (series) 36
Nano 4
Nappi, Rudy 76
Nash, Ilana 145
Nash, Roderick 104
NBC television network 68
Ned Nickerson 42, 78
Nelson, Portia 67
Nelvana and Marathon Productions 77
Nero Wolfe 6, 139
the Network 52
"Never Violence" 127
New Line 77
New York Zoological Society 98
Newark Airport 59
Newman, Kim 190, 196
Nickelodeon 86
Nielsen ratings 143
Nightwing 190
Nikolajeva, Maria 126
Nolan, Lloyd 75
Norris, Frank 110
Novy, Marianne 125
Nye, Russel B. 151

Oedipus 19, 26, 27, 30, 32, 33
Oedipus complex 22–24, 26, 30
Old Lady Squeamish 4
On the Road 123
"The Open Boat" 110
Opie, John 104
O'Rourke, Meghan 20
Oscar 120, 122–124, 127–130
"Ozymandias" 56

Palmer, Jerry 149
Parry, Sally 37, 41

The Partridge Family 73
The Passing of the Great Race 98
Peerce, Larry 69
Penny Parker (series) 43, 44
Perry "Slim" Robinson 28, 31, 64, 66, 82
Pete Crenshaw 16, 138, 140, 142, 147
Pete Jones 71, 80
Peters, Ingo 133
The Phantom 109
Phil Cohen 40, 80
Pinchot, Gifford 88, 104
The Pleasure of the Text 33
Poe, Edgar Allan 6, 7, 137
Pomeroy 151
Popowich, Paul 78
Poppy Ott 136, 137
Pound, Ezra 55
The Power Boys (series) 4, 13
Prachett, Terry 168
Prescott, Norm 70
Princess Leia Organa 135
Princeton University 148
Progressive Era 15, 87–90, 92, 93, 95–98, 102–105
Psycho 74
Pussy Galore 162
Pyrhönen, Heta 124

Q (Christopher Cool) 150, 151, 159
Q (James Bond) 151, 157

The Racer Boys (series) 13
The Radio Boys (series) 13
Ralph Parson 109, 111
Random House 132
Rasmus 16, 120–130
Rasmus and the Tramp 16, 120–130
Rasmus and the Vagabond see *Rasmus and the Tramp*
Reading for the Plot 27
The Red Cloud 95, 100
Redhood 190
Rick Brant 10, 11, 13, 148, 169
Riis, Jacob 92
Robin, the Boy Wonder 190
Robins, Kevin 9
Rocky Beach, California 139
Ron Weasley 133, 135
Roosevelt, Theodore 88. 90, 96, 104, 108
Rosa Klebb 164
Rosenberg, Bruce A. 149, 150, 152, 156, 162
Roth, Marty 39
Routledge, Christopher 122, 128, 129
The Rover Boys (series) 4, 8, 13, 43
Rowling, J. K. 168
Ryan, Tracy 77

Sam Radley 73
Samuels, Ken 78
Sanders, Hugh 67
Sandman 185
Sandy Allen 13
Saraga, Esther 125
Scheimer, Lou 70
Scribe, Eugene 133
The Secret at Shadow Ranch (Nancy Drew) 41
The Secret Files of the Diogenes Club 190
The Secret of Skull Mountain (Hardy Boys) 43
The Secret of the Old Clock (Nancy Drew) 37, 38
The Secret Warning (Hardy Boys) 43
Selby, Sarah 65
Shakespeare, William 3
Sherlock Holmes 6, 7, 81, 137, 138, 169, 171–173, 176, 178, 189, 196
Shields, Arthur 64
Shigeta, James 70
Shirley, James 3
Shirley Flight 146
Shopton, New York 90, 94
Shore Road 65
Sidaris, Arlene 73
"Silver Blaze" 169
Simon, Neil 83
Simon & Schuster 76, 77, 83, 143
Sinclair, Upton 92
Sinfield, Alan 174, 175
The Sinister Sign-Post (Hardy Boys) 10
60 Minutes 72
The Sky Trail (Tim Murphy) 108–110, 116, 117
The Sleuth 66, 71
Sloan, Michael 72
S.M.E.R.S.H. 155
Smith, Paul 8–10
Smolinske, Seth 135
"Sole Survivor" (Hardy Boys television) 69
Sonnenfeld, Barry 86
Sony Pictures 86
South Pacific 68
S.P.E.C.T.R.E. 156
Speedman, Scott 78
Spice Carter 155, 159, 164
Spiderman 192
Spielberg, Steven 51
Spin & Marty 63, 69
Springsteen, R. G. 66
Star Trek (series) 105
Stephanie Plum 6
Stevens, Craig 75
Stevenson, Parker 73, 74, 76, 79
Stevenson, Robert Louis 196

Stickland, Andrew 172
The Sting of the Scorpion (Hardy Boys) 76
"The Strange Fate of Flight 608" (Hardy Boys television) 81
Stratemeyer, Edward 7–9, 62, 63, 65, 68, 70, 72, 76, 82, 90, 108, 133, 138, 139, 158, 192
Stratemeyer Syndicate 7, 8, 20, 36, 40, 47, 78, 90, 132, 133, 136, 141, 143, 144, 147, 148, 150, 195
Superman 109, 113
Sutherland, Hal 70
Svoboda, Frederick Joseph 122
Swanson, Kristy 2
Swift Industries 86

Tagged for Terror (Hardy Boys) 51–53, 56–57, 61
Taliaferro, Charles 150, 157, 158, 162
Tanner, Joy 78
Ted Scott (series) 11
TEEN *see* Top-Secret Educational Espionage Network
Ten Little Indians 83
The Terminal 51
Thompson, Jill 196
Thoreau, Henry David 93
The Three Investigators (series) 13, 16, 43, 132, 133, 136, 137, 139–142, 147, 180
The Three Musketeers 133, 134
The Three Wise Men *see* The Wise Men
Thunderball (James Bond film) 162
Thunderbirds 80
Tiger Beat 75
Tim Murphy (character) 108–118
Tim Murphy (series) 16, 108, 114, 118
Titus Jones 139
TOAD 147, 156, 161
Tolkien, J.R.R. 168
Tom Quest 4
Tom Sawyer 137
Tom Sawyer 137
Tom Swift (character) 4, 15, 87, 90–104, 169, 180
Tom Swift (series) 86, 87, 90–105, 143, 148, 151
Tom Swift and His Electric Rifle 100
Tom Swift and His Electric Runabout 94
Tom Swift and His Submarine Boat 91
Tony Prito 40, 70, 80, 81
Top-Secret Educational Espionage Network (TEEN) 147–149, 154, 155, 157–159, 161, 164
Tower Mansion 26
The Tower Treasure (Hardy Boys) 20, 23, 24, 32–34, 37, 40, 43, 63, 64, 69, 79, 82
transcendentalism 93

The Treasure Hunt of the S-18 (Tim Murphy) 108, 109
Treasure Island 64, 196
The Treasure on the Tracks (Hardy Boys) 194
Trial by Fury (Christopher Cool) 148, 153, 161
Trigger Berg 136
Trixie Belden 13, 43, 171, 177
Tuffy Bean 136
Twain, Mark 123
20th Century–Fox 68, 69
Twilight 19
Tyler, Josh 86, 103

Umphlet, Wiley Lee 137
the uncanny 30, 194
Underworld 59
United Air Lines 116
United States Forest Service 88
Universal Studio 72–74, 76, 77, 79–83
Utnapishtim 4

van der Osten, Robert 104
"The Vanishing American Hobo" 123
Variety 68, 76, 86
The Venture Bros. 187, 190, 191, 196
Vicki Barr 13, 43, 132, 146
View-Master 71
The Viking Symbol Mystery (Hardy Boys) 81
Vilnoff 10
Vlad the Impaler 75
Volpone 4

Wade, Jay C. 146, 156
Wagon Train 143
Walby, Sylvia 172, 177
Wall-E 86
Walt Disney Corp. 62, 63, 65, 66, 68, 72, 82, 83
Wanda Kay 71, 80
Wannamaker, Annette 47, 126
Warnock, Robert 83
Wayne, John 44
Weaver, Dennis 75
Welch, Bill 63
Westcom Entertainment Group 77
Wexler, Paul 65
Whitman (publisher) 141
Whitman, Stuart 75
William, Paul 75
Wilmot, John 3
"Wipe Out" (Hardy Boys television) 69
The Wise Men 134
Wonder Woman 109
Woolf, Michael 152

Word of Disney 72
World Trade Center 54
Wycherley, William 3, 4

The X Bar X Boys (series) 13, 43
X Marks the Spy (Christopher Cool) 144, 148, 159, 163

Yaeger, Patricia 59
Yellowstone National Park 88
Yummi Toyama 155, 164

www.ingramcontent.com/pod-product-compliance
Lightning Source LLC
Chambersburg PA
CBHW032055300426
44116CB00007B/750